AUTISM WITH SEVERE
LEARNING DIFFICULTIES

HUMAN HORIZONS SERIES

AUTISM WITH SEVERE LEARNING DIFFICULTIES

A Guide for Parents and Professionals

by

Rita Jordan

A Condor Book
Souvenir Press (E&A) Ltd

First published 2001 by
Souvenir Press (Educational & Academic) Ltd.,
43 Great Russell Street, London WC1B 3PA

Reprinted 2002
Reprinted 2005

ISBN 0 285 63599 9

Typeset by Rowland Phototypesetting Ltd.,
Bury St Edmunds, Suffolk

Printed in Great Britain by
Creative Print and Design Group (Wales), Ebbw Vale

Contents

Dedication

To Katie Thomas (neé Berry) who was my inspiration and model in working with this group and who, sadly, did not live to see this tribute. She will be remembered in the lives of the individuals for whom she worked so tirelessly.

Preface

Autism is undoubtedly a 'trendy' topic in education and, to a lesser extent, social care, both in the UK and internationally. The Internet has over 200,000 web pages on autism, and education systems around the world are being challenged to meet the needs of this apparently growing – and until now often unrecognised – group. There are no doubt many reasons for this, including (one hopes) the desire to understand and make life better for all those with autistic spectrum disorders and their families. Another reason, however, is the fact that understanding others who are different from us helps us understand ourselves and the processes of normal development. In that context, it is not surprising that interest focuses on those who have what is termed 'high functioning autism' or Asperger's syndrome.

In the past, the needs of this high functioning group with autistic spectrum disorders were attributed to emotional and behavioural difficulties (if any kind of meaningful attribution was made), and such children and adults were often either not diagnosed or misdiagnosed. It is also true that, in relation to autism that is accompanied by additional learning difficulties, this group is now recognised as being far larger than was ever conceived. Thus, it is entirely appropriate that the last ten years has seen a greater focus on this group reflected in the literature. However, there is a problem in that this change of focus is now in danger of creating an equally unjust neglect of those who have the dual disability of autism and severe learning difficulties. Just as parents of children with higher functioning autism once looked in vain at books on autism for a reflection of their own child's difficulties, so parents of children with autism accompanied by severe learning difficulties now feel themselves (and their children) marginalised by the media attention now given to the higher functioning group.

In 1978 I was co-author of a book for children with profound and complex learning difficulties, who were then just becoming the responsibility of Education departments rather than Health (Kiernan, Jordan & Saunders: *Starting Off*, Souvenir Press – now out of print). That was a pioneering book in the UK in its recognition of the needs of this group and the positive way they could be met in education, no matter how profound or complex the difficulties. It was, however, a book of its time. Many of the children depicted in that book were children with autistic spectrum disorders, whether or not they had a specific diagnosis, yet none was identified as such. The book also described and advocated an approach to the education of these children, based on applied behaviour analysis, which was then the dominant approach to the education of children with severe learning difficulties. Although some elements of behavioural approaches remain in many special schools in England and Wales, they have largely given way to both cognitive and interactive approaches, and, furthermore including all children within the National Curriculum has had a profound effect. In the USA, behavioural approaches have remained dominant to a far greater extent and, ironically (given the behavioural assumption that diagnostic status has no bearing on the education to be provided), many are now re-marketed as specific approaches for autism.

All these factors have played an important part in the decision to write this current book. The most important influence, however, has been the worrying tendency for battles, that I assumed to have been won, to reappear. Sixteen years ago, before the advent of the National Curriculum in England and Wales, I was part of a professional body, representing those working with children and adults with autism, that was concerned about the assumptions (then current in the educational establishment) that children with autism did not have needs separate and distinct from those of other children. The emphasis then was on children with autism accompanied by learning difficulties because it was assumed that this represented the majority of children with autism. We produced a booklet aimed at influencing that perception in the educational establishment as well as providing some practical guidance for professionals (AHTACA, 1985).

Our understanding, knowledge and skill have improved dramatically since those days, as has the educational climate in which we all operate, and AHTACA has produced an updated version of that booklet (2000). Yet the issue it sought to address has, apparently, not gone away. A recent review of special education by a renowned special educator (Farrell, 2001) contains the following statement, in a confused argument about the role of categories within education:

'. . . *teaching approaches commonly employed with pupils who have severe learning difficulties can also be used effectively with pupils who are autistic'*(sic) p. 4.

Apart from the lack of respect shown by the attribution 'autistic', in contrast to pupils *with* severe learning difficulties, this statement would not be unexceptional. It is true that there can be a useful sharing of approaches between those geared for children with autism who also have severe learning difficulties and those for children with severe learning difficulties alone (Jordan, Macleod & Brunton, 1999), but there is an important caveat. The sharing of approaches can only be effective if there is an understanding of the specific needs of the children with autism. The most effective schools, in fact, seem to be the ones that put those needs to the fore and then find (unsurprisingly) that these special approaches are of benefit to others. In other words, the best approach is the opposite to that suggested: rather than ignoring the needs of these special children because (once they have severe learning difficulties) their 'specialness' is not recognised, *basing their approach on those special needs* will help teachers understand and meet the needs of many other (if not all) children. The context of the statement made by Farrell shows little understanding of this, or how and why autism affects learning and development in children with additional severe learning difficulties, at least as much as in other children.

Perhaps it is presumptuous of an author to suggest that her book is timely, but, for all the reasons given above, I believe that to be so. As detailed in the text, there is a group of individuals who are most dependent on others for their current and future quality of life, and yet may have the poorest prospects of influencing and managing their contact with others. It is a much quoted truism that the measure of civilisation is how the most vulnerable and powerless are treated, and there is a good case for classifying individuals with autism and severe learning difficulties as among the most vulnerable in our society. A parent wrote to me recently in some despair: in spite of decades of special education, he saw no brighter future for these individuals than what he described as 'benign prisons'. That is a bleak view of what has been achieved so far but, sadly, it is not so far from the truth. However, I believe that with our growing understanding and resources we could do better.

That represents the rationale for writing the book: the hope that it will once more assert the needs and rights of this neglected group and suggest some ways in which we can move beyond this bleak view of their future. I have seen many examples of encouraging and even inspiring practice: we just need to learn to share that more widely, not to be side-tracked by divisive claims for particular approaches, and to be ready to defend the needs of these vulnerable children against those who would ignore them (through ignorance or ideological conviction).

References

AHTACA (1985). *The Special Curricular Needs of Autistic Children*. London, AHTACA.

AHTACA (2000). *The Special Curricular Needs of Children with Autistic Spectrum Disorders*, London, AHTACA.

Farrell, P. (2001). Special education in the last twenty years: have things really got better? *British Journal of Special Education, 28, 1*, 3–9.

Jordan, R., Macleod, C. & Brunton, L. (1999). Making Special Schools 'Specialist': a case study of the provision for pupils with autism in a school for pupils with severe learning difficulties. In G. Jones (Ed.). *GAP: Good Autism Practice. Occasional Papers, 1* Birmingham, University of Birmingham School of Education.

Kiernan, C.C., Jordan, R.R. & Saunders, C.A. (1978). *Starting Off*. London, Souvenir Press (Currently out of print).

1 Implications of the Dual Diagnosis

A seven-year-old girl kneels on the floor of a busy open-plan nursery; let's call her Amy. It is an opportunity class, established for children with very special needs (who were, before 1971, excluded from education as being 'ineducable'). There are twenty such children in the class, together with their normally developing pre-school brothers and sisters. There are also a large number of adult 'helpers': a ratio of approximately one adult per child with special needs. Many of the children are multiply disabled with a range of physical and sensory difficulties in addition to their severe or profound learning difficulties. In spite of that, most are happily and purposefully engaged in some enjoyable 'task' with their adult helper and in the company of the other children. But not Amy; she represents my first encounter with the children who are the subject of this book, those with autism and additional severe learning difficulties.

Amy rocks back and forth on her knees, wailing in the most pitiful and haunting way and (when not physically prevented by the watchful helper) hitting her head violently with her hand, plucking frantically at her hair, picking her skin until it bleeds, and poking her eyes. Occasionally she reacts ferociously to the attempts of the adult to restrict her self-injury or direct her to a task and then she bites and scratches the adult or any unwary child who has strayed within her reach. In her two years at the nursery there is no discernible improvement. Some days she is more distressed than others; rarely, is she calm, and never at peace. Staff feel she has gained nothing from her time at the nursery, the only possible benefit being the regular two-hour break for her mother.

Meanwhile, her sister also attends the nursery. Sarah is two years younger and she is mobile, very mobile. She trips round the nursery on her toes twirling furiously and suddenly swooping to tear something from the wall or a painting easel, or to toss toys and equipment into the air in abandoned glee. As adults hurry in her wake trying to repair the havoc and prevent further damage, she becomes more hyperactive, appearing to enjoy the chasing involved and the way she is able to cause so much disturbance. Eventually, a determined adult may succeed in anchoring her to a chair and engaging her in a task. Surprisingly, she then shows considerable skill and dexterity. When these attempts to engage her in work started she would resist violently, but as time went by she accepted being led to her task each time and (if the adult was delayed or distracted by something else) she would take the adult's hand and drag her or him to the table at the appointed time.

There's another child, let's call him Roy, among the twenty with special needs who is not settled into the group. He has Asperger's syndrome (although in the early 1970s, of course, it was not recognised). He can walk and talk (insistently and incessantly) but has almost as much difficulty as Amy and Sarah in directing his attention to the activities planned by the adults. He has an autistic spectrum disorder and, in spite of his very obvious differences from Amy and Sarah, there are some special needs he has in common with them. His autism is interfering with his learning but he does not have general learning difficulties, so his needs are not the focus of this book. He is mentioned here to illustrate that it is not the degree of learning difficulty that is crucial in determining special needs, but the degree of autism. Most of the children in the nursery (apart from the normally developing children) have significantly more severe learning difficulties than he has, yet they are more able to relate to their helpers and to the other children and so they are more able to participate in the educational process. Unless the adults learn to adapt their style to allow him to begin to learn, he too may show increasing developmental delay, but that will be secondary to his autism.

While our knowledge about autism and our approaches to it have changed, these three examples still represent key features about the population of children on which this book focuses.

Autism and general learning difficulties may occur together

There have been, and continue to be, many misconceptions about the relationship between autism and severe learning difficulties. When Kanner first identified a new syndrome of autism in 1943, he thought that all the children were fundamentally intelligent, but that their intelligence might be masked by the autism. Although the example of Roy, above, illustrates that autism can indeed make it hard for the child to learn and thus may lead to learning difficulties, autism itself is not responsible for producing general intellectual impairment, which is what is meant by the term 'severe learning difficulties' (sld) or 'profound and multiple learning difficulties' (pmld). We know this because it is possible to have severe autism and yet to have normal or even advanced levels of intellectual functioning.

Once someone is skilled in working with children with autism, we also find that intelligence tests are just as reliable for them as they are for others, so it is usually possible to measure general ability and degree of autism separately. When this is done in young children there is no clear direct relationship between the two; the most severe learning difficulties are not always accompanied by the most severe degrees of autism. As children get older, however, it is easier for those without significant learning difficulties to use their general intelligence to learn the skills necessary to overcome some of the problems caused by the autism. Thus, the more able are more likely (although not invariably) to become less autistic as they get older. In this way, it is the learning difficulty which is causing the child to remain more autistic rather than the autism which is causing the learning difficulty.

Kanner's original assumption, then, was wrong. However, that idea persists because of the anomalous behaviour often seen in autism. It is common for development to be uneven and even for there to be splinter skills that are highly developed in relation to the child's general level of functioning. There is something about the purposeful way in which the child often pursues his or her own interests that makes one think that if only one could 'scrape away' the autism, the child's true ability would be revealed. But autism is not like that. It is a way of developing, and so it is integral to the way the child experiences and understands the world. Good teaching and an appropriate environment can enable the child to function adaptively within their autism, but we cannot remove the autism without removing the person. We do not do the child any favours by failing to recognise the full extent of all the difficulties that need to be overcome and we should be very wary of assuming that the child's *best* level of functioning represents that child's *true* level of functioning across all areas.

The notion that it was the autism that made it seem as if those children also had learning difficulties was (and still is) one expressed by some parents and professionals who are working with the children, for the reasons outlined above. Yet, alongside that myth, was a parallel and opposing myth that was more likely to be shown by professionals without direct experience of this group. That was the idea that 'autism' was just a fashionable label for 'severe learning difficulties' and that it was sought by parents who did not want to face their child's 'true' difficulties and/or who wanted to procure better facilities and resources for their child. This is of course equally fallacious. One can have autism without any additional general learning difficulties and indeed while having superior general levels of intelligence. It is also very clear from the examples given at the start of this chapter that children with autism, even where they do have additional severe learning difficulties, are different from those with sld without autism; they have different needs and thus need different approaches.

The triad of impairments in autism

Wing and Gould (1979) in their Camberwell study were the first to recognise and demonstrate that autism and sld could occur together. They found that children and young people who shared a number of key features formed a distinct group that was clearly distinct from others with sld. The shared characteristics fell into three areas of social development, which came to be known as the 'triad of impairments' that characterise autism. Current diagnostic systems are based on this triad. Jordan (1999) argues for a slight modification to produce the following description of the three areas of developmental difference in autism. The examples that are given are of the kinds of behaviour of children with autism and additional sld that can be found in each area of development.

There are, of course, no particular behaviours or even lack of single behaviours by which autism can be recognised. The kind of behaviour shown in each area of difficulty will depend on the child's personality, level of intellectual and linguistic functioning, experience and teaching, and can change over time. It is qualitative differences in these areas of development that distinguish autism, but this must be judged against what would be expected for their level of intellectual functioning. The more severe the learning difficulties, the less functional behaviour will be expected and there will be a consequent increased difficulty in recognising the autism.

Social development

The level of social skills and social understanding is out of keeping with the child's general level of functioning. This does not mean any single way of behaving, and Wing (1996) has identified different types of social impairment in autism. Once again, these are not fixed characteristics and the child may change over time as a result of development or education, usually moving towards being less withdrawn and more socially active. Amy can be taken as a typically withdrawn child, who was placed in the worst possible environment, given her need to withdraw, and hence her high levels of distress and inability to learn. Such children can make little or no sense of others and find the kind of stimulation they present (speech, touching, attempts at eye contact) both confusing and stressful, even painful. They react by trying to withdraw and can be calm when left to themselves in a quiet environment but become very upset at any attempt at forced interaction. That is not to say that they should be merely left alone, but that the way we intervene must take account of the very real difficulties being experienced and not assume it is just a matter of modifying behaviour.

Sarah, on the other hand, represents a child who started as withdrawn but is moving into a 'passive' stage. Thus, she does not seek social interaction, but she has begun to accept it and, once it is predictable and the demands made are clear, even seek it. She can enjoy doing something with someone, although she would still be likely to withdraw from any attempt at 'pure' social engagement, which she does not understand. At this stage she is typical in being able to respond to adults but not to other children, who are far more unpredictable. In time, she may learn to interact passively with her peers as well, and this process can be aided by supporting the other children in their attempts at intervention.

Roy, the little boy with higher functioning autism (or Asperger's syndrome), could be seen as illustrating Wing's third category of 'active but odd'. He is keen to make contact with others (especially adults) but he does not know how to interact with others and repeatedly gets it wrong. It is possible for a child with autism and sld to fall into this social category but it is more unusual, at least when young. Attempts at social engagement are liable to be misunderstood and, unless there is specific knowledgeable help, early attempts at social interaction may be stifled. For example, one social game that is appreciated by most mobile children with autism is 'chase'. The child with autism may learn a strategy of thumping others and running off in order to be chased but this may well be mistaken for aggression and squashed rather than developed. Sometimes, around puberty, a young person with autism and sld will start to become interested in interacting with others in a way s/he has not done before, but the additional learning difficulties make it even harder for them to succeed, in learning these social interaction rules, than the abler person with autism.

Communication

All levels of communication are affected in autism, regardless of level of language ability. It is this mismatch between language and communication which is both unique to, and characteristic of, autism and which it is hardest for parents and professionals to understand. For all other groups, if they have or are given some means of communication, they are able to use it to communicate a wide range of functions—to make requests, to protest, to comment, to deny, to seek information, to express emotion, to seek mutuality and so on. Spoken language, when it comes, rests on this foundation of communicative understanding and skill and can enrich and extend it, but language is normally so embedded in communication (at least in its roots and in its spoken forms) that dictionary definitions often refer to language as a form of communication. Yet this is not so in autism. Parents with non-speaking children will commonly feel that, if only they could talk, they could say how they were feeling or what they wanted. Those who have speaking children with autism know that sadly it is not so simple as that. Of course, it is easier to work with children with language, and the child has a potentially valuable tool for learning. Yet mere possession of language (or some taught alternative such as sign) does not ensure that the child with autism will be able to use it either for communication or for thinking, and therefore learning.

As with the social area of development, there is considerable variation in the communicative behaviour of children with autism. One significant variable is the possession of language. Genetically, there is a relationship between language disorders and autism, so children with autism may well have a specific difficulty with language acquisition; they will not be diagnosed with such a difficulty, especially if they have sld alongside their autism, because it will be considered that the other diagnoses are sufficient explanation for the lack of language ability. It is true that sld make it more difficult for children to acquire language (which depends on a cognitive base as well as specific language learning), but autism will not of itself lead to language failure. It is likely that the combination of a lack of communicative underpinning due to the autism and a lack of cognitive underpinning due to the sld may contribute to the fact that children with autism and sld experience difficulty and delay in acquiring and understanding speech and some (up to 50%) remain without language through life. However, among children with the same degree of sld and autism, there are still differences in that some acquire some useful language and others do not. It is likely that that difference is due to the presence or absence of specific language difficulties, so that at least some of these children will need to be taught alternative forms of communication.

The communication difficulties in autism are not confined to language acquisition, however, but are seen in difficulties in understanding gestures, facial expressions, social signalling through eye pointing, body postures and communicative distances. They are also seen in problems in establishing joint attention with others and understanding about shared and separate perspectives on the world. Thus there is an interaction with the social problems outlined above and the child's willingness to engage in social interaction will be an important variable in their motivation to acquire and understand modes of communication. As with everything in autism, the picture is a complex one. For children with sld but no autism, the priority will be to teach the child some means to communicate and to build up their understanding of the world to have something to communicate about. Children with autism and sld will need this as well but the priority for them will be to build up their understanding of what communication *is*; without that understanding, they are unlikely to be able to use the methods of communication, even if we are able to teach them. It is a sad fact that many children with autism and sld may be taught a large number of signs, for example, but they only use them when prompted to do so, as a sort of learned routine, rather than as a tool for influencing their world and improving their quality of life.

Flexibility in thinking and behaviour

Difficulties in being flexible in thinking and behaviour are a feature of both autism and sld, so here the effects are additive. However, the thinking of those with autism is different in that it is harder for them to develop a sense of themselves as learners or to understand what they do or do not know. Thus people with autism and sld are dependent on prompts from others or from the environment in order to learn and remember, and it is hard for them to learn spontaneously or to apply what they have learnt to new situations. This means that most of what they do is habitual and they rely on one action to cue the next. If they are interrupted in an activity or a routine or if their normal routine fails in some way, they either have to start again at the beginning, or become very disturbed and distraught and at a loss as to how to get round the problem. People with autism and sld, then, easily acquire 'learned helplessness' –

relying on others to prompt them through tasks, and being at a loss when conditions change or the prompter is absent.

This means there is always a kind of tension in teaching skills to people with autism and sld. On the one hand, learning is most effective when it is one-to-one with the teacher who can structure the task to obtain the maximum learning. Yet, almost as soon as this has been achieved, the teacher (and this might be a parent or carer) needs to begin the task of teaching the child to go beyond the very cues that have been so successful in the teaching. This will have variable success, depending on the level of the learning difficulties, and there will be some with very profound learning difficulties who will not be able to manage independent learning but will always depend on a facilitatory structure to promote their learning and quality of life. However, for all this group, it is important to be aware of the fundamental nature of this difficulty in flexibility, so as not to misinterpret these difficulties as deliberately provocative or challenging. People with autism need support in order to change or adapt their behaviour, and this applies to the inhibition of problem behaviour as much as to the generalisation of skills.

The importance of the autism diagnosis in determining special educational needs

When confronted with a child with very severe or profound learning difficulties, it is not uncommon for professionals to feel that it is these general learning difficulties that constitute the child's main area of need, and that the importance of the autism in determining special educational needs is thus made peripheral. This attitude not only exists in professionals whose main experience is with sld, where the view might be thought to arise from ignorance of the effects of autism, but can also be seen in autism-specific services. Sometimes, there is the view that the learning difficulties are so great that it is a 'waste' of autism-specific teaching and resources to direct them to this group. This raises issues of equity and equal access, which should have been resolved by the 1970 Education Act (Department of Education and Science, 1970) and all subsequent legislation, but unfortunately is still an issue, when resources are limited.

However, it is not just a matter of recognising that all children are entitled to relevant educational access, but of recognising what is 'relevant' in each case. It is certainly true that (as with children without autism) the more severe the accompanying learning difficulties, the harder it will be for the child to make progress and to benefit from the teaching. Yet that does not mean that autism-specific teaching is in any sense 'wasted' on this group or is not needed. The abler people with autism are far more likely to have the opportunity to live relatively independently of others, whereas this is a group of individuals who are almost certain to remain dependent on other people for both their current and future quality of life.

Thus, teaching them basic life skills, as would be appropriate for children with sld without autism, will have limited success, and will be even more limited because the autism may well mean that the child is not able to benefit from the teaching. If the child is fearful of others or over-sensitive to the stimulation they provide, they may well react with behaviour which others find difficult to tolerate and which has the effect of driving away the very people the children need to support their learning. This in turn will also have severe effects on their future quality of life. In fact, it might well be argued that autism-specific teaching is *more* rather than less important for this group.

While sharing certain characteristic difficulties in development, people with autism, are all also very different from one another. Even among the population of children with sld as well as autism, there will be significant differences in how individuals learn and make sense of the world. Thus, taking account of the autism does not mean treating the children with autism and sld in exactly the same way. There will be some generalisations that can be made about the most effective ways of teaching such children, but there will also be significant individual effects. There is no single curriculum or teaching approach that will suit all the individuals in this group. The autism diagnosis is just a signpost to direct the teacher or carer to the fact that the causes and functions of the behaviour that is seen may be different to those for the same behaviour seen in those without autism. This will help the process of finding the correct and most effective approach for that child, but it will not tell the teacher or carer exactly what to do in each case. It will still be very important to get to know the individual and to recognise the effects of that individuality in determining special educational needs. That is one of the reasons why it is important for there to be a key worker for each child, who understands about autism but also knows how that autism is expressed in that individual and what his or her strengths and support needs are.

Autism is a difference, not a delay
'Severe learning difficulties' is an umbrella term which does not carry a lot of information about how that individual thinks and learns; all that can be said is that there will be significant delay in acquiring developmental milestones and in reaching learning objectives. The effects of the general sld, then, will be a quantitative one whereas the different medical conditions underlying the sld will affect the quality and process of that learning and development. Children with autism and sld are likely to show a developmental pattern that is both deviant and delayed; it is the deviance due to the autism that will have the greatest impact on teaching and learning but neither aspect can be ignored.

An example will illustrate the importance of paying attention to both the autism and the sld in understanding these children and meeting their needs.

How a child with autism and sld develops
When Peter was born, he appeared to be a normally functioning child, in spite of a difficult birth with a long time in the birth canal and the consequent fear of possible effects from the lack of oxygen. There were no obvious abnormalities and he cried lustily at birth, but very little after that. He was the second child of the family and to begin with his parents were grateful that he appeared to be so undemanding. It was true that he did not seem to sleep much but he only seemed to cry in response to discomfort (hunger, pain or a dirty nappy) and never simply to demand attention. It was a little worrying to his parents that it was not possible to comfort him through contact, as had been possible with his older brother, but, since there was always an obvious

'cause' for his crying, it was a relatively simple matter to meet his needs.

As he developed, however, there were further sources of worry. His lack of interest in others began to be very obvious and seemed to be increasing rather than diminishing. When held he seemed to resist the hold, often arching his body away from the contact and always looking through or past the person trying to make contact with him, whether this was an adult or a child – including his three-year-old brother.

His mother was breast-feeding him as she had done his brother but, although she found it difficult to specify in what way, she found the experience with Peter far less satisfying. He took as long to suckle but that seemed to be because of general slowness rather than the bursts of sucking followed by pauses that had characterised the feeding process with his brother. His mother did not understand the significance of this, but she was aware that it was far harder to feel 'connected' to Peter as she fed him and she found herself with time to read books and newspapers at the same time, in place of the absorption she had felt with her first child. She talked about this with her husband and with friends but was reassured that it was different with a second child and that she was probably just more confident now and able to take things for granted. Later, after diagnosis, she would look back and examine her own behaviour over this period with anxiety and some guilt in case it was her behaviour that had created her child's difficulties in becoming attached.

In fact, of course, the reverse is true. It was her child's failure to cue her normal and natural responsiveness that was at the root of the problem; she was ready to interact with her child, but this instinctive behaviour needed to be triggered and sadly in this case it was not. If it had been possible to detect the autism then, the mother might have been supported to interact with her child more deliberately, but this would have needed specific training and support, even then, because it would not be the normal process and would feel unnatural for that reason.

Eventually, Peter's difficulties became more tangible and his mother sought help from the health visitor and then her GP. At the first developmental test, there were sufficient signs of both delay and oddness for Peter to be referred for further testing. Deafness was suspected but eventually ruled out when Peter showed extreme sensitivity to the turning pages of a book (which he liked to flap rapidly between his hands, rocking his whole body and squealing with delight at the same time), while ignoring attempts to attract his attention with rattles and toys. He sat up at the correct time and showed good hand-eye co-ordination but he took a long time to crawl and when he did so he did not use his knees but scuttled around the floor with minimal contact— using fingertips and toes only. He began to show extreme rages at any frustration and would cry for hours in a state from which there seemed to be no way of rescuing him and where there was no way of comforting him.

His turning away from others now seemed more deliberate and he would often close his eyes and block his ears when others were trying to interact with him. He would react with what seemed like a mixture of pain and fear when taken shopping or to any busy place with bright lighting and lots of noise. He continued to sleep very little but no longer was happy just to lie there. Sometimes he would wail; sometimes he would bang his head against the headboard of the cot until his mother could bear it no longer.

He had developed no speech sounds or babbling and did not point either to indicate his needs or to draw attention to something. In spite of no other sign of using or understanding language, he would sometimes (often when alone, but able to be overheard) come out with a short phrase perfectly articulated with the exact intonation used in the original, usually from a TV commercial or an overheard phrase said with emphasis. Altogether it became clear that the child had significant difficulties despite the best parenting from loving parents.

When the dual diagnosis of sld and autism was made it was suggested to the parents that Peter's main problem was his difficulty in learning and his autism was described as being 'autistic features', thus implying to his parents and others that these were in some way secondary and peripheral. This, allied to the fact that the only facility offered was a nursery attached to a school for children with sld, determined where Peter was placed, rather than any detailed or informed assessment of his special educational needs. A statement of his special needs was made, but the parents had no reason to query the placement, since they had accepted that the sld were paramount and the school had good resources and seemed approachable and helpful. The parents were also exhausted by this point (Peter was now three and a half) and were pleased to hand over some responsibility to people whom they saw as 'experts'.

Schools for children with sld can be very good environments for children with autism and sld (Jordan *et al.*, 1999), but this is only so if the needs of such children are recognised and there is some expertise in the school for meeting those needs. That was not the case in the school which Peter attended. He might have been able to benefit from the lively atmosphere of the school, if he had been given initial support and training in tolerating this busy atmosphere and in learning the survival skills he would need in that environment. The school, however, understood 'equality of treatment' to mean treating all the children in the same way rather than finding individual ways of ensuring 'equality of access' for all. Thus, their view was that Peter would need to learn to adjust and that this would best be achieved by insisting on him participating fully in the life of the school in the same way as the other children, including attendance at assemblies, toleration of group teaching, interesting and varied visual displays (usually related to past learning experiences rather than what was required at present) and spoken instructions, repeated with increasing insistence (and often rephrasing) when met with failure to respond.

All the school practices were perfectly sound for most children with sld, although there may have been children, other than those with additional autism, who would also have benefited from a more individually based approach. As will become apparent from future chapters in this book, however, they are not likely to be helpful for children with autism, especially for those like Peter with additional sld. In such an environment he became increasingly stressed and disturbed and this began to show in challenging behaviour, first at home (as is often the case) and then at school.

Not only was his behaviour becoming more disturbed, but he was also failing to learn, and the parents became increasingly dissatisfied with what was provided and the level of support they received. They joined a group of parents of children with autism and began to see autism-specific services as the only way forward. The school by this time was also finding Peter's challenging behaviour difficult to accommodate, since it proved unresponsive to their normal behavioural techniques for managing difficult behaviour. The relationship with the parents had broken down with a lack of trust on both sides, the school characterising the parents as being unable to accept their child's learning difficulties whereas the parents characterised the school as failing to recognise their son's autism. At a review meeting, when Peter was seven, it was mutually agreed that the school was no longer able to meet Peter's needs and a specialist placement was sought.

It took some time for this to be arranged, since most specialist places have waiting lists. When Peter was eight he was excluded from the school following an incident when he badly head-butted a member of staff, resulting in her hospitalisation. This made it more difficult to find a suitable placement and Peter ended up at home for eighteen months, with a few hours of home-tutoring a week. His behaviour during this period became beyond the management of his parents and he was given tranquillisers that further reduced his capacity to learn and to cope, while doing very little to make his behaviour more manageable. By the time a place became available, Peter was coming up for secondary transfer and, in view of his now extremely difficult behaviour, a 52-week residential school was sought and obtained.

Peter's parents were by now not only exhausted but thoroughly demoralised and deskilled. They tried to maintain their involvement with their son but his school was a long way away and they did not by this time feel confident of their own capacity to look after their son. Peter settled into this school and did reasonably well, although perhaps not as well as he might have done had his true needs been addressed from the start. His learning was now completely dependent on the structured environment provided by the school and as he moved into adulthood it was clear that he would need a similarly structured environment for the rest of his life. The final outcome, then, is not tragic, but nor is it ideal either for Peter or for his family. It is hard to say how different the outcome could have been. After all, Peter has significant special educational needs arising from both his autism and his sld. What it does illustrate is that it is not sufficient just to pay attention to the sld and that good well-resourced facilities for children with sld are not necessarily sufficient for children with autism.

Summary

Autism is being used in this book as a shorthand for 'autistic spectrum disorders', but the population addressed by the book are those with autism and additional sld. In spite of many misconceptions over the years, it is now clear that autism can co-exist with general learning difficulties and sometimes these will be severe and even profound. Common to all individuals with autistic spectrum disorders are a triad of developmental impairments, but the way these are expressed will vary significantly with individual differences. It is important to recognise the implications of both the autism diagnosis and the sld when determining special educational needs; it is also important to know the individual and how they learn and make sense of the world. Above all, it is important to recognise that autism leads to a difference in development, not a just a delay, and approaches for children with sld (no matter how effective for children without autism) need to be adapted to take account of that difference.

Further reading

JORDAN, R. (1997). *The Education of Children with Autism.* Paris: UNESCO Guides for Special Education.
PEETERS, T. (1997). *Autism: From theoretical understanding to educational intervention.* London: Whurr.
WING, L. (1996). *The Autistic Spectrum: A guide for parents and professionals.* London: Constable.

2 Characteristic Behaviour and Development

In Chapter 1, two sisters with autism and sld, Amy and Sarah, were briefly described. Although it was clear that they had aspects of development in common, it was also clear that the triad of impairments that characterise autism had very different expression in each girl. The main effect of autism is that it interferes with the process of socialisation by which cultural meanings are transferred across generations. Apart from the different personalities, levels of general and linguistic ability and different experiences, children with autism will also differ from one another because each one will have had to make sense of their own experiences for themselves, without the benefit of this cultural transmission. We recognise autism as a developmental disorder, but we need to think about what this means when understanding individuals with autism.

The fact that autism is a developmental disorder has three main consequences for how autism is seen in any individual. These are discussed below.

Compensation

When one meets a child (or even more so an adult) with a developmental disorder, whatever the age, one does not see a list of the 'symptoms' of that particular disorder. Rather, one sees how that person has lived with the disorder, adjusted to it and compensated for it. When considering autism, then, one does not see a textbook account of autism but the *effects* for that individual of having lived with autism throughout his or her life. As is often the case in autism, it is perhaps helpful to take the analogy of a sensory disability, such as congenital blindness. If one is blindfolded, one can get some idea of how the world appears to the blind person, but it is a very imperfect notion. Blindness is not sightedness minus sight; congenitally blind people will have developed alternative ways of understanding the world around them and will do better at, for example, finding their way around than those who are sighted but who are wearing blindfolds.

In the same way, people with autism are not the same as people with social understanding who have failed to acquire social skills for some reason, or who have withdrawn after some trauma. When we see something, for example, we cannot avoid seeing the meanings our culture has transmitted. We have to work very hard to step outside our cultural and habitual mode of seeing, and it is normal for us to 'see' the world according to the meaning we expect to see; it is very hard to see it in any other way. Just as it is hard to imagine how the world appears to the congenitally blind, it is even more difficult to imagine how the world would appear to those with autism, who do not share perspectives with others, and so do not learn (or only learn with difficulty) to see the world as others see it. For them, the way the light shines on an object may be of greater significance than the particular identity of an object, and the same object may not be recognised under different degrees of illumination. Or it may be that the shape of an object is more 'visible' than its function or its social meaning. Many children with autism, for example, find it easier to do a puzzle picture upside down so that they can concentrate on the shape and not be distracted by (to them) meaningless or distracting pictures.

What does this mean in practice, when living or working with individuals with autism? Well, the main implication is that apparently bizarre or puzzling behaviour does have meaning and function for the child with autism, but that meaning is not necessarily the one normally attributed to it. We must avoid 'reading' behaviour too literally. Sometimes, as in the case of the puzzle above, understanding that the child has a unique perspective helps to explain their apparent highly developed skill in a particular area, compared to a generally low level of functioning. It also explains why a child may show a great ability to concentrate on something they themselves find fascinating, yet find it impossible to concentrate for more than a few seconds on a task selected by others. Just as we may not be able to see the attraction of the railway track or bit of fluff, so they will have problems in understanding our focus of interest in the task we have set.

It also offers a more useful perspective when dealing with some kinds of difficult behaviour. For example, we may see a child with autism behaving in a way that, in another child, would be a clear example of aggression. Of course the effects of the behaviour may be the same; it may hurt as much and we will need to control it, just as we would with any child. But we stand a much greater chance of managing the behaviour successfully, if we try to understand the meaning and function of the behaviour for the child, so that we can work out how to avoid its occurrence or how to teach a more acceptable alternative.

It is in fact very rare for a child with autism to display aggression as we normally use the term, although they can certainly show difficult and even violent behaviour which might be considered aggressive if seen in someone else. Yet the child with autism seldom, if ever, directs his or her violent actions with purposeful intent of hurting another. Rather, the violent act may result from blind panic, when something unexpected or frightening occurs, or from frustration, when something that is expected fails to materialise, or a learned habitual response fails to produce the expected result. The person with autism is reacting without planning or deliberation, so is not going to be deterred in the future if the behaviour is punished, and will find it impossible just to inhibit what is for them a 'natural' response. We have to try to understand the behaviour, not to condone it, but so we can prevent future occurrences.

Transactional effects

Autism is recognised, in part, by the way it makes us feel when interacting with the person with autism. It affects the development of the child, of course, but it also has effects on parents, teachers, carers, brothers and sisters, classmates and indeed anyone who is involved with the child. The effect is marked but also intangible, so that other children, for example, may not be able to say what is wrong, but know instinctively that the child with autism is 'odd', 'different', 'strange'. The effect is enhanced if the child has no obvious abnormalities, as is usually the case in autism, although those with additional severe learning difficulties may show some signs of whatever has led to their general cognitive impairments.

Having a child with any form of disability has an effect on parents, and there are well identified stages in adjustment, when the parents may grieve for the 'normal' child they have lost. With all other forms of disability, however, no matter how severe, there is comfort to be had from being able to help one's child and seeing the results of one's efforts, no matter how slow the development. It is hard for parents and there are times when the pain returns (as other children pass examinations, get jobs, leave home, get married and so on). Each milestone may be a reminder of the loss, but for parents of a child with sld without autism, there are also compensations. The very dependency, that may be a source of grief, can also provide compensation in the knowledge that one is still needed and has an important role in furthering the child's development and adding to the quality of his or her life. Then, as other children reach adolescence, there may be comfort in knowing one can help keep the child secure from many dangers, and many parents even come to appreciate the particular attributes of their child with sld and feel they gain from seeing the world through these eyes of innocence and the joy that is obtained from simple pleasures.

Some of these compensations apply to the child with autism and sld, but others are cruelly denied. Most telling of all is the fact that, in spite of his or her devastating disability, there may be no obvious way of helping your child, and professionals you turn to for advice may be equally bemused. It may even be that other people, in their ignorance, blame the parents for their child's condition. It is hard to imagine a crueller situation than to be told your child has autism, but then to be given no way of helping your child, and to find that the steps one takes intuitively may not work and may even appear to make things worse. That is the true devastation of autism. The very skills and natural nurturing tendencies that make one a good parent of other children or a good teacher or carer may not only not work with the child with autism but may further upset the child or cause more withdrawal or fear. It is not surprising if parents then become desperate to get help for their child and so become vulnerable to all kinds of claims, especially when there is a delay following diagnosis when nothing appears to be happening and the situation is deteriorating.

There are also particular difficulties in autism that are hard to understand and can be very hurtful (especially to parents) when we use our normal frame of reference. One such difficulty is the failure to develop trust. Children with autism do not develop an understanding of people as people, so they do not learn to trust people (such as parents) in the way that is so important in normal development. They have to put their trust in things and ordered events that they can understand and rely on, and that is why they become so attached to routines and so distraught when routines are disturbed. The effects of this on parents is illustrated by the example below.

In a parent workshop, a particular mother had three children, all of whom had some degree of special need and two of whom had an autistic spectrum disorder, the youngest one having autism and additional sld. In spite of all the difficulties she had to face, this mother was a determined, cheerful person who nearly always had something positive to contribute to the group in terms of strategies she had developed and problems she had overcome. However, one day she came to the group in a very distressed state with great scratch marks down one side of her face. She explained what had happened.

She had developed a routine with her youngest son every Tuesday: they would go swimming together in the afternoon, stop on the way back outside a shop with a green and white awning and buy an ice-cream, and then go on to collect her other children from school. On the day before the workshop, the two parking spaces outside the shop were taken, the first time this had happened. As she approached them, then, the mother said, 'We'll have to park across the road to get you your ice-cream' but, as she turned the steering wheel, her young son let out a screech and leaned forward and scratched her down the side of her face. She was hurt physically, but also, more deeply, emotionally. 'I always get him his ice-cream, I was going to get him his ice-cream, I told him I was going to get him his ice-cream, why couldn't he trust me?'

That mother had to be helped to understand that her son was not judging her as untrustworthy; he could not trust her because he had no understanding of her as a person worthy (or unworthy, for that matter) of trust. He had to rely on what he could understand—not her, not her words and not (although he might have done if older or with less severe learning difficulties) her characteristic behaviour; he put his trust in stopping outside the shop with the green and white awning. So, any deviation from that, in his eyes, meant that he was not going to get his ice-cream, no matter what anyone said or did. Once we understand that, we can help to give him a more manageable item to trust, since we cannot control parking spaces in life. He was taught to exchange a picture of an ice-cream for his ice-cream until the picture came to 'mean' ice-cream. Then, in a situation where giving the ice-cream must be delayed, he can be given the picture and learn to trust that the ice-cream will follow. It also meant that he had started a process of communication which could be used for many other situations and expanded.

It is not just parents who experience hurt and dismay in their interactions with their child with autism, however. Professionals also can become very disturbed and suffer a sense of becoming de-skilled, when their professional skills, developed over many years of successful practice, no longer seem to work with the child with autism. Professionals may react by feeling that working with a child with autism is just too difficult for them or insufficiently rewarding, they reject the child as being inappropriately placed in their setting or leave that setting themselves. They also need help to understand that their professional skills are not wasted, but need to be adapted to meet this new challenge. They may not be able, as they have with others, to rely on developing a relationship with a child before expecting to teach the child anything, nor to teach through that relationship. They will have to learn how to teach without that relationship, but will find that the relationship may develop through the teaching. As is often the case in autism, we often have to do things 'back to front'. Trying to relate to someone who does not know what you are for seldom works, but once you have demonstrated your use (through teaching them how to do something in which they are interested), they can learn to share information and pleasure with you.

Secondary 'handicaps'

Often what is seen in terms of behaviour, or missing behaviour, in autism is not a direct result of the autism itself but a secondary effect of missing out on experiences necessary for development. Humans are born with very underdeveloped brains and with very few instinctual behaviours. This means that most human behaviour and understanding is learnt in the early years through a process of socialisation. In autism, it is this process of socialisation that is disturbed and consequently much of this early learning is missing or takes a different and unusual form. In the past it has been difficult to determine exactly how children with autism develop as babies, other than from parental report.

How parents perceive their babies depends on many factors such as their experience of typically developing babies, their expectations, and their capacity to observe behaviour. Early development is often reported to be 'normal' and this may be the case, but on closer examination it sometimes turns out that there have been differences that may not have seemed significant at the time but that can have a long-term effect on development. Severe learning difficulties, of course, will produce more noticeable effects on early development but they can then serve further to disguise or mask the more subtle effects of the autism.

The existence of video cameras and the growing library of films of mothers interacting with their young babies (often without any idea at that stage that their child has autism, although severe learning difficulties are usually apparent from an earlier stage) has had a great effect on our understanding of the importance of these early interactions and how they may go wrong in autism. There are also some studies in early interaction in laboratory settings that have enabled more systematic investigation of the effects of mother and child factors on the development of early interaction and how this may be disturbed in autism (Hobson, 1993; Trevarthen *et al.*, 1996). It is important to note that this is very different from earlier (completely mistaken) views that autism is somehow caused through the inadequacy of mothering. It is not the mother's behaviour that leads to the disturbed behaviour of the child, but rather the child's failure to engage with the mother which leads to the loss of these invaluable opportunities for learning.

A particularly instructive video is of a mother with twins, one of whom later turns out to have autism (they are not identical) and the other does not, but at the time of the video the mother does not yet know that anything is wrong. She has set aside time to play with each child and she is ready (biologically and psychologically) to do this. Playing with your baby is one of the few instinctual behaviours we have, so that we are not taught how to do this and we are not consciously aware of the triggers needed to start us off and to keep it going. The trigger that elicits the play behaviour in the mother is in fact eye contact. Thus, the mother picks up her little typically developing baby, makes eye contact readily and goes into her routine. Watching such routines, it is apparent that this is an extremely rich learning experience, but it is worth considering some of the key aspects of development that are fostered in such interchanges.

Emotional sharing
Empathy does not develop through a conscious process of working out that other people are happy/unhappy and so on; it develops from shared experience of emotions, and we are biologically adapted to have those experiences. If a baby is crying in its cot, we can lean over with wide eyes and a smile and begin to nod (with or without saying anything) and mostly the baby will stop crying and begin to smile back. The baby is programmed biologically to do this and, indeed, if the baby wants to continue crying s/he has to close her/his eyes or turn away to resist this pull to respond to the nodding smiling face with a corresponding smile. Equally (although, one hopes, less likely), if the baby is smiling happily in her/his cot and we lean over with a deep frown, the baby will respond with a down-turned mouth and eventual tears. The facial muscles that are involved in these changes of facial expression have effects on the emotional experience of the baby—through the mediation of hormones. When we smile, for example, we release endomorphins which have the effect of

making us feel happier (hence the therapeutic value of smiling and laughing). Thus, an inbuilt mechanism to mirror certain facial expressions (which we know is present in the newborn from a few days—if not hours—old) has the effect of ensuring that we also share emotional experiences with our interacting partner. This is the precursor to bonding with that individual and also learning about the experience of emotion (seeing our own feelings reflected in the face of the other) and empathy. As we know, it is a key defining feature of autism that people with autism have great difficulty in establishing empathy with others or in understanding emotions, their own or others.

Turn-taking
Turn-taking is one of the most obvious features of early mother-child interactions. Even when the baby appears to have little behaviour to contribute to the interchange, mothers pause to allow the baby's contribution. This might only be a look or a gurgle or even a burp, but it is responded to by the mother as if it had meaning and were a valuable part of the interaction. In time, of course, treating the behaviour of the baby 'as if' it were a meaningful communicative behaviour makes it become so and the baby learns to take a turn in an interaction and to learn the cues that mean it is her/his turn. Often these will have been exaggerated, such as the rising pitch of the mother as she leads up to a pause. Eye gaze and the characteristics of an 'expectant' facial expression contribute additional cues to the baby that a contribution is needed. Even able people with autism who develop good structural spoken language have difficulties in turn-taking in conversations, never recognising when a pause occurs (and, thus, often interrupting others) and not supplying pauses in their own contributions so that they appear to talk 'at' rather than 'to' others.

Cause and effect
The interaction between mother and child not only involves each taking a turn but each having a noticeable effect on the other. The human face is amazingly expressive and adaptable, providing rich sources of feedback to the infant on her/his own actions.

Mother/baby interactions emphasise this learning, with the mother copying the relevant actions and expressions of the infant, feeding them back to the infant, exaggerating and amplifying them and building them into meaningful and predictable routines. In this way, the baby develops a sense of her/himself as an agent having an effect on the world and able to initiate as well as respond to the environment. This sense of agency is part of self-awareness, and involves an emotional connection with one's actions and their effects, being a precursor to creative and spontaneous actions, to control and monitor one's own behaviour (executive functions) and to develop memories of one's own involvement in events (personal episodic memory). Russell (1996) and Jordan (1999) both see problems in this sense of agency as a crucial aspect of autism and people with autism certainly have problems with spontaneity, executive functions and personal episodic memory.

Modulation in levels of arousal

This important aspect of interactions between mother and infant has only recently received much attention in relation to autism, yet it is a feature of such interactions that has been studied extensively in relation to the effects of maternal depression, for example. In most cases of interaction, mother and baby are beautifully tuned into the arousal level of their partner, and this 'tuning' is performed by both. If the mother is 'over-eager', for example, the baby will perform actions (closing eyes, turning away) to reduce her/his own level of stimulation and so avoid getting over-aroused. If, on the other hand, the mother is suffering from a post-natal depression and consequently understimulates her baby, the baby tries to increase arousal by seeking stimulation – leaning forward more, actively seeking eye contact and so on. If mother remains depressed for a long period, then the baby remains in a chronic state of under-arousal which itself has an effect on development. However, the developmental effects are not just those of under- or over-arousal itself, but the learning involved in making the adjustments to behaviour to maintain an appropriate and even level of arousal. In autism, this learning seems not to have occurred, so that people with autism suffer from states of both under- and over-arousal without any spontaneous mechanisms for adjusting their own levels of arousal to fit the circumstances. Sometimes they may use external ways of doing this (such as holding an object pressed into the palms of their hands to reduce arousal) or revert to primitive methods such as looking away from eye contact or blocking ears.

Having examined the developmental importance of this early playful interaction between mother and child, let us return to the mother of twins who, having engaged successfully with her non-autistic son, now turns to her baby with autism. She is equally ready to engage, but, sadly, her baby is not. He is unable to give her the eye-contact trigger she needs in order to go into her instinctual pattern of play behaviour. She does not understand about the trigger, so she cannot override this but merely keeps on trying to make eye contact, ducking and diving in her attempts, but all to no avail. At the end of ten minutes of this unsatisfactory struggle, mother gives up and returns her baby to his cot. The baby does not appear to mind, but it is not just a pleasurable experience that has been lost. Think of all the missed learning in terms of emotional sharing, turn-taking, cause and effect and modulation of levels of arousal. Ten valuable minutes have been missed now, but this loss is multiplied by other ten-minute sessions in the day, by day, by week, by month, by year. What can start as a very small and apparently insignificant difference, such as an inability to gain eye contact, can, in this way, be transformed into a large developmental difference.

Similar missed opportunities for early learning can lead to equally devastating developmental consequences. Thus, children with autism are seldom able to adapt to the intentions of others, so that they do not play with others, unless taught or at least prompted. Once again, it is not simply a matter of missing out on current pleasurable occupations but of the developmental consequences that may ensue. When we see a child who engages only in solitary play, then, we see someone who is missing some of the learning opportunities that they need, perhaps even more than others. Once more, they miss shared interests and emotions, turn-taking, cause and effects on others, plus the practice of social roles (mother and father, mother and baby, teacher and pupil,

Batman and Robin), the language that accompanies these roles, and many of the social rules and adjustments that govern social interactions (such as politeness, adjustment of language to fit context, and sharing).

Perhaps, even more importantly, in failing to engage in social interactions with brothers and sisters or their peers, they also fail to engage with emotions (jealousy, spite, humour) that can be labelled in context and tied to mental states which the child is currently experiencing. It is not then surprising if children with autism grow up without an understanding of the language of mental states or how to use them in predicting the behaviour of others. It is difficulty in this domain that is referred to as a problem with developing a 'theory of mind' in autism, but this may not be a cognitive failure as such, rather a failure to engage in the opportunities for its acquisition. This view is supported by the fact that other children who miss out on these learning opportunities also exhibit these 'theory of mind' difficulties; this is true of deaf children born to hearing parents, some children with severe language and learning difficulties and even children with conduct disorders who do not play readily with other children or do not attend to the language accompanying these interactions. Typically developing children also show earlier development of a theory of mind (that is, they understand about mental states) if they have a brother or sister up to six years either older or younger than themselves and if they have a parent who talks about emotions as they are being experienced.

All of this can present a depressing picture when one considers all the learning opportunities that are missed by the child with autism. If the child has additional sld, the chances of them 'catching up' on all this missed learning is clearly further reduced. Yet the knowledge that many of the characteristics of autism are not irreversibly 'inbuilt' into the condition, but arise as secondary effects, provides in fact a hopeful message. The more we understand about how these aspects of development normally arise, the more we should be able to provide the teaching experiences necessary for the child with autism and sld to learn these skills and understanding. If we are able to start early enough we may be able to prevent some of these secondary effects occurring at all and in any case we should be able to implement some compensatory teaching.

Is it ever too late?

As has been shown above, when dealing with a developmental disorder, it obviously helps minimise difficulties if effective intervention occurs as early as possible. Yet there are numerous examples where recognition of an older child's or even adult's real difficulties, followed by intervention to meet those needs, can produce remarkable and lasting benefits. In the past, the literature was rather depressing in terms of outcome – suggesting that little could be done other than providing a protected environment. A combination of greater understanding of the nature of the disorder and better strategies for working with such individuals has transformed the picture. We now know that people with autism and sld continue to learn and develop throughout life and many can learn even complex skills, if we can find the right way to teach them for that individual. The growth of information technology has increased the opportunities for this to happen.

At the same time, it is important to recognise sensible and appropriate goals for individuals at different stages of life. The goal of interventions should always be functional for the individual in terms of current and future quality of life. A means, and understanding, of communication, for example, is a priority for the individual with autism and sld at any stage of life. What that means of communication should be, however, may change over time. It is important, as later chapters will show, that we provide a means of communication from as early as possible, that does not depend on the child developing spoken language. If the child reaches adolescence without developing speech, then it is more sensible and useful to concentrate on this alternative means (such as symbols or signs) for their own expression of communicative intent, while it will still add to the person's quality of life if we continue to try to develop their understanding of speech.

In social development, also, we need to address difficulties in understanding and tolerating others throughout life. Yet we also need to think of the balance of the programme that we provide for adults in this area. Social skills are always going to be an area of great difficulty for this group and an area of development in which they are likely to gain limited success. In continuing with a social development programme into adult life, therefore, we need to be very clear that what we are doing enhances, rather than detracts from, the quality of life of those adults. It may be important, for example, that they learn to be comfortable with other people and to co-operate with those who are supporting their lifestyle. It is far less certain that it is in their best interests to continue to go through a formal social skills programme, however, which may just add to their overall confusion and distress.

Whatever decision is made must depend on individual need but it is just as problematic to go on providing a form of social skills teaching, regardless of the benefit to the individual, as it would be to deny such a programme to someone who could benefit. To understand this dilemma we need to think of our own most difficult subject at school and how much relief we felt when we could at last stop struggling with it. Imagine if, instead of being allowed to leave it behind and get on with those aspects of learning that we enjoy or which are useful to us, we are made to continue with it throughout life, until we have reached a standard which, realistically, we will never manage. Imagine the depression and frustration this would cause and how it might interfere with our actual success in other areas and our feelings of self-worth and efficacy. Of course, social understanding, like understanding of speech, is important to continue to develop, because it does impinge on so much of the individual's life. What we need to think about is how we can arrange a quality of life for adults with autism and sld that is not dependent on them developing social skills themselves.

Summary

Given that autism and sld are both developmental disorders, specific developmental processes are clearly important in understanding the conditions. Severe learning difficulties mean that all aspects of development are also delayed but autism means that development will not only be delayed, but deviant. Understanding the behaviour of an individual with autism and sld, then, depends on understanding how that behaviour has been shaped by the processes of compensation and secondary handicaps and also the transactional nature of development. All this means that early intervention has the most likelihood of success in preventing adverse developmental influences but people with autism and sld continue to develop and can benefit from effective intervention throughout life. The principles underlying programmes of intervention at any age should be that it is geared to individual needs and promotes current and future quality of life.

3 Fostering Social Interaction

Social difficulties in autism

Social interaction is one of the key areas of development through which autism is recognised. Problems in this area of development have particular behavioural manifestations when the child has both autism and sld. A central problem in autism is in the difficulty in processing social information, although there is uncertainty as to whether this results from more basic difficulties in processing information (of which social information is just a particular example) or whether it is this difficulty that leads to other problems in processing information (one route for this being the secondary effects of the social difficulty as given in Chapter 2).

Whatever the developmental route, it is clear that people with autism do suffer difficulties in processing social information, which interacts with any learning difficulties and affects further learning in two fundamental ways. Normally we process social information at speed, through special dedicated pathways in the brain. If there is disturbance or failure in these pathways, then the person with autism will have to use other pathways for general cognitive processing in order to process social information.

This means such processing will be far slower than is normally the case and it will also mean that the person with autism (unlike the normal case) will be unable to process social information at the same time as other information. If we now add in the effects of a learning difficulty, where general cognitive processing is slower and more limited, then such effects on development and functioning are amplified. The child with autism and sld will then have great difficulty in processing any social information, will require far more time to do so and, if they are required to do something else at the same time will not be able to do so at all.

The implications for an educational system that relies on personal teaching, and teaches in social groups, will be obvious, but will be followed up in later chapters. Since education usually takes place in a social context, there will also be management problems affecting children's access to all aspects of the curriculum.

The message for all forms of teaching (at home or at school) is that tasks need to be taught with minimal social information to process. It may seem natural to us to sit facing a child to teach her/him to do up a button, or draw a line, but for the child this may simply be too distracting; coping with our encouraging facial expression and 'helpful' gesture (neither of which are intelligible to the child with autism) will just distract the child from the relevant cues to which s/he needs to attend to complete the task. If we then offer comments in the form of verbal prompts (or nagging), this will add yet another level of confusion and potential distress, making it even harder for the child to do what we are urging her/him to do. Teachers and carers learn to work from behind, with minimal language, and try to structure the task so that it is visually obvious what needs to be done, without the need for prompting or further social or physical guidance.

When trying to teach social responses, on the other hand, we need to focus on that, so that no other cognitive demands are made. If we are trying to get the child to play a simple game with others, for example, we will need to make sure the child with autism is first taught to perform the 'game' on his own or (if that is impossible) one-to-one with an adult. Only when the child has mastered the game itself, will it be possible to teach her/him to play it with others.

Direct teaching of social skills will also be required since there will be many aspects of social development that will not occur spontaneously and many compensatory strategies that will be needed. There is the further practical difficulty that teaching a social behaviour appropriate to a child at some point in her/his life (e.g. teaching her/him to accept and return embraces so that s/he no longer rebuffs her/his mother) may take so long that by the time it is achieved it is no longer appropriate (the child is a teenager).

Social interaction inevitably involves two people. If people with autism have a problem in socially interacting with us, then do we not have an equal problem in socially interacting with them? We are unlikely to make much progress, therefore, if we only concentrate on changing the behaviour of the person with autism. We need to change our own behaviour as well, and to create environments that foster social interaction.

Setting social priorities
There is a danger in looking at all the missing social skills in autism and developing teaching programmes to teach each one in turn. This might be seen as a deficit model, and is not only depressing but also inefficient. The key difficulty is in teaching social skills without social understanding. If we just try to teach these missing skills without the child understanding what s/he is doing or why, our chances of success are low; even if the child learns to do what we are teaching, the skill may never develop beyond a habit. In that sense it will only happen when it is prompted or cued and it will not generalise to new situations. It may also place the child at risk, as will be seen below. We stand a better chance of giving the child a more functional skill if we can assist the child in understanding what the behaviour is for and how it relates to other situations.

Nevertheless, there are ways of behaving in social situations that are so important in terms of allowing the child (and the family) to lead anything like a full life, that the child may need to be taught these as habits, while continuing to work on the understanding. As we saw in Chapter 2, the children's social difficulties often prevent them participating in the very situations they need in order to develop their social skills further. Fear and confusion never reduce, because the child never has a positive experience of these situations. A priority, therefore, is to teach basic 'entry' skills which allow this participation, and then to use positive experiences as opportunities for further learning.

Experiences, such as that relayed by Park (1986), show how a behavioural programme can be useful if it uses something that is meaningful to the child to draw his or her attention to social stimuli, which otherwise would have little meaning. It is common, for example, that children with autism and sld do not pay much attention to other children (except in a negative way, if they interfere with them) but begin making relationships with adults—especially those in charge in a situation. One reason for this is the very pragmatic one that it is the adult who is more likely to be the one in charge of things (deciding on activities, distributing snacks), in which the child with autism is most interested, and whose function s/he understands. Thus, a way of getting the child with autism and sld to attend to other children is to redress the power by putting other children in charge of choosing activities from time to time or in distributing snacks and other rewards.

It may be necessary to develop some rules that have a wide currency, such as 'there needs to be a communicative partner in any communicative exchange', although this may have to be continually demonstrated in practical contexts. This should help the child learn not to sign under the table or give a message to an empty room, although it may take the child with autism and sld a lot of direct teaching to develop a general rule from all the many instances of the rule you will have to teach. There may also be a point in teaching the child social rituals for greeting others or apologising, even if the child does not fully understand what is going on, because that will help others develop a more positive view of them. Yet there is little point in teaching the child something like waving 'bye-bye', if the child is unable to recognise the social signals of someone's departure or someone's wave, that would make the response appropriate. If the child will always need to be told to 'wave bye-bye', then the point of doing so will be lost. We have to try to teach meanings, wherever possible, rather than meaningless rituals.

We can characterise the setting of priorities as teaching directed at:

- removing any barriers to the child's interaction with others
- helping the child understand the function of social acts.

Dangers in 'teaching to deficits'
One problem with identifying a particular missing skill or 'deficit', and then teaching that, is that we are so focused on that skill, that we forget about the total situation. As an example of

this an adolescent boy of seventeen (Keith) attended a specialist school in London. He had severe autism and sld, but had made good progress with a structured curriculum, and was due to move on to a social education centre for adults with learning difficulties in the following year. He lived at home, and one of the problems with his transition to adulthood would be a greater problem in obtaining effective transport arrangements. The social service transport could not keep to the timetable of the taxi that took him to school, and this would present particular problems for his parents' work arrangements. It was agreed with the parents that a priority for his educational programme at school would be to teach Keith to use the public transport system (in particular, the Underground train system) to get from his home to the social education centre and to return.

Such a programme clearly involves many aspects of learning. There were all the tasks needed in finding the correct platform, purchasing the ticket, identifying the correct train, waiting safely on the platform and so on. These took a while to teach but were relatively straightforward compared to a significant difficulty in Keith's social behaviour, which was interfering with successful completion of the programme. Like many people with autism, Keith was very reluctant to share his space with others and so would not join others on a seat nor tolerate others joining him. Even then (the 1980s) this difficulty alone made using the Underground train impossible. Thus, teaching Keith to tolerate others joining him on a seat, and teaching him to go and sit next to others, became a key focus for his training programme at school.

Staff were inventive in their methods, getting relatives and friends to act as stooges in parks and other public places where they modelled and prompted Keith to tolerate others coming to sit next to them on public seating and teaching Keith to join others on such seats. Once that had been accomplished in open spaces like parks, it was generalised to the Underground train, with staff once more modelling and prompting the correct 'joining' behaviour on the train. Because it was impossible to make people (other than the stooges used in the original training) join Keith on empty seats, it was inevitable that later sessions concentrated on getting Keith to join others, already seated on the train.

So focused were the staff on training this, they forgot to put themselves in the shoes of the learner, or to see how others might interpret the behaviour they were in fact teaching.

After some six months or so of intensive training, it was decided that Keith was ready to make the journey on his own. Staff watched unobtrusively as he walked to the station, purchased the correct ticket, found the correct platform and waited appropriately on the platform, without dancing about near the edge as he had done prior to teaching. So far, so good. The train came along, Keith entered the carriage and the train progressed into the tunnel. It was only as the train drew away that the staff noticed that the carriage that Keith had entered was empty, apart from an elderly lady, sitting alone on a double seat. The events that followed, with hindsight, seem inevitable. Keith did what he had been trained to do; he joined the lady on her seat. The lady interpreted this behaviour (given the choice of alternative seating available) as threatening and, in a panic, pulled the communication cord, which stopped the train. This led to transport police investigating the incident and the staff, unable to gain access to the train which was now in the tunnel, were unable to intervene on Keith's behalf. Keith had a little speech but not to a level that would have enabled him to answer these hostile questions, or to understand what he was supposed to have done wrong. Of course, he had in fact done nothing wrong. He had done what he had been trained to do for the last six months.

When the staff were eventually able to rescue Keith, he had become severely traumatised by all the uproar and shouting, and had begun to lash out at the policemen as they tried to arrest him. It took almost a year to get him back to the stage where he was able to attempt the Underground train again. During that year, he had a more balanced programme, stressing the choice of when to sit alone and when to join others. It is easy to see that that is what should have been done from the start, but at the time staff became caught up in teaching the missing skill they had identified, and the broad context was lost.

It is not just that focusing on a deficit can lead us to neglect the broader picture. Another problem comes from the inappropriateness of some of the 'rules' we may derive in order to address an apparent deficit. Such a rule is 'always look at the person you are speaking to', derived from the observation that children with autism and sld may not look at the person talking to them—a fact that most people find disconcerting. Such rules may seem sensible and natural, but they can be misleading and their operation may be socially *dis*abling, since the child will not know the purpose of looking, and will not be able to time gazes appropriately.

The result is that the child with autism and sld who is taught to look, as a habit, without understanding, will learn to stare. They will often then look at others instead of their work, which is inefficient but, more alarmingly, as they grow older, their staring may make them vulnerable. The only two conditions (in Western societies at least) in which people stare deep into the eyes of others are as a sexual overture or as an expression of aggression. Both interpretations will make the person with autism and sld vulnerable, since they will be giving an unintended message, and will have no skills in dealing with the consequences. That is not to say that we should ignore the problem of the child not looking but we should address it in ways (as indicated in later chapters) that teach the purpose of looking and not just a meaningless performance.

Taking part in groups
Children with autism will have problems with self-reflection and indeed awareness of themselves either as individuals or as part of a group. They will need to be taught directly to act as part of a group beginning from a base of response to group commands; their understanding, however, is likely to remain well below the concept of 'group identity' that is needed if the child is to benefit from the group in the transition from child to adult. Early teaching will be to teach (through direct prompting) that the child should obey (or attend to, whichever is appropriate) when addressed by name (usually the easiest one to start with), by 'you' when accompanied by a direct look but not when the look is directed at someone else, and by the many different titles which are relevant. Such membership titles (each of which will need separate teaching) include titles such as 'the girls/boys', 'the blue group',

'the class', 'the school', 'the children', 'the family', 'the next person in the queue' and so on.

Recognising oneself as belonging to a group is one thing; enjoying and benefiting from group membership is another. In many cases the child with autism and sld may never develop friendship groups with peers. There will then be a need to compensate for the lack of those social skills that are gained through such peer relationships. Teachers may need to teach directly some of the 'transition skills' that groups of friends impart to aid the transition from childhood to adulthood. Thus they will have to make clear that some rules are sacrosanct (such as safety and health rules), while others (such as not eating between meals) may need to be 'bent' if the child is ever to fit in with society. Support through the sexual and emotional changes of adolescence will need to take account of the fact that the normal sources of reassurance and support, provided by friends, will be absent.

Video is not normally very useful as a teaching medium for children with autism and sld, since it can be almost as difficult to interpret as real life. Still videos (as with instant photographs) can be useful, however, in drawing things to such children's attention and helping them recognise social cues. There are exciting possibilities in the use of the more innovatory aspects of Information Technology, but these are still at the design stage. The major problem with computer-assisted learning is always the transfer to real-life situations, but interactive video, multimedia approaches and virtual reality may make this more likely. Certainly, communication aids via the computer can offer a very useful alternative to those who do not develop speech.

Fostering interaction

One aspect that can be addressed by education, as was suggested above, is to ensure that secondary handicaps do not occur because the child's social difficulties exclude him or her from the very situations that are needed for social learning to take place. Imitation of the child's spontaneous actions can be an effective strategy for getting the child to start to communicate. It helps individuals with autism to pay attention to others and to learn that they can modify their behaviour. The teacher or parent starts playing a game whereby they copy the child's noises or actions, timing the imitations and the pauses so that the child begins to notice and turn-taking is established. Some children with autism may resist this intrusion into their 'private' actions at first, but in time most accept it, and begin to like the fact that they have a way of controlling what the adult does. Once this is well established, the adult can begin to change the action or noise a little to see if the child can be persuaded to imitate that, and so begin to acquire the very useful skill of imitation.

Early intervention programmes in the UK now often focus on developing the interactive relationship between parents and the child with autism and sld, since this relationship is such an important precursor to others. 'Music-Assisted Communication has been used for this (Wimpory *et al.*, 1995; Christie *et al.*, 1992) but there are also approaches that train parents to develop these interactions for themselves. The Hanen method (Sussman, 2000) was developed for use by speech and language therapists in Canada. It has since been adapted to fit the needs of children with autism and is being used by professionals to help parents build and sustain early interactions with their children, in spite of the difficulties of the children. Parents come together for training in understanding their children and in ways of working with them. Home visits are then made and sessions videoed and used for further training that draws attention to interactions that are effective, and help the parents gain confidence by building on those.

There are a range of techniques in use in the UK now which have documented long-term gains in children with autism, based on this mutual enjoyment of interaction, using child-initiated actions. Good pro-social behaviour can be developed through play, as will be explored in later chapters. A more systematic teaching approach is that of 'Intensive Interaction' (Nind & Hewett, 1994). This has been used with individuals with profound and multiple learning difficulties who were not formally identified as having autism but whose behavioural description leaves little doubt that that was the case. The basis of the approach is to re-learn the basic earliest social interactions by slowing, simplifying and emphasising them to the point where some pleasurable response is obtained from the individual. This is then built upon to put the individual in charge of the interactive routine and thus enable him or her to stop, continue, extend or change it at will.

The Option approach or 'Son Rise' programme (Kaufman, 1994) was developed by parents in the USA and is based on a very similar idea as intensive interaction, except that it is an intensive home-based programme rather than one which is normally part of a special school curriculum. Like intensive interaction it is said to 'work' by going with the child and incorporating the child's actions into an interactive format which, like early dyadic interaction (between mother and child), puts the child in charge. Two 'success' stories are well documented (Kaufman, 1994), but there has been no systematic evaluation beyond an observational report (Jordan, 1990).

Music-assisted communication is now widely applied in the UK, and uses live music to emphasise and reinforce pro-social behaviour in pairs of either a child and the child's key worker, or a child and the child's parent. The music must be live, so that it can be continuously responsive to the child's actions, but in some situations the teacher or carer him/herself produces the music (usually by singing), when no music specialist is available. This has its problems but may also have advantages in drawing the child's attention to the actual interacting individual. It is not clear here whether the music is particularly relevant to the gains shown, or whether it is repeated structured interaction that 'works', and this is being investigated. Children with autism can often appreciate the structure of music, whereas they do not understand spoken language, so it is likely that music itself may be helpful in this way.

Teaching about emotions
Children with autism will need to learn about the emotions of others and of themselves, in situations that make the meanings clear. Mirrors can be used to draw the child's attention to their own emotional expressions that are unambiguous (so that the teacher does not mislabel them for the child) and to the contexts that have led to them. This means we have to be really careful about getting children to sing songs like 'If you're happy and

you know it clap your hands' through prompting a child who may not be happy at all, often quite the reverse. We may not be comfortable singing 'If you're miserable and you know it clap your hands' but this would be much better if it were indeed a truer reflection of how the child was actually feeling.

Drawing attention to a child's own actual and current emotion is far more effective than teaching the matching of schematic drawings of facial expressions to some label such as 'happy' or 'sad', which is unlikely to be related to knowledge of real situations. It is only once children have learnt to recognise and identify their own emotional states that they can begin to recognise those emotions in the facial expressions of others. Teaching that a stereotyped expression means 'happy' or 'sad' is misleading, and likely to make children more confused if they try to generalise their matching skill to the real world.

Understanding one's own emotions is also a precursor to managing their expression. The child will need to be taught ways of managing extreme emotional reactions, but it is important that the child be allowed the right to express emotions, and it is inappropriate expression rather than the emotion itself that needs to be tackled. It is inhumane, as well as ineffectual, to try to suppress emotional outbursts. What the teacher or carer needs to do is to recognise the emotion (and to help the child to do so), and its legitimacy, while giving the child a more acceptable mode of expression. And the 'new' way will have to be at the same developmental level as the old way, and—if it is going to act as a replacement—provide as much satisfaction for the child (in terms of its effect).

Example

Liam was a child with autism and sld who reacted to any frustration by head-banging. Parents are sometimes advised to ignore such expressions of frustration, on the grounds that attention might lead to the child increasing the behaviour in order to get attention. It is true that this may happen, and the child can come to recognise that head-banging can be an effective way of gaining control over others. Nevertheless, it is not safe to ignore, since the long-term consequences of head-banging, in terms of detached retinas and consequent blindness, are too severe. Unless the child knows another way of expressing frustration, ignoring is also unlikely to be effective in reducing the head-banging in reaction to frustration. The only effective long-term strategy is to teach the child another way of expressing frustration, and to do so in a way that does not give the child attention for the head-banging itself. At the same time, of course, we need to look at the conditions that led to Liam's frustration to try to reduce these conditions, by teaching Liam more skills or adjusting the environment to remove the source of frustration.

In this particular case, a situation was chosen where the source of Liam's frustration was clear. Liam had physical and visual impairments as well as his autism and sld, and he had a favourite object (a small wooden doll) which he liked to hold in his hand and twiddle in and out of his fingers. From time to time he would drop the doll and be unable to locate and retrieve it by his own efforts. In this situation he would scream and immediately start to head-bang until the doll was restored to him. He also head-banged in other situations, as is often the case when the child has a limited repertoire of behaviours to express a variety of emotions and in response to many different situations.

But this was a very good situation with which to start a programme of teaching him another way to express his emotion of frustration. The reasons for the frustration were not only clear, but Liam also gave a cue (his scream) to the imminence of his head-banging. Thus his mother could intervene to prevent the head-banging and prompt another response, without fear of rewarding the head-banging. The act that was chosen as an 'alternative' expression of his frustration was banging on a drum with his hands. The drum was placed in such a position that it also prevented Liam from gaining access to the floor with his head, should his mother not reach him in time to prompt the hand, rather than head, banging. The alternative act was at the same kind of level developmentally, and produced the same kind of immediate effect, as the behaviour it was meant to replace. Because it was at a simple developmental level, there did not need to be any period of training before prompting the child to perform the drum-banging.

It took three days of very constant vigilance on the part of his mother before Liam learnt to beat the drum in this particular situation rather than trying to head-bang. This was partial success, but it is not a good long-term solution because a drum will not always be available. However, giving Liam another way of expressing his frustration meant that he was then in a calmer state to begin to teach him a way of communicating his loss (of the doll), than if this had been attempted while he was still agitated by his frustration. As Liam took to the drumming, he began not to scream, which was welcome by the family but was a threat to the programme because there was no longer a signal of his frustration. It was, therefore, a priority to teach Liam to communicate (rather than just express) his frustration. He was taught to drum (which he was already doing as an expression of his emotion) and then to pass his mother (or whoever else attended to him) a tactile symbol that he was being taught means 'help'. Once he was beating his drum, waiting until someone came and then handing over the symbol (which took several months of teaching), it was judged Liam was ready to learn another way of attracting attention other than drumming. He was taught then to clap his hands once (otherwise hand-clapping can get out of hand and may itself become a form of self-injury, as an expression of frustration) and then wait and hand over his 'help' symbol as before.

At the same time as teaching the child more acceptable ways of expressing emotions, we need also to harness their emotions in their learning. As with all other groups, meaningful enjoyable experiences enhance learning, and, if we can also make these social, we shall improve social functioning. Teaching should aim to create the mutual enjoyment of tasks, through strategies such as working alongside the child rather than directing him or her, or joining in with what the individual is engaged in. For the most withdrawn, the teacher may need to use desensitisation techniques to enable the child to tolerate this, or the early interaction games as indicated above.

Helping the child to interact socially

Sharing attention

Apart from the problems, such as in Liam's case, above, of gaining attention before communicating, sharing attention is a vital precursor to engaging in social interactions. Children with autism and sld rarely attempt to share toys or direct an adult's attention by pointing or looking at objects, and nor do they automatically turn to what the adult is looking at, pointing to or holding up for the child. They appear to understand the use of the other person as a 'tool', and may often indicate something they want by pulling or pushing an adult (or part of an adult, such as a hand) towards the object they want, but cannot get for themselves. What they do not seem to understand is that the other person has a perspective of their own that could be shared or directed.

In order to start the process of social interaction, therefore, the child needs first to be taught to recognise attempts to gain their attention, and to respond to that. Before they can do this, however, they may need to learn to share the attention of others and to obtain and direct it where appropriate. It will be easier for the teacher or carer to join in with the child's focus of attention at first, rather than expect the child to recognise and join the attentional focus of the adult. It is a similar process to the early interactions between mothers and normally developing babies, where the mother comments on the activity the baby is engaged in ('It's a ball. Look it rolls! Wheee! There it goes! Mummy rolls the ball. Jamie roll the ball!' and so on), and does not expect the baby to change focus to a predetermined topic the mother wants to 'discuss'. The same sensitivity that the mother displays to the baby's interests will need to be used with the child with autism and sld beyond the age when this comes naturally, and will have to be a teaching style that influences all attempts to engage with the child socially, at home or at school.

This is especially true for the nonverbal child, where an effective teaching strategy is often to join in the activity in which the child is already engaged. This is the basis of intensive interaction, the son-rise programme and music-supported interaction, as shown above. It can be applied to all aspects of the curriculum, however, and not just to specific sessions for encouraging social interaction. If the child is painting a picture, for example, the teacher might also make his or her own picture, sitting alongside the child, instead of merely directing the child with instructions. This makes it easier to gain the child's attention in a relevant way, and has the added advantage of providing an ongoing model of what the child is to do without continually prompting or nagging the child to keep on task.

Preventing withdrawal
When children with autism and sld appear not to be interested in others, it may be because they do not know how to relate to others, and the methods described above for encouraging interaction should be used. It may be, however, that the problem is not in relating to people as such, but due to a preference for their own self-absorbing activities. This becomes an issue in enabling social interaction, nevertheless, if the stereotypic ritualistic activity is used as a way of shutting oneself off from others. Even if that is not the original motivation, stereotyped responses do eventually help to isolate the child from others and reducing ritualistic behaviours may be a necessary first step in helping the child interact with others.

Just as with other children, children with autism may also become depressed, and may even have a greater liability to depression as they move into their teens. Thus, if a child with autism becomes more withdrawn into self-stimulatory behaviour and this goes on for a prolonged period, it is worth considering that the child may be experiencing a period of depression. It can become difficult to receive treatment for this when the child has sld and cannot voice his/her own concerns, but not all withdrawal is due to autism, especially if the child had previously been more sociable. Medication alone is seldom the answer, but the child may need the help of a short period of medication to help lift the child's mood, while educational and behavioural methods are used to help the child develop renewed interest in others. Certainly children should not be denied treatment for a depressed state simply because they have autism.

Some of the approaches given above (such as the son-rise programme and intensive interaction) do not let the child use his or her own stereotypes (mechanical repetitiveness) to withdraw, but insist on joining in with his or her chosen activity, albeit in a loving and accepting way. Some specialist schools also take charge of the situation and use educational activity to prevent withdrawal in a process known as 'Intrusive Teaching'. There may be initial resistance on the part of the child to such direction but, if the teaching is consistent, alternatives are usually accepted, and the child often comes to seek these teaching sessions and the regular contact from an adult. That is not to say that the child should never be allowed to withdraw. In conditions of stress (and many teaching situations—especially if social—are of their nature stressful for the child with autism and sld), the child may only be able to function overall if allowed 'time out' to engage in stress-reducing activities. It may, however, be necessary to structure these periods, so that children know what they have to do before such a 'time out' period, and the duration in which they will be allowed to withdraw. If children are simply permitted to withdraw at will, there is a danger that withdrawal will come to dominate, and the child will find it increasingly stressful to join in with others.

Free times and playtimes present a particular problem for children with autism. These are often the times of maximum withdrawal, and contact with peers in such unstructured situations is likely to be both unpredictable and frightening. It is a mistake to expect children with autism to join in with others in free or 'play' times, without an extensive programme beforehand to teach the skills that are needed. Other children also need training so that they can learn the best way of engaging the children with autism in play activities. The most effective management of such times might be to facilitate a period of play with their peers and then to allow a period of withdrawal. It is better to have a brief and successful time together than to try to prolong it to the point where play breaks down and the child with autism becomes stressed or distressed.

Friendships

It is unlikely that children with autism and sld will make true friends without considerable facilitation, although they will have preferences as to their companions, and staff should be sensitive to these when constructing social groups. As the child moves into adulthood, there is the question of how far the child's 'choice' to be alone should be respected, and how far the staff should continue to try to develop and encourage friendships. The principle is that staff should try to ensure that the child's choice is a real one. They should not be avoiding others because they are frightened or confused by others, or because they lack the social skills to engage them. Nor should they be alone simply because they have no positive experiences of what a friendship can bring. It is only when we are sure we have helped them successfully to understand others, have taught them how to relate to others, and have given them some positive experiences of being with others, that we can be sure that being alone is a choice we should respect.

In order to develop friendships, the child needs, therefore, to have experiences of doing things s/he enjoys with others. Within such experiences, children with autism need to be taught specifically to attend to others, to recognise their own and others' pleasure, to act with others and to join in with them in co-operative play activities that involve skills of shared attention, turn-taking and mutuality. However, these skills are not going to be easy for the child with autism and sld to acquire, and many may never be achieved at a functional level. Nevertheless, having fun together contributes to current quality of life and is likely to contribute to future quality of life, so it is a goal worth pursuing, regardless of outcome.

If the child's peers all share the same difficulties, the chances of forming successful friendships are further reduced. This is one area, therefore, where integration with others without autism (whether or not they have learning difficulties) is likely to be most beneficial. Even so, just placing the child with autism and sld alongside others is unlikely to ensure any degree of integration, and may in fact lead to less social contact with others (Jordan & Powell, 1994). Roeyers (1995) has developed ways of enabling normally developing peers to play with children with autism, but clearly the degree of additional learning difficulty will also be an important factor to consider when choosing likely playmates. Whether the chosen peers are normally developing children or children with sld but without autism, the most favourable situation for developing play is one of 'reverse integration'. This is where the chosen 'other' children come into the 'autistic' setting to play or work with those with autism, rather than expecting the children with autism to adjust to new settings as well as new people and expectations. In some schemes these playmates are then able eventually to take the children with autism back into their own setting, where now the children with autism already know how to interact with those children and just need to learn to do so in this new setting.

Children with autism and sld may never gain the social and emotional maturity to have a friend in the deepest sense. Yet they have been shown to benefit from being with others and to learn to exhibit many aspects of 'friend' behaviour. Even a superficial friend may be valuable and serve as a gateway both to a wider social life and to further social understanding.

Teaching and caring relationships

The processes of education and care are based on the idea that the adult facilitates and mediates the learning experience for the child. Where the child is disturbed or confused by this social interaction, then this will have tremendous implications for teaching, whether of academic skills or of self-care skills in a home setting. Most teachers and care staff operate on a model that is true of parenting: the first priority is developing a relationship with children and then that is used to stimulate and motivate the children to further learning. Yet in autism that relationship can seldom be built in isolation, just through contact, and so adults cannot wait on the development of their relationship before they begin to work with the child.

As is often the case in autism, as we saw in earlier chapters, we may need to do things in reverse as it were. By working regularly with the child on some task or activity the adult may find that the relationship grows as the child develops some understanding of how that person functions and therefore what to expect. Most children with autism will eventually develop relationships with those who make themselves predictable and will learn best from such familiar people.

There is a danger, that unless we also teach for independence, that the child with autism and sld may become 'overdependent' and even exhibit what has been called 'learned helplessness'. They may begin to depend on the adult for confirmation that their responses are appropriate, and to wait for the adult to initiate the next stage in any problem-solving process. This sometimes reaches the point where they will not take any action, physical or intellectual, without prior approval. This can be exacerbated by sole use of behavioural teaching methods where the child learns only to respond when given the correct cue and then demands the expected 'reward' to mark the end of the action. As later chapters will show, teachers especially need to be alert for this and use a variety of techniques to foster different styles of learning and to move towards independent problem-solving.

Where children with autism and sld have problems learning from others, nonsocial ways of learning can enable the child to make progress, without waiting for social relationships to develop. The use of computer assisted learning for some aspects of the curriculum provides a good example of this asocial learning environment. This provides a good learning environment for children with autism but it should not preclude teaching towards social understanding. There should also be a parallel programme of teaching the child how to learn in social contexts.

TEACCH (Schopler & Olley, 1982) is an approach developed specifically for pupils with autism that does not preclude direct teaching but also allows for independent learning opportunities. In this programme the child is put in charge of his/her own timetable that is coded in a way that indicates where a task is to be done and with what degree of supervision or help. As long as there are opportunities to foster social skills and understanding, this can be an effective way of utilising the child with autism's strengths and of preventing the stress and confusion of too much social stimulation.

Summary

Social difficulties are a key feature of autism and are exacerbated by additional learning difficulties, which make it harder for the child to work out social information cognitively. Social skills are also difficult to teach since the rules are often implicit and need to be flexible to cope with changing and particular contexts. Children with autism and sld will need carefully structured approaches that help them manage in social situations and learn to relate to, and learn from, others. In some aspects of teaching, the difficulties may be circumvented by allowing the child to learn in nonsocial situations, while at the same time fostering social development through a variety of experiential situations which are carefully managed to control for stress and confusion. Peers can be useful 'teachers' in social contexts, but they will need some support and training to make this effective. Friendships are unlikely to be deep, but can serve a useful role in enabling the child to have fun, and in preventing secondary handicaps developing as a result of social isolation. A severely withdrawn child may need directed help in overcoming this, whereas periods of managed withdrawal are a necessary part of a programme of socialisation which, of its nature, is likely to be highly stressful for the child with autism.

Further reading

NIND, M. & HEWETT, D. (1994). *Access to Communication*. London: David Fulton.

4 Systems of Communication

Communication and language

When parents of a newly diagnosed child with autism and sld are asked about their teaching priorities for their child, it is common for them to emphasise speech. 'If only he could talk', they will often say 'he could tell us what he wants and what is upsetting him'. Language and communication are so closely bound together in normal development that it does not often occur to the parent that speech alone is not the answer. Parents of children with autism who do develop speech soon realise, however, that the speaking child with autism may still not be able to communicate, to express needs, or to explain what the matter is when s/he is upset. Speech in fact may become a barrier to communication in some cases, with the child talking incessantly, leaving no space for communication. The child may even begin using speech as a form of self-stimulation that shuts the child off from communication, rather than contributing to it.

Language, of course, is an important developmental skill and can help the child develop in all other ways, so it is important that we do try to develop it, wherever possible. But whether or not they can speak, children with autism always have problems with understanding and using speech in context, and they also have problems understanding all other aspects of communication. This means they will not be able to 'read' facial expressions, to understand why the voice goes up and down and why one word is stressed rather than another. They have problems understanding the meaning of body postures, of gestures, of indicative pointing, of eye signalling and all the rules of conducting a conversation. All this is true, regardless of the child's level of general intelligence, but the child with additional sld will have extra difficulties in trying to work out all these meanings in the way that children with autism (deprived of a normal intuitive understanding) need to do.

Communication is a priority both for its own sake and because it is a fundamental skill for providing access to other learning. Those with autism will need to learn what communication is about before they can learn to use whatever system of communication they have, whether this is spoken language or some alternative form that they have been taught. Parents, and some staff, sometimes worry that if children are given an aid to communication, such as a sign or symbol system, then they will 'give up' on speech and settle for this 'easier' system. Although specific language-teaching may also need to be encouraged, there is no evidence that this preference for sign or symbol ever occurs in a child who would be otherwise capable of speech. Of course, if the child has a specific language problem (as is often the case) then language learning may be very difficult, if not impossible, especially in conjunction with sld. Yet all the evidence shows that if children are taught how to communicate with whatever system they are capable of using, then they are far more likely to develop speech and to use it meaningfully, than if they are denied a way of communication while speech training is stressed.

Parents are also often under the impression that their child fully understands speech and so they see the lack of expressive speech as almost 'deliberate'. They certainly often feel that the child does not 'need' another system such as pictures since s/he 'understands perfectly'. In the first place, even if the child does understand speech, that does not mean that s/he can produce it at will and the use of another system may actually help the child begin to speak. In the second place, the feeling that the child fully understands speech is usually not a true reflection of the child's abilities but comes from the child responding readily to cues and routines. This can be tested by using totally different words when giving a habitual instruction and watching the child obey the expected, rather than the actual, command. For example, the child may be told to go to bed just as s/he is putting on his/her coat to go to school or to clean his/her teeth while being handed a hairbrush. That is not to say that understanding cannot be developed, but that is best done through positive teaching for meaning, rather than through making assumptions about the child's level of understanding.

The nature of communication
In order to foster communication in children with autism, it is necessary to understand what communication is and how it relates to language. There are four basic conditions that are necessary for communication to occur. These are:

- *Something to communicate **about***
  The child must not only have needs, desires and concepts (which children with autism have as much as other children), but must also be aware that they have them, which may not be the case in autism. Initial teaching, therefore, must build up this self-awareness of needs and desires, and must help develop shared concepts to which communicative forms (such as language) can be attached.

- *Something to communicate **with***
  This is usually the most obvious focus of teaching, especially when the child is not speaking. Speech may be the ultimate goal, but it is vital that the child be given a way of communicating as soon as possible and that we do not wait until language develops (or fails to develop) before we start teaching the child how to influence the world through the use of some shared system. Visual systems are likely to be the most effective (unless the child has an additional visual problem), although some may need to use actual objects.

- *Something to communicate **for***
  Communication does not occur unless the child has a reason for communicating. In many families the child may react so badly if things are not just how s/he likes them that parents learn to anticipate and meet their child's needs almost before the child knows s/he has them. As an example, a teacher is visiting a family to see why the child, who is communicating well at school, using the symbol system he has been taught, is failing to generalise this to the home. As the teacher sits talking with the mother, the time for the child to come home arrives

and the mother frantically gets the right Thomas video in place, and the banana and drink on the table, in front of the television. The mother has learnt that if this is not done, her son will become so distraught that the evening will be ruined for all the family. Yet for that boy with autism and sld, there is no reason for him to communicate and so he is unlikely ever to do so, unless this situation can be changed.

However, a reason to communicate not only requires needs that are not anticipated but also an environment that is responsive to the child's attempts at communication. Most home environments do provide that because they are naturally involved with the child and get to understand the odd ways the child may be trying to communicate. Brothers and sisters, as well as parents, can often 'interpret' the child with autism and, once this is happening, the child's response (even if it is a little bizarre) can be modified to make it more generally communicative. The important step is making the child aware of communication and this cannot happen if no one recognises what the child's behaviour means, as can sometimes happen at school. As will be seen below, even where the child is not communicating, interpreting behaviour 'as if' it were communicative can be the best way of helping it to become so.

- *A communicative **partner***
  The child with autism has no intuitive grasp of the importance of other people and needs teaching to understand that communication does not just depend on the child learning some words, signs of symbols as a kind of ritual; there must also be someone who receives and understands these 'messages'. Without specific teaching of this aspect of communication, children with autism can be found mumbling words that no one can hear, pointing in empty rooms, signing under the table, and standing forlornly with a symbol in an outstretched hand, but directing it at no one.

As can be seen from those features above, they are separate from the particular means of communication, whether or not that is spoken language. If the child does not develop spoken language naturally, its development may be fostered in different ways, but teaching for communication should progress, using whatever the child is already using or can easily be taught to use. Communication is the normal motor for developing language and so fostering communication will not only enable the child to have more control of his/her environment, become less frustrated and begin to learn more effectively, it is also the best way to help develop language itself.

Adults or older adolescents, who do not speak, may never learn to do so (apart from a few words), in spite of years of teaching, but all can learn to develop a system of communication that can transform their lives. They may even be able to learn a written form of the language they may never learn to speak, since written language is often easier than spoken language for these children. This in turn may lead (especially with modern forms of communicative technology) to computer-generated speech or visually displayed speech.

Problems in language and communication

Language difficulties

Spoken language may well be a problem, then, when there are additional learning or language difficulties. A significant number of individuals with autism and sld remain mute and will have difficulty in learning all language forms, especially as they have to do so without an understanding of communication to support the learning. There may be failure to appreciate communicative intent so that 'common sense' is never applied to work out what is really meant. This difficulty is not easy to understand and the child's misinterpretation is often attributed to obstinacy or wilfulness or a lack of motivation. Unlike teaching language to any other group, therefore, the teacher of those with autism must teach the difference between what the words mean and what the speaker means, since children with autism interpret expressions literally and never make inferences beyond the actual language used. They never question the purpose behind a command or ask for clarification if they do not understand; it is almost as if they have no expectation of understanding and just use language as cues to actions, sticking rigidly to certain set language forms to serve as these cues.

One young boy with autism and sld was very interested in a particular TV game show where contestants were given the cue 'Ready, steady, go!' before they could answer. This boy then transferred this to his own behaviour and would (or could) not answer any question or proffer any comment until given the prompt 'Ready, steady, go!'. This rigidity in what words mean extends beyond such cues to speech. The child will often only recognise one form of words as having a particular meaning and can get very anxious if this is altered. For example, the child may have been agitating to go outside and mother says 'Off you go then' and lets him out. The next time that boy wants to go out, his mother may have completely forgotten the exact words she used last time. This time she says 'OK. You can go out', but instead of going the child agitates more. His mother is getting a bit impatient now and will say things like: 'Aren't you going to go?' 'I'm not holding this door open indefinitely you know.' 'Come on Raoul; stop messing around and get out into the garden.'

With each change in expression (especially with those he does not understand) Raoul becomes increasingly agitated and may end up escalating into a full tantrum, perhaps even becoming violent and/or destructive. For his mother this is puzzling and infuriating. She thought she had identified what her child wanted (as indeed she had) and was doing her best to comply. Even if she realised that the form of words was important, she would probably have difficulty recalling exactly the form she had used before and so this is a very difficult situation to manage. That is one reason why it may be helpful to have another system (symbols or signs) running alongside speech, even when you are sure the child understands speech, because use of the same sign or symbol can be a constant that allows some variation in what is said or the tone of voice in which it is said.

Problems in processing language can occur even when the child does understand and use some speech and even when the child scores well on language tests. Children with autism may often perform better in test situations than in real life because test demands are explicit and clear, sentences used are often short, and there are no confusions with other (or changing) meanings that come from accompanying gestures, such as winking or smiling, that often indicate that the language used is not to be interpreted literally. Sarcasm and metaphors are examples of everyday use of language which is completely baffling for the child with autism and often leads to distress. A young boy with autism and sld was having some inclusion experience in a mainstream infant classroom. Although integrated activities were set up and prompted by the accompanying learning support assistant, the child was still very dependent on that support and seldom did anything spontaneously with the other mainstream children. One afternoon, however, the child with autism teamed up with a determined little boy with Down's syndrome and the two of them had a great time tipping out all the bricks on to the floor. It was not behaviour the teacher would normally have allowed, but the children were so enjoying doing it together and egging each other on that the teacher (very wisely) felt the social learning outweighed the 'naughtiness' of the activity. However, she did eventually feel that she should intervene, and he went up to the two boys and said 'Look at all this mess!' and then, looking directly at the two children 'You are a pair!' The boy with Down's syndrome just looked sheepish and giggled, understanding (in spite of his sld) that he had been naughty but that the teacher was not really cross. The boy with autism, on the other hand, became distraught and started shouting 'I'm not a pear! I'm not a pear!' The spellings indicate the different interpretation that had been made but the problem comes from not just misunderstanding the language itself but from not being able to pick up any of the other clues that would lead to the correct overall interpretation.

Equally puzzling are apparent instructions ('You do that once more . . . !') which are meant to be the opposite (i.e. prohibitions), so that the poor child is completely bewildered when s/he *does* do it again and then gets into terrible trouble as a result. Even more common in English is the use of indirect commands which are phrased as questions or choices, although they are meant as nothing of the sort. The teacher who asks the child with autism 'Can you bring your book to me?' should not be surprised (and certainly not angry, since the child is not trying to be awkward) if the child says 'Yes' but does not move.

A young woman with autism (who has very good language and does not have additional learning difficulties) turned up at a school for children with autism, where she was due to give a talk to parents. As is often the case in such schools, the entrance to the school was 'guarded' by the school secretary who said to the young woman with autism, 'Would you like to sign the visitor's book?' Now this young woman with autism is rather clumsy and does not enjoy writing, especially in such 'registers' where she is never sure exactly what information is required, what goes where, and whether she can manage to write in the small space provided. Not unreasonably, then, she responded to what had been presented as a choice by saying (politely, as she had been taught) 'No thank you'. The secretary, however, became very agitated and irate at this response, shouting and gesticulating and saying, 'You can't go into the school unless you sign. Everyone has to sign the book. Those are the rules.' At this point a member of staff who understood autism arrived on the scene and was able to avert what otherwise might have become a nasty incident, as the young woman with autism herself became very disturbed and panicky. What is a pity is that a member of staff (albeit a non teaching member) in a specialist setting had not been better trained in the problems faced by people with autism. Part of the problem is, as in this case, that people may be able to make appropriate adjustments when faced with children without speech (as was true of most of the children in this school) but forget to make adaptations when faced with someone with apparently good speech. Being able to speak in autism is a poor guide to comprehension.

Apart from all the nonliteral uses of language which cause problems in autism, just dealing with long strings of language can present problems where a short phrase, with a pause, will not. Adults with autism who are able to reflect back on their childhood often talk about the problems they experienced in processing speech (Williams, 1996; Gerland, 1997). They speak about the way in which they could start off understanding what was being said, and then the words would all start to sound jumbled up, and it would appear as if the person were speaking very fast and shouting. This is what a language-processing problem can feel like. If you are not processing the speech in meaningful chunks, but relying on processing each word as it comes along, then you have to try to hold all these words in your working memory in order to get to the meaning of the whole phrase or sentence. You can start off doing this with the first words, but it may take you longer to process each word than it does the person to say it. After a few words, then, the unprocessed words 'pile up' as it were and then flood through. The experience of this is of the words speeding up and the speech changing in pitch (i.e. appearing louder). Adults need to learn to speak in short meaningful phrases and to leave processing time between each phrase. This is the kind of speech that is triggered naturally when faced with a young child without speech, but the problem comes when the child has speech and so this way of speaking does not come naturally, and has to be specifically trained.

Apart from the structure of the language, children with autism and sld have problems with the way language sounds. They are able to hear intonation patterns in speech, for example, but they cannot attach pragmatic meaning to them and so they just become 'noise' that distracts from and interferes with the meaning of what is said, rather than adding to it. They have similar difficulty in using intonation patterns appropriately in their own speech, which then sounds either very monotonous or robot-like or has widely (but often, inappropriately) variable intonation patterns.

Understanding communicative gestures

Many problems in communication result from a deviant pattern in the development of an understanding of communicative intent and the development of speech roles (Jordan, 1989). It is also clear that many are rooted in the direct perceptual problems which precede, and perhaps initiate, that deviant pattern, including problems in the development of joint attention and early communicative gestures such as pointing in order to comment. In autism, then, there is a difficulty in interpreting communicative gestures, such as 'look at this', indicated by holding an object up for inspection, pointing or eye-pointing. Many of these form the fundamentals of communication and have begun to develop in normal development by six months. At this time, if an adult holds up an object within the baby's view, the baby will automatically look at it, knowing instinctively that this is meant as an object of joint regard. By twelve months normally developing babies will hold up objects themselves so that they can join with adults in this shared attention. An adult who is not aware of what is going on may attempt to take the object from the child at this stage, thinking that is the intent behind the baby's action. The baby then has to snatch it back; the 'game' is not about giving and taking at this stage, but about sharing attention. It is this shared attention that helps the child understand what words mean, as objects of joint regard are named and pointed out to the child.

The fact that these are normally such early occurring behaviours in young children mean that they are often assumed to be automatic by adults. Adults (parents and later, teachers) will continue to hold up objects they want to label or talk about ('What's this?' 'Look! It's a teddy.') and not understand that the child may not be directing his/her own attention to the correct item. If the child is focused on a bit of fluff, and the adult apparently tells him/her that it is a 'ball' 'bottle' or whatever, then it is not surprising if the child gets confused or develops a private understanding of what words mean. Even where the child is focused on the correct object, he or she may not be attending to the item as a whole or the correct 'bit' of the item selected by the adult. The adult may be saying 'red', meaning to draw attention to the item's colour, but the child may be focusing on the way the window is reflected on an item's shiny surface, so that 'red' in the child's mind comes to mean that shiny reflection. Present the same red item in a dim light, then, and its 'redness' disappears, whereas a shiny blue object may be happily identified as 'red'. This does not mean that the child cannot see the difference between red and blue, but that he or she does not understand which particular aspect of his/her perception is being labelled in this way. Such difficulties can accumulate and have a significant effect on the child's overall language and cognitive development.

The solution is for parents and teachers to analyse their instructions to children with autism, and to identify those aspects that are assuming communicative knowledge that the child may not have. Once that has been done, the next step is to achieve the discipline of giving explicit instructions of what the individual is actually to do, instead of relying on implicit understanding of communication. They will not only need to be told where to look to achieve joint attention, but also that holding items up is a signal to direct attention to that object, as is pointing. Beyond that, adults need to start by joining the child's focus when labelling items or actions, since, as was seen in the last chapter, this will be easier for the child than expecting him or her to adjust to the adult's focus. This requires imagination and sensitivity on the part of the adult since there are no universal clues to the way in which the child with autism is interpreting the world; we cannot say that it is light reflection that all children with autism will notice, for example, or even that the same child will always be responding to this aspect of perceptual stimulation. We need to try to see the world through the child's eyes at that particular time, which is, of course, difficult. We should remember, however, that this is just the task that we are setting the child with autism, when we expect them to adjust to our interpretations and perceptions, so the effort we spend in doing this will be very instructive in what we need to do when it comes to helping the child make the adjustment.

Clearly, the communicative gestures that relate to reference will have most impact in teaching situations, but parents may be more concerned with teaching some acceptance of gestures of comfort and affection. Direct teaching of the meaning of a gesture may be helpful, especially to the more verbally able child. Thus the adult can explain that putting an arm around someone means you like them a lot or means that you want them to feel better when they are sad. This can be accompanied by a brief demonstration, and if this is done sufficiently often the child will gradually come to accept the gesture and may even seek it.

Other children with more severe additional learning difficulties might need a programme in which the adult gradually introduces touching and affectionate gestures by building on what the child is doing and finds enjoyable. Such programmes form part of teaching approaches such as intensive interaction (Nind &

Hewett, 1994). Particular problems may arise in relation to comfort gestures. This is not only a source of particular anguish to parents when their child rejects comfort when hurt, but it can lead to a child failing to report pain or accidents, for fear of getting what, in their eyes, is a form of additional assault through hugs and cuddles. Teaching parents to direct their comfort gesture more directly to the child's hurt ('kissing better', for example) can make it easier for children with autism to understand and accept what is going on, especially if they are able to understand a rationale for the action, such as 'saliva contains antiseptics which can help make the wound better'.

Nonproductive, pedantic, literal use of language

Because of the failure to understand about communication, whatever language or alternative system is possessed tends to be used for a very narrow range of purposes, mainly to make requests and, in the more verbal, to talk obsessively about some aspect of especial interest (Wetherby, 1986). It is often echolalic (parrotted) and non productive, in the sense that it does not build on what others have said, nor does it relate to the context but tends to reproduce familiar learned patterns of speech. The individual with autism will try to understand what the words mean rather than what the speaker means, s/he will interpret idioms or sarcasm literally and so may miss the point or even become distressed. Practitioners will need to address these problems by direct teaching of conversational skills (turn-taking, active listening, topic introduction, maintenance and change) and attempting to make contextual knowledge explicit. For those with the most severe difficulties, it may even be necessary to teach explicitly about synonyms and to make sure that the child has a concept (through sorting activities) before attaching a label, to avoid rigid narrow conceptual categories. Otherwise, the child may appear obstinate when s/he does nothing when instructed to 'Hang up your coat!' if the child's understanding is that the object in question is an 'anorak' rather than a coat.

Whereas communication is the normal precursor to language development, in autism, language may develop without the child having any idea of how to use it for communication, or any understanding of how speakers can use it pragmatically to create a variety of meanings beyond the literal meaning of the words and sentences. Most children will pay more attention to what they think the speaker intends by what is said, than to the literal meaning of the language used; children with autism are blind to that intention and focus on the literal meaning, regardless of how absurd or unlikely that may appear to be to the onlooker. Children with autism, for example, are the only group to respond to commands such as 'Wipe your feet on the mat!' by laboriously taking off shoes and socks in order to do so. Autism is also the only condition where the means of expression does not lead automatically to the communicative use of those means, and the teacher will have to teach communicative functions directly, whether or not the child can speak.

Reading—hyperlexia and abnormal development
Some individuals with autism, even with additional sld, will exhibit what is known as 'hyperlexia' where they are able to read mechanically beyond their level of understanding. Parents and teachers should be careful always to check for understanding of what the child can apparently 'read' and look for opportunities to demonstrate the purpose of reading. This is most easily accomplished (as well as tapping into the child's likely source of strength) if the child is encouraged to read factual texts rather than fantasy stories. The child with autism may find it easier to learn to read than to listen to stories or to tell them from picture books, so the normal stages in progression may not apply. The relative facility with written language, however, may mean that this can be used as a bridge to spoken language, as well as providing a way of getting needs met. Computer-assisted learning can be used to add to a child's means of communication and often symbols (which can be very confusing in their meaning and their visual detail) are better replaced by written words which anyone can understand. Many children with autism and sld will benefit most from a communication board that contains some pictures, some symbols and some written words, according to the child's abilities, interests and needs.

Educational uses of language

As well as having considerable problems with expressive speech, children with autism and sld will have particular problems related to the way language is used in education.

● There may be failure to appreciate communicative intent so that 'common sense' is never applied to work out what is really meant. This can make such children seem obstinate or disobedient when in reality they simply do not understand what is intended. It can be a source of confusion with other children, as well as with adults, and may make the child with autism the butt of teasing and ridicule.

● For many of the reasons given above, it may be difficult for the individual with autism to follow verbal instructions, especially if these are expressed in indirect 'polite' forms. There need to be ways of delivering the curriculum through media other than verbal instruction. Such means should be flexible to meet individual needs but are likely to include: the visual presentation of tasks, structure in the classroom that indicates when, where and how tasks are to be tackled, physical guidance, without accompanying speech, for teaching skills, and ready access to computer-assisted learning (CAL). However CAL may be a retreat, to avoid the difficulties of social interactive learning, and so training to learn alongside others needs to continue in parallel.

● Many questions asked in teaching contexts are not 'genuine' (in the sense that they seek information that the questioner has not got); rather, they are asked to test the individual's understanding or to encourage greater individual participation, or to issue instructions. Individuals with autism may mistake these educational uses for the proper use of questions and use it as a model for their own repetitive questioning. They will then be doubly confused when such behaviour is restricted or punished and they neither understand other ways of achieving the same functions nor the meaning or function of 'genuine' questions. There are other reasons why children with autism may ask the same question over and over, but these are discussed below, under problems in communication.

- A failure to appreciate the nature of conversations and the model that staff, especially, often give of discourse, may lead to the child learning inappropriate ways of interacting with others. Teachers will usually determine the topic of a lesson and either ignore attempts to divert him/her from that topic or redirect such attempts back to the chosen one. A straight copying of this didactic style, however, will lead to the child choosing the topic without regard to its appropriateness to the listener's focus of attention or the immediate context, and therefore producing bizarre irrelevant comments. It will also lead directly to pedantic, over-explicit styles, to ignoring signs of listener-inattentiveness or boredom, and ignoring contributions from others that do not fit the listener's predetermined goal for the 'conversation'. 'Real life' communication skills need to be taught in functional contexts to counterbalance these 'educational' uses. Children with autism and sld will also need to be taught directly how you learn to recognise pauses in conversation or how you should give them, and recognise (by use of eye-contact and body posture) when others are ready to contribute to a conversation. Without such teaching they may stick to the lessons learnt in a school context, but holding one's hand up in a restaurant is more likely to get the attention of the waiter than to signal a wish to contribute to a conversation, and waiting for others to raise a hand before giving way as a speaker is not going to work outside an educational or formal group setting.

The dimensions of communication
Programmes sometime fail in autism because the child is being asked to learn more than one thing at the same time, and finds this confusing. This is especially true in communication teaching where the child's grasp of the situation is so poor and most adults have little idea of the complexities involved. The TEACCH programme (Watson, 1985; Watson *et al.*, 1989) has provided a useful breakdown of the dimensions involved in communication,

and supports the idea that only one dimension should be taught at a time, in order to maximise chances of success. The five dimensions that are proposed are:

- *Form*

This tells you about the means of communication you are teaching the child. You need to note whether the child is to use speech, signs, symbols, pictures, objects of reference, or written language. The form also tells you the level of each of these modes of communication, single words or pictures, for example, two or three word phrases, sentences and so on.

- *Vocabulary*

This applies to new words, pictures, symbols or objects, depending on the form.

- *Communicative function*

This describes what the communication is for. It covers things I ike requesting objects, requesting routines, making comments, protesting, seeking information, negating, greeting, saying farewell, asking for help, expressing emotion and so on.

- *Semantic meaning*

This describes the semantic category—object label, agent of action, action, descriptor and so on. It is often difficult for parents and non language specialists to understand the difference between this category and communicative functions. Speech and language therapists can help develop this dimension of communication, but many teachers ignore this dimension and are still successful in teaching communication. In practice, therefore, the semantic meaning is often conflated with the communicative function without adverse effect. However, it may be that the child's understanding of meaning is at the prerepresentational stage and then it is important to get the child to the stage where a symbol can be used. Thus, at the first stage of meaning (the sensory stage) objects are just perceived as having sensory properties so, for example, a cup is just something to be licked or flicked, not to 'stand for' a drink. A child at this stage needs work to bring him/her to the next stage of meaning (presentation), whereby a particular cup, for example can come to 'mean' a drink. Then there is the further stage of 'representation' whereby any cup can 'mean' a drink. At this stage the cup functions as an 'object of reference'. This is also the stage at which symbols can be introduced. Finally, there is the stage of 'meta representation' whereby the child can use an arbitrary language. There is now a programme to teach the early stages of this meaning-making called COMFOR (see Noens and Van Berckalaer-Onnes, 2004), which is soon to be available in English.

- *Context*

This is an important dimension of teaching in autism that cannot afford to be ignored, however. Like other aspects of their learning, children with autism and sld do not generalise communication easily from one situation to the next. Just because they can ask for something at tea with their mother does not mean they can ask for the same thing at dinner with their father, and so on. Each aspect of the context needs to be taught and generalised. Most specialist teaching, at least, does pay attention to the dimension of context as well as that of form and vocabulary. Parents, however, do not always understand that the skills of the speech and language therapist are more profitably used assessing the child's language and communicative abilities, devising a programme to develop these abilities and then working with parents and key staff (i.e. staff in daily contact with the child) to help them carry out the programmes. Working in isolation with a therapist may make it seem as if the child is making good progress, but this has little longterm benefit if the child can only perform for that therapist in that situation. Programmes should either involve teaching in the functional context where the behaviour will be used (the preferred option), or there will need to be specific teaching for generalisation of the skill.

Form, vocabulary and context are usually taught, but the one that is often missed is the dimension of communicative function, which is the one that defines the difficulty in autism (the one concerned with communication itself). The reason this dimension is so often neglected in teaching may be that it is so much a natural part of normal social situations that it is difficult to isolate it as a dimension and even more difficult to think about teaching it.

Teaching is also less likely to be successful if more than one of these dimensions is taught at a time. This can be overlooked as a factor, especially when one of the dimensions is 'communicative function' which comes so naturally to most of us, without any need for direct teaching.

Example

A ten-year-old girl with autism and sld (Jacint) had developed single-word speech, although a symbol-based communication board was available to her, as she sometimes appeared to have word-finding problems. Finding the symbol helped her find the word and express it. Jacint attended a school for children with sld where there were a number of children with additional autism but where staff had no specialist training. Her teachers had (with the help of the speech and language therapist) understood her need for the symbol system as well as speech, and were happy with the way she was able to use it to ask for something, as long as they had anticipated her needs and there was a symbol in her book. However, there were times when she wanted or needed something that had not been anticipated and then, being at a loss to communicate this, she would become distressed and sometimes would hit her head with her hand, bite her hand or throw things to the floor. There was also a problem in that her communication book was becoming unwieldy and attempts to categorise it (under headings such as 'food', 'work items', 'clothes' and so on) had been unsuccessful, since Jacint (and even some staff) had problems in remembering the classification. It was clear that it would not be possible just to add to the book indefinitely.

It was decided, therefore, to teach Jacint to ask for help, as a first step, and then to move to separating her communication symbols into separate 'topic' books. She could then be taught to ask for these by name (making the categories visual and thus easier to remember) and so go on to find individual items within each book. It was also decided to have a sustained teaching effort directed at getting her to vocalise the words without the prompt of the symbol, to see if familiarity would overcome the word-finding problem. However, it was recognised that this latter programme would take a while, and might not be completely successful even then, and meantime there was the problem identified above. Staff were anxious (with some justification) that if Jacint continued to be frustrated in her attempts to communicate, she would become used to reverting to her former habits of self-injury and/or destructiveness to get what she wanted.

Existing symbols for 'help' were complex, both visually and conceptually, and it was decided that, rather than teach such an arbitrary symbol that others would not necessarily understand, it would be better (and perhaps easier) to teach the written word 'help'. In spite of the speed with which Jacint had picked up symbols in the past, however, there was very little success in teaching her to use this written 'symbol' to ask for help when she needed a symbol. Staff were convinced that the problem lay with the fact that this symbol was in writing, whereas she was used to picture symbols. That may have been a factor, but an advisory specialist in autism suggested that they first consider the possibility that the problem was not in the change of fonn per se, but in the fact that Jacint was being asked to learn a new form (writing, instead of pictures) at the same time as a new function (seeking help). One solution would have been to change the written symbol to a picture one, but it was felt to be better educationally if Jacint could learn to move on to writing, and it would also be easier when it came to finding new symbols for all the needs she was now expressing.

If Jacint was to use the new form, everything else would need to stay the same; she could not, at this stage, therefore, learn to ask for help at the same time. Instead, some of the picture symbols she was already used to using frequently were changed to written symbols. This was done in stages using boardmaker (computer software) to construct picture symbols with a word beneath at first. The word was gradually increased in size, while the picture was reduced and then the picture was hidden beneath the word, so Jacint got used to responding to the word and only when in difficulties did she lift the flap and peep at the picture. Jacint took to this readily and within a term the bulk of her commonly used symbols had been transferred to written symbols.

Now was the time to introduce the new function of 'help'.

Situations were engineered so that Jacint needed a symbol not in her repertoire. In this situation, before she get upset and frustrated, she was given the written word 'help' and prompted to give it to another member of staff who then supplied her with the new symbol. Situations needed to be engineered where different symbols were required, so that she was not associating 'help' with the object wanted but with the process of obtaining a symbol for the wanted object. Once more, she responded fairly well to this teaching and in the space of a few weeks had learnt to use 'help', vocalising 'help' as she handed over the written word. The use of 'help' was then generalised to other people in the same situation and then to other situations. For example, she often became upset when getting ready for PE when she could not get her socks positioned 'just so', with heels in the correct place so that there would be no wrinkles as she put them on. Rather than ask for help, she would fling both socks and shoes across the room, unless staff happened to notice and could preempt this by helping her. Once more, two members of staff were needed—one to watch for the right moment to offer her the 'help' symbol and to prompt her to give it to the other adult, who was to provide the help. In time, Jacint was using the written 'help' sign in a variety of settings and the overall result of the programme was that Jacint developed (rudimentary) reading skills and eventually single-word speech, without the need for symbol or written prompts. It was as if the written language system made the spoken one more accessible, although such a positive outcome cannot be guaranteed.

Summary

Most children with autism and sld will have some difficulties in acquiring language and understanding at least some aspects of it but, regardless of whether or not the child can speak, the main problem in autism is communication. Communication and language each have their own structure and the child's difficulties with each aspect needs to be identified if language and communication skills are to flourish. Parents and staff need to monitor and modify their own use of language to try to make it more accessible to the child and should use visual forms to communicate with the child.

Unlike other children with sld, who may also need teaching in order to develop means for communication, children with autism will need to be taught communicative functions and what communication is about. The dimensions of communication should be tackled one step at a time. There are specific problems in language and communication in autism but these are best dealt with, not by trying to suppress them, but by understanding their function for the child and helping him or her develop towards meaningful communication.

Further reading

NOENS, I. & VAN BERCKALAER-ONNES, I. (2004). Making Sense in a Fragmentary World: Communication in People with Autism and Learning Disability, *Autism: The International Journal of Research and Practice*, 8, 197–218.

WATSON, L. (1985). The TEACCH curriculum. In Schopler, E. & Mesibov, G. (eds), *Communication Problems in Autism*. New York: Plenum Press.

WATSON, L., LORD, C., SCHAFFER, B. & SCHOPLER, E. (1998). *Teaching Spontaneous Communication to Autisitic and Developmentally Handicapped Children*. New York: Irvington Press.

5 Teaching Language and Communication

Getting started

It may be necessary in some children to teach awareness of concepts and needs as well as a means for communication and to provide an environment that fosters communication. For children for whom it seems impossible to find anything that they want (at least enough to 'work' for), then we literally have to teach them to want something. For this, we use the feature of autistic functioning which is that people with autism like predictability and to do what they do. Thus, if at the same time, and regularly, and frequently, we present some activity or stimulus, the child will not only come to expect that thing but will want it (and can thus be trained to ask for it).

Using the child's own responses

Starting the communicative process, by imputing meaning to the child's noncommunicative expressions, is the basis of normal language and communication development. One boy with autism and sld found it difficult to eat breakfast first thing in the morning, but, by the time he reached school, he often became very upset and started to self-mutilate. Having looked at many different possible triggers for this behaviour, and having discussed the situation with his parents, there was a strong suspicion that the boy was, in fact, reacting to hunger. He may not have meant to tell anyone that he was hungry when he started to cry and hit himself each morning, but, if parents or staff have worked out that that is probably what is wrong, they can treat his behaviour *as if* that were what it meant.

Each time he starts to cry (and before he starts to hit himself—timing is crucial) parents or staff can say 'Oh! Are you hungry?' and then offer food. Then the boy can be prompted to communicate that need in a different way (giving a card with a picture of food on it, for example, or giving an 'object of reference' such as a spoon or plate). The success of this programme relies on the staff working out accurately what it is that the child would want to be communicating in that situation, at that time, if he knew how.

As indicated above, the priority for a child who is not communicating (whether or not there is any speech) is to get the child started in doing so. Communication is learnt through doing it, so practice (through prompted example) is much more important than instruction. Even when the child can speak, but especially when s/he cannot, a simple symbol approach is a good way to start, since the necessary actions can be fully prompted whereas speech cannot. Eventually, the goal is fully reciprocal communication but it is best to start with something both meaningful and rewarding to the child. Request is, therefore, the best communicative function with which to start. It is easiest to demonstrate and it is by far the easiest for the child with autism and sld to master.

Teaching pointing

There will be the need to give priority to communicative gestures over vocabulary, and the most important of these is pointing. Children with autism and sld often do not point at all, unless specifically taught to do so and, even then, they will only point to request rather than to point things out. The chapter on social development explores ways of developing joint attention, out of which pointing for comment can be developed. This section concerns the development of pointing for request—a very important first step in communication. Children need to develop some form of language (whether this is speech, sign, symbol, objects of reference or written language) so that their ability to communicate about things beyond the 'here and now' can be developed. Yet teaching the language prematurely, before the child understands anything about communication, can add to the confusion. Children may start to use a sign for 'biscuit', say, to mean 'give me' and so use it for anything they want, not just biscuits. Or children may not understand the reference of any of the signs they have been taught, just thinking they have to do something to get what they want, not understanding the rules for when you do one thing rather than another. In such cases, children then often run through their complete repertoire of signs in the hope that they will eventually hit on the right one, but no real learning about communication takes place.

Teaching pointing, however, needs to be done with care. Unless the child is taught to make eye-contact at the same time, the pointing itself can become another meaningless ritual and the child may be found pointing to empty rooms, expecting what s/he wants to appear as a result of the point alone. It is important, therefore, to teach pointing with looking. Steps in this teaching process, then, may be as follows:

- If the child already tries to grab (or grabs the teacher's/parent's hand and 'throws' it at the desired item), then take the situation when this is about to happen.

- Interrupt the 'grab' (or the throw) sharply, with a restraining hand.

- If the restraint is abrupt enough and is done as the child is grabbing (but has not yet picked up the item), this should cause a momentary glance at the person causing the obstruction, even in individuals with autism.

- As soon as the child glances, the adult removes the restraining hand, allowing the child the take the item, while saying 'Oh! You want a—Go ahead!'.

- If this is continued on a regular and consistent basis, children will come to look as they reach towards the desired item, almost 'as if' they are asking permission.

- At this stage, the 'grab' can be shaped into a point, first a point that touches the item and then pointing at a distance.

- This can then be extended to a variety of contexts.

- Once children are pointing regularly in this way, then they can be taught signs and symbols (or words) to enable them to ask for things that are out of sight.

Using systems for communication

PECS

A system like the Picture Exchange Communication System (Bondy & Frost, 1994) provides a structure for the kind of teaching programme used with Jacint (above). It is not necessary to use all the stages, and teachers should remember that the purpose is to develop the child's communication. There have been some examples of over-rigid use where a child has asked for a drink (by saying 'orange') and then been made to go and fetch a symbol before being given the drink; such rigid interpretations are clearly absurd and carry the danger that the child's spontaneous communicative attempts will be lost. However, used critically and appropriately, it highlights two important features of using symbol systems effectively with children with autism:

- *Spontaneous use of communication:* The child is taught to exchange the symbol for something s/he wants spontaneously rather than becoming dependent on someone saying, 'What do you want?' 'Show me what you want!' 'Point to what you want!' and so on. In PECS there have to be two trainers, neither of whom says anything. The situation has to be one where the child clearly wants something and is used to having it freely available. Some PECS training suggests a preliminary phase of training this exchange by holding up desirable items (pieces of apple, for example) and then prompting the child to give a symbol rather than take it. This does seem to work in many cases, but carries the danger that the child is being taught to ignore natural communicative signals such as people offering you things. It also teaches more about conformity (i.e. you must pass a symbol, rather than snatch) than it does about communication. It is better to choose a natural situation and teach in a natural way. Such situations occur readily in home or residential settings. Imagine breakfast time at home where the child loves Frosties and is used to being helped to dress by Dad and to coming down to find his Frosties waiting for him on the table. This day, however, as he comes down there are no Frosties but instead Mum is standing by a Velcro board attached to the fridge. Her hand is held out flat, next to a symbol of Frosties (a part of the packet, a small empty packet, a picture or whatever the child will instantly recognise), which itself is attached to the board by Velcro. Without saying anything, and before the child can react to the fact that the Frosties are not out on the table, Dad prompts the child physically to cross the room, take the symbol from the board and place it in his mother's hand. As soon as the symbol hits her hand, Mum comes to life, says 'Oh! You want Frosties' and quickly gets his bowl of Frosties (previously prepared) and gives it to her son.

The child may be bemused, but has his breakfast and so is content. This process is repeated day after day, but with Dad gradually reducing his prompts, until the child is crossing the room, getting the symbol and placing it in his mother's hand by himself. Once that is routine, Mum gets a bit more awkward. She starts to drop her hand until it is by her side. Then she starts to move away from the board until eventually the child is having to chase his mother round the kitchen to give her the symbol. At that point it is clear that the boy understands the process and is ready for the next stage of introducing another symbol, perhaps at another time. Eventually, the child can make a choice from a full menu of choices from a board or a book, and can even build up to phrases to express choices.

- *Use of a menu:* The other important benefit of the PECS format is that it introduces the child to the idea of a 'menu' of choices. As in the example above, the child learns the boundaries of the choice available. This can make management of the communicative teaching much easier. When teaching a child with autism to use signs or symbols, there usually comes a time when the child has learnt the sign or symbol and asks for the item all day long. This is a problem whatever is being requested, but is particularly difficult if it is something to which you do not want the child to have unfettered access (sweets, perhaps or the same *Thomas the Tank Engine* video). If you just ignore the child's requests (or appear to do so by saying things like 'Not now', 'No more', 'Later', and so on) then the child is quite likely to give up on this form of communication and revert to screeching, kicking or whatever ways s/he had developed in the past for getting what was wanted. A 'menu' makes the rules clear—you can choose, but only from what is on offer. This is a very valuable lesson to teach the child from an early age.

TEACCH

While a system such as PECS can be useful in teaching the child with autism and sld to express a choice, it is also important to give others a way of communicating with the child. Communication is a two-way process and, unless we demonstrate its use ourselves, there is a danger that any system (PECS or MAKATON [Walker, 1980] or whatever) will just be used to control the child's responses and not to add to mutual communication. TEACCH (Treatment and Education of Autistic and Communicatively Impaired Children: Watson *et al.*, 1989) provides a way for adults to communicate with children using the same system of symbols, words or objects of reference that the child is using for his/her own expressive communication.

The essence of this is that children with autism and sld find verbal instructions difficult to interpret and remember. Parents and teachers should use pictorial timetables to communicate to the child what is going to happen and what the child should do. TEACCH involves systems that help the child move from one activity to the next as well as ways of helping the child realise when they have finished a task and what to do then. Other uses of TEACCH are explored in later chapters, but in terms of communication it helps make adult intentions and task demands explicit and clear, and reduces the anxiety and stress that come from a child not understanding what is happening and not being able to predict or plan ahead, without this visual structure. TEACCH also includes very good observational formats for collecting information about the child's functional communication and ways of interpreting the child's behaviour in communicative terms (Watson *et al.*, 1989) and has good systems for joint parent/teacher planning in setting communicative goals.

Choosing alternatives to speech

A considerable proportion of children with autism and sld, as indicated above, will need to be given alternative (or at least augmentative) ways of communicating. Although the particular values of PECS and TEACCH are given above, and both systems have good track records of success, it is more important that the system chosen fits the child and the situation, rather than adheres rigidly to any set system. There are pros and cons of different alternative or augmentative communication systems but it should be remembered that non-iconic signs (i.e. ones that do not look like what they represent) are almost as difficult as spoken language, while written language (especially through computer-assisted communication) may, unlike in normal development, be more easily acquired. In general, children with sld and autism do best with pictorial symbols, whether realistic photographs, boardmaker or Makaton symbols, although for some (with visual problems or profound learning difficulties) objects of reference may be needed.

The teacher and parents (for decisions on the communication system to use must, above all else, involve a joint view) cannot base the decision purely on the child's preferred medium (visual, for example) without taking the communicative environment into account. The very essence of communication is that it is a shared system and, while there can be some individual variation within a class or family group, there must be a system that is understood and used by all the adult members of the communicating group at least. If a child learns to sign, that might be very appropriate if all staff and most family and friends can also be taught. However, even then, the child may be signing away in a burger bar but no one understands, so either a teacher or parent has to intervene or the child gets frustrated and 'gives up' on this system. Both scenarios destroy the child's sense of the efficacy of the sign being used, and may mean that earlier ways of getting what you want – grabbing, screaming, pulling others, for example – return. Giving the child a picture of a burger and chips may not be so advanced in terms of language use, but it may do a better job in supporting communication as the assistant happily hands over what is wanted in response to the picture. It may be, of course, that a system of sign can be augmented by pictures for certain situations, or vice versa; the needs of the child are paramount.

As a general guide, the following points will help with the decision:

- *Intelligibility* for the naïve user: i.e., will others be able to use and understand the system without the need for training? Others can be trained, but (as seen in the example above) this is not always successful or even feasible.

- *Portability* and ease of use: i.e., will the system be able to be used in a variety of contexts (including the outdoors or the swimming pool) without the need for elaborate or cumbersome equipment? This is obviously especially relevant for systems depending on the use of technological equipment, but also has implications for symbol and picture systems.

- *Compatibility* with the user's level of linguistic, cognitive, sensory and physical functioning: i.e., is the proposed system within the individual's capacity to acquire? It is hard for the person with autism to understand the purpose of communication so it is important to have a system the person can readily understand, especially when there are additional sld.

- *Usability* within present or projected future environments: i.e., does the system allow the individual to communicate with those who currently affect that individual's quality of life (and those who are likely to be significant in doing so in the future)? Most people with autism and sld, for example, are unlikely to use or understand sign at a level that would allow them to participate in signing communities for socialisation. If the person is always likely to need a personal assistant, then that person can presumably act as an interpreter, yet it puts a limit on education if independent functioning is always to be hampered by an inadequate communication system.

- *Normalisation* i.e., is the system one that encourages inclusion into society, or does it increase the likelihood of further segregation and isolation? A part of this would be the consideration of whether the system could be used as augmentative to speech in the hope that speech development would be facilitated by its use, or whether the system was purely an alternative to speech. As discussed above, this would limit (but not preclude) inclusion opportunities.

ICT—facilitated communication

ICT (Information and Communicative Technology) grows apace, so there is little point in giving current systems which might be out of date by the time the book comes to print. Nevertheless, most people with autism find the computer-learning environment very facilitative and there are an increasing range of communication aids which can be of great benefit to individuals with autism and sld, even if they were developed originally for those with motor problems. In the UK there are centres which develop these aids and where children (and some adults) may be referred for assessment of their communication needs and ways of meeting them through ICT. Sometimes these centres operate within the auspices of the local educational authority; sometimes they are in hospital settings and accessed through occupational or speech and language therapists.

There is also a particular form of facilitated communication which makes claims about 'releasing' the hidden potential of people with autism; this is to the extent that the claim is that autism should be redefined as a motor disorder. Facilitated Communication is the name given to a particular form of prompting a child to point to letters or words either on a communication board or with a special computer (Biklen, 1990). The rationale for the approach was that autism is really a motor disorder and that the person with autism knows what he or she wants to say but cannot execute the motor movements to speak or to type or point independently. A facilitator helps the child to do this by assisting the withdrawal of the pointing finger after it has made a point (or tapped a key) and repositioning it for the next point. In this way many remarkable (and some disturbing) texts have been claimed to have been 'written' by mute children with autism.

Clearly it is not an adequate explanation of autism when many children with autism can speak and type independently. Nearly all scientific investigations of the phenomenon also have shown that it is the facilitator who is (unconsciously) guiding the person with autism and who is thus the true author of the texts produced. After a lot of initial interest, then, Facilitated Communication (FC) is no longer much used, except in a few centres which have persisted, in spite of the negative scientific evidence.

Although it would be cruel to 'put words in the mouths' of children with autism instead of trying to give them a real way to communicate, there have been some useful side-effects from the use of FC in autism. It has reinforced the fact that many children with autism, even with sld, can be taught to read and type and use that for communication. It has also reminded staff that many children with autism do have additional motor problems and often need help in planning and executing movements. Finally, it has provided a context in which staff and/or parents can sit with their child and enjoy a teaching task together. These positive aspects should be used, while being aware of the dangers of the unintentional guidance which may produce misleading results.

Assisting listening ability
Enabling children with autism and sld to listen to what others say and to take account of what others say in their own speech is more difficult. There are some games which can help with this process, but they do depend on the child having speech and a working memory that will hold at least three or four items. The 'supermarket' game has each child saying, 'I went to the supermarket and in my basket I put some—'. The first child completes this phrase with his or her own choice ('sweets' for example) but the next child must now complete the phrase by repeating what the first child said ('sweets' in this case) and then adding his or her own choice. This goes on round the group, with each child having to listen to what has gone before and take account of it in their own answer. Of course, group numbers will need to be small if the task is to be manageable, and the game may have to be introduced by having picture cards to register what each child has said and to reduce the demands on memory.

A common difficulty for children with autism and sld is story time in school, which may involve sitting and listening to verbal information at a speed and of a length that the child cannot follow. Nor are the children usually clear about what is meant by 'listening' and they will see it as the same as 'hearing', rather than realising that it involves an active process of trying to make sense of what is heard. Where there are additional problems of hyperactivity, as there often are, it is of little use to exhort children to 'sit still and listen'; they may need something to do or at least fiddle with, if they are to be able to listen. Helping children understand that listening is an active process, and helping them tolerate sitting to listen to a story, can start with giving them toy characters or puppets and teaching them to act out the main themes of the story being told. For children with written language skills, the structure of a story can be made more explicit by teaching them to pick out all the words that refer to the main character (e.g. Tom, he, his, him) and underline or highlight them in a certain colour. Then other characters can be highlighted using their own colour. Yet another separate colour can be used to highlight the actions of the main character and so on. In this way children can build up a visual 'map' of the key characters and events in a story that helps them realise what a story is 'about'.

Conversational skills
Conversation requires spontaneity, turn-taking and reciprocity. Not surprisingly, these are all very problematic in autism, thus true conversations are very difficult for the child with autism and sld. The child has to keep track of the conversation, to monitor its progress, and actively listen to the contributions of others, in order to match his/her own utterance in terms of topic, relevance, style and timing. This is a complex array of skills which is difficult for children with autism and sld, even when their language skills are sufficient. Some of the outward forms of conversational behaviour, however, can be taught. Children can be taught to take turns by having something to pass round to indicate each speaker's turn. The more able can be taught rules for entering conversations and ways of changing topic politely, and even ways of closing conversations, although that is more difficult. One way

of tackling the problem is to teach sufficient skills to enable the person to begin to participate in simple routine 'conversations' with others, of the kind that are often seen between mothers and their babies. Just as the mother does then, such 'conversations' do not depend on the child having much (or indeed, any) language, and music and singing may be used to add to the facilitatory structure. It is only through active participation that the child will really learn to develop conversational skills and express then fluently.

Talking about events
The cognitive difficulty in doing this will be discussed in later chapters. Here we just examine briefly the problem children with autism and sld have with stories and with 'talking' about what they have been doing. Although most children with autism do not have an interest in stories, others can become very obsessional about particular stories, especially cartoons, or videos, and demand to have the same ones told over and over again. It is not clear what the fascination of these particular ones are (*Thomas the Tank Engine* videos seem popular with children with autism the world over, for example), but it may be that the characters are simplified human-like characters who do predictable things and have definite characters (one is always 'naughty', another 'trustworthy', for example), so that they are less confusing than stories that relate to real people or which are ambiguous about people's motives and beliefs.

Helping children with autism talk about what has happened to them and what they have been doing needs to be tackled in a slightly different way. We can borrow from the techniques of normal child-rearing and mimic (and emphasise and adapt) the way in which parents normally help their children learn to talk about themselves, through a process of first going over events in a structured way, and then prompting them to talk about it in a structured way to others. The child can respond with symbols rather than words, of course. The structure used consists of questions that help the child see that one needs to talk about a character (who?), an event (what?), a time (when?), a consequence (what then?) and an emotional/experiential reaction (how?). The child is helped to build up this topic-comment structure of a narrative through a careful scaffolding of this kind. For children with autism and sld the scaffolding may need to be more emphatic, and, once more, may need to involve visual symbols.

Some key problems in language and communication

Pronoun confusion

Children with autism and sld find it difficult to understand the way in which personal pronouns such as 'I/me', 'you', 'he/she' change according to conversational roles and whether one is speaking, being addressed by others or being talked about. The most common confusion is that they refer to themselves as 'you', 'he' or 'she' or by their proper name, mirroring the way they hear themselves addressed by others. The first person pronoun ('I'/'me') only refers to the self as a conversational role, or an experienced agent or recipient of action. Individuals with autism will have little understanding of conversational role and, without an experiencing sense of self, may not express this agent or recipient role either.

General work to help children build up a sense of themselves performing actions, through reflection and instant photographs of their own role within activities (Powell & Jordan, 1992), will help in the acquisition of this pronoun. However, this may not always be possible where the learning difficulties are very severe. In a more direct way, the child can be taught to label his/her own assertive acts, using the 'I' pronoun, even if this is only in imitation at first. For example, they can be prompted to say 'I stand' as they stand, 'I wave' as they wave, and so on. They may be helped to do this with photographs or with the written words on cards. The understanding of 'you' can be fostered by helping the child attend to situations when 'you' is used to refer to people other than the child in a very explicit way. With children with sld as well as autism, it might be better to allow the use of names instead of pronouns to avoid confusion.

Echolalia

Copying what is heard (from others, videos or TV) either immediately or after an interval of hours, days or even years (delayed echolalia) is a common problem in when children with autism and sld start to speak. This should be seen as a positive development rather than something to eliminate, because it often leads to more productive language and it usually has at least some communicative purpose. Thus, immediate and delayed echolalia may be interpreted as ways in which the child with autism is either trying to communicate or is 'playing' with language in the sense of analysing and recombining it; such an interpretation allows the teacher and parent to try to build on this process. The first step should be to determine exactly how the echolalia is being used and the form it is taking. This includes noting the situations in which the echolalia is occurring and how close it is to the echoed utterance. This is easier when the echolalia is immediate and the 'model' utterance is directly observable. Analysis of delayed echolalia may need to infer the utterance being echoed, but it will still be helpful to analyse the communicative functions being served by the echolalia and to try to determine the conditions that are triggering it.

The first question to ask is 'What is the child communicating?' At the very least it indicates that the child has recognised a need to take a 'turn' in a conversation. At a more advanced level, the child may persist in the echoed utterance until some end has been achieved, and this will demonstrate the child's purpose. Other questions to ask concern whether there are any changes in the form of the delayed echolalia over time or whether there is evidence of failure to understand being the cause of the echo? Often a child with autism and sld will echo a command they do not understand, whereas they will obey one that they do.

Treatment depends on the answers to these questions. Where the child shows little understanding of what is being said and little functional use of the echoing in a communicative sense, the priorities would be:

- to improve the child's understanding of spoken language,
- to increase the proportion of spontaneous utterances,

● to introduce planned variation of the echoed utterances that could be taught to the child specifically as functional ways of achieving particular communicative ends.

Long pauses and the slowing of interaction have also been shown to be effective in increasing the proportion of spontaneous utterances compared to echolalic ones. The likelihood of spontaneous speech is also increased by not putting pressure on the child to speak, but continuing with the 'conversation' with the child, regardless of the type of participation by the child, or whether there is any participation at all.

In order to develop the communicative value of the child's echoed utterances, it will be necessary to impute communicative intent to the delayed echolalic responses. The teacher or parent would begin by getting the child to echo (using the same delayed echolalic phrase) immediately. Once the child had begun to echo the phrase immediately on a regular basis, then echoing that phrase would be made a condition for the item/object requested (e.g. 'Do you want a biscuit?'). If the child is using (or has been taught to use) this phrase readily as a request, the teacher or parent would look for other situations where the child's needs are clear and where such a phrase might be adapted to fit a similar communicative intent (e.g. 'Do you want go out now?'). Finally, the teacher or parent might shape the child's 'comment' into a more conventional request form (e.g. 'Can I go out now?').

Summary
Children with autism and sld will need direct teaching and enabling environments in order to develop both language and communication skills and understanding. For many, an alternative mode of communication will need to be taught as an alternative or precursor to the development of speech. Visual systems will generally be most useful but the actual system chosen will depend on an analysis of the child's strengths and weaknesses and the characteristics of the situation. There may need to be a mix of methods and the overall purpose of improving communication should not be forgotten.

Further reading

WATSON, L., LORD, C., SCHAFFER, B. & SCHOPLER, E., (1989). *Teaching Spontaneous Communication to Autistic and Developmentally Handicapped Children*. New York: Irvington Press.

6 Play Skills

The role of play in development
The very term 'play' suggests that this is not a serious aspect of development; indeed, it is often thought of as the opposite to work. When considering the learning needs of a child with autism and sld, therefore, and all the many important life skills that need to be taught, difficulty in learning to play may not be given a high priority. That, however, would be a mistake. It has been suggested that play is in fact the 'work' of the child and it is through play that the child develops most, if not all, the skills that will be needed to tackle the more 'serious' aspects of life. It is through play that the child learns:

● to solve problems
● to learn about the effects of their own actions on the world
● to learn about the properties of objects
● to learn about others, about social roles and appropriate behaviour to go with those roles
● to learn about the joy of learning and
● to learn the vital social skills of co-operation and competition.

In solitary play the child explores the world, finding out about its properties but also finding out about him/herself. The child develops a sense of self-efficacy and an understanding about things he or she can affect, and things that are impervious to the child's actions. The child learns to differentiate him or herself from objects and to know when stimulation comes from the inside or the outside. S/he develops a sense of events that are caused with intent and events that occur 'accidentally', 'inadvertently' and beyond one's control. The child notices the patterns of occurrences and through all this learning comes to attach meaning to the world and to his or her own place within it. It would be hard to think of a more valuable base for future learning.

In social play, the child learns about other people but also learns more about him or herself. Our sense of ourselves comes partly from our sense of agency as an actor in the world but also from our relationship with others, our adjustments to them and their reactions to us. Left to ourselves we develop our own idiosyncratic view of the world and this narrowness is never challenged or extended. We become ritualistic, always doing things in the same way and becoming resistant to change. With others we not only learn the obvious skills of waiting our turn, compromising and negotiating, co-operating in tasks we could not tackle alone, but in the process we learn about others' perspectives of the world and how to adapt and accommodate to the demands of others. Above all, we learn to share emotions and imagination, to have fun together and so to increase our pleasure and to share our pain, and so reduce it.

Lack of flexibility in autism

From the description of the benefits of play, given above, it can be seen that many of the characteristics of children with autism and sld might stem from difficulties in engaging fully in play. Children with autism and sld are frequently described as 'ritualistic', meaning that they develop routines on which they then come to rely, so that disturbances in those routines may lead to stress and even challenging behaviour. The skills that are learnt also seem to be less adaptable than in other children so that they have problems in transferring what they have learnt in one situation to another. Much of the learning of children with autism and sld is habitual; they rely on the same cues being present in order to remember and 'trigger' the response.

Non-autistic individuals learn what it is to have intentions through early interactions in which they notice and respond to the effects they have on others, and direct their behaviour towards producing those effects and collaborating in joint intentions. From those joint intentions comes not only awareness of how to direct one's own behaviour towards ends, but also that this is a feature of the behaviour of others also. Children with autism and sld have difficulties in reading the intentions of others but they also have difficulty in developing intentions of their own. It is as hard for them to project themselves forward to make their behaviour goal-directed as it is for them to remember personal events (projecting themselves backwards). It is noticeable that it is only when their own obsessional interest is involved that this can serve to make their behaviour focused towards achieving certain ends; it is cognitively difficult for them (i.e. it is not just a matter of lack of motivation) to direct their behaviour towards some goal that has been set by others.

When play is seen in children with autism and sld, however, it tends to be solitary and stereotypical. Such children engage in simple repetitive actions, or stereotypies, which may become even more dominant at times of stress. The more profound the additional learning difficulties, the more likely are stereotyped and self-stimulatory activities and this is even more so when there are additional sensory disabilities. Much of the play, then could be characterised as self-stimulatory and includes:

- visual stimulation of flicking or spinning objects
- auditory stimulation of clicking, tapping or making repetitive sounds
- taste stimulation of licking or ingesting all manner of substances
- tactile stimulation of feeling particular textures
- proprioceptive stimulation (sensations from muscles and the position of joints) of odd gestures of the hands or odd body postures
- vestibular stimulation (sensation from the balance organs of the inner ears) of balancing on narrow ledges, swinging, climbing or spinning themselves.

Difficulties with play (especially functional and symbolic play) feature in diagnostic criteria for autism and lack of pretend play is often seen as a defining feature of autism. As with so much in autism, however, it is not so much that the child with autism and sld cannot play in the way that others do, as that play and interests do not develop spontaneously. If they are directly taught, in an attempt to compensate for the missing skills, the play tends to remain limited to the kinds of play and interests that have been demonstrated by the teacher (Libby *et al.*, 1998). However, as will be seen below, recent work has challenged this pessimism and there have been successful attempts to teach symbolic play to children with autism and sld that have enabled generalisation beyond the test materials and trained routines (Sherratt, 1999).

The relationship of the cognitive difficulties in autism to play behaviour

Perception

There are many reports of inconsistency or fluctuating perception in autism and a mixture of perceptual or sensory integration difficulties. At a practical level, a child with autism and sld may be over- or undersensitive to particular forms of stimulation, which may lead to extreme reactions (to certain noises, or touching, for example, that may appear as painful) or lack of reaction (to pain itself). It also helps to realise that perceptions may vary from one extreme to the other, even within the course of a day, although it may then be more difficult to find a solution. It is also important to be aware that integration of stimuli may not only be difficult of itself but may require extra time.

If the child with autism has perceptual disturbances, this may affect play and exploration of the world in a number of ways. Some aspects of a stimulus may be more noticeable than others and the relationship of one feature (such as colour or shape) may not be integrated with another, resulting in difficulty in relating to the object as a whole. There may be a special attraction to certain functional characteristics of toys so that the most attractive aspect of a toy car may not lie in its representation of a real car (which may not be at all apparent to the child with autism and sld) but in the way its wheels spin round. Noises made by certain toys or by other children playing may simply be too painful for the child with autism, who may block his/her ears and withdraw from contact. Responsiveness to others may be very slow and this will disrupt all forms of interactive play (including early lap play with the mother) so that play partners, unless specially trained to wait and give adequate time for a response, will become discouraged and give up.

Attention

When teachers describe a child with autism and sld as having a 'short attention span' they usually mean that the child will fail to concentrate on the tasks the teacher has set. Children with autism, however, can usually sustain attention or concentration on their own chosen 'play' activities for a long time so there are probably other reasons why they do not sustain play with other children. It may be a problem of motivation, where the child does not understand the purpose of the game nor understand the reactions of others. However, attentional problems in autism are not all due to this kind of motivational problem and there may be genuine difficulties in sustaining attention, especially when the child is young or the learning difficulties are very severe. It is also clear that children with autism and sld have problems in switching attention and may take a long time to do so; as above, the danger is that the play partner will not wait long enough for a response and the play opportunity is lost.

As well as problems in attending to social play, attentional problems (this time in selective attention) may affect all aspects of play. If perceptual difficulties mean that certain aspects of toys and objects are attractive, selective attention problems make it difficult for children with autism and sld to switch to other aspects, and their attentional focus becomes fixed. Their well-documented problems in joining in with the attentional focus of others (i.e. developing shared attention) mean that their attention cannot be directed by others. This in turn means that they do not make the same interpretations of their experiences as others are making of theirs and communication difficulties mean that different perceptions are never shared. Thus, they may never develop an interest in the functional properties of objects, as pointed out by others in play, but develop instead their own fascination with certain aspects of the appearance of toys and objects (even people).

There are many reports in the literature of people with autism attending to detail but not being able to see the whole. This is undeniably true in some instances but it appears to relate to what is seen as meaningful rather than an invariable feature of cognitive style. It was also thought that individuals with autism were unable to attend to more than one stimulus at a time, but this is probably a developmental delay rather than a deficit. Many individuals with autism and sld, however, will be unable to attend to two sources of information at the same time, which means that instructions or commands only serve to enhance (rather than direct) the actions the child is already performing; unless this is understood, the child may be seen as 'disobedient' rather than having a problem with processing. This too affects their capacity to join with others in play routines.

Memory

Children with autism and sld often have fairly good rote memories and good recall to detail alongside an inability to give the gist of a story or event and an apparent failure to remember what happened to themselves even a short while before. Memories in children with autism need to be cued or prompted in some way and there appears to be no way in which individuals with autism can search and produce memories spontaneously. They may not 'get used' to stimuli, so that they often enjoy the same experience over and over again (replaying a section of a video, repeatedly lining up objects or throwing objects out of the play area), much to the irritation of families and potential play partners. It is as if they enjoy the predictability of repetitive actions and stimuli and fail to be bored by them. This may be because they have difficulties in establishing memories of themselves performing actions, although that is not certain.

On the other hand, children with autism and sld (unless they have additional physical impairments) are often good at playing with large motor toys and have good procedural knowledge for skills such as bicycle-riding or climbing.

Solving problems

In common with many others with learning difficulties and especially those with poor language skills, children with autism and sld display poor metacognitive skills (being able to think about their own thinking and so plan, monitor and control it). These difficulties mean that children with autism often learn in a rote way, adhere to learned responses in certain situations and are at a loss if the response does not work. They find it very difficult to inhibit their actions and will persist with habitual responses even when these are known to be wrong or when they are punished. They cannot model their own intentions, which leads to apparent motivational problems and they rely on others or the situation to cue their actions. It also means they will have difficulty making choices or even understanding what a choice is (since that depends on modelling alternative actions) and an inability to benefit from 'incidental learning' where particular responses have not been trained.

All this means they can show problem-solving skills where the problem is readily seen within a particular task. They can do jigsaw puzzles (especially upside-down so there is no picture to distract), often unscrew screws, pick locks and even dismantle domestic equipment (perhaps in search of the transistor at its heart), for example. However, there are few play activities that involve these particular skills. What they have problems with are all aspects of team games, where responses have to be inhibited (as the child waits the appropriate time and/or conditions for the required response), controlled and monitored. One cannot take part in a team game without being aware of one's own actions in relation to others and theirs in relation to you. You also need to make decisions and choices based on the current state of play and need to have a sense of your own intentions in relation to the goal and to monitor the intentions of others. Children with autism and sld can participate in games with clear explicit rules that do not change as the game progresses, and one of the few social games they enjoy is 'chasing'. Even here, their social difficulties mean they may not know how to initiate such a game in an acceptable manner, often hitting others and running away in the hope of being chased.

Computer games can be an exception to their difficulties with problem-solving games. However, they manage these primarily because there is no social content to process at the same time and the rules of the game are made very explicit. Choices also tend to be explicit and limited (do this or this) and the consequences of actions are visual and clear, allowing for fast learning. Mostly computer games will be solitary but they do present an opportunity to encourage social participation, especially if the game is set up so that more than one player is necessary.

Acquiring concepts

Children with autism and sld do not seem able to see the meaningful patterns in the world around them and have difficulty analysing stimulation and abstracting the features that lead to concepts being formed. Sometimes this is described in the literature as a difficulty with abstract concepts and certainly the learning difficulties may make some abstract concepts difficult to acquire. However, the real problem (certainly in relation to autism) does not lie in the abstract quality of the concept. Most people with autism (including those with additional sld) find some forms of abstract concept, such as those involved in music, maths and science easier to grasp than everyday concepts. This is because these abstract concepts are acquired through specific explicit definitions (science and some aspects of maths) or involve a medium (music) whose structure they understand. Children with very severe learning difficulties of course will have problems with some of these concepts, but that is not to do with the autism.

In autism the problem with acquiring concepts is to do with the difficulty in abstracting relevant features from their experience to form a fuzzy concept of the object, modified in turn by future experiences. To them each experience appears to be unique, and so their concepts are equally tied to those instances: they think about a particular object they have experienced rather than developing an 'idea' of that object. Of course the effect will be more noticeable when it comes to abstract concepts, since, for example, a judge in a wig and gown is more misleading about the concept of justice than a particular chair is about the concept of a chair. Yet all these rigid concepts will inhibit thinking and will be harder to elaborate and link together than would be more flexible concepts.

This style of thinking also has a profound effect on the development of play. The point about these rigid concepts is that they are also particular to that individual's experience and so cannot be shared. If you cannot share a concept, then you cannot join with others in games that involve such sharing, which are all forms of imaginative play. Of course, that is not to say that these cannot be taught, if they are made explicit, but it is not going to happen spontaneously. On the other hand, the ability to appreciate the structure of music means that they can often play musical games, and music can be used to structure play activities for them.

Integrating thinking

Children with autism and sld do not seem to set up models or schema of events they are engaged in, or of stories they are told. They do not attend to overall meaning or see the pattern through which things are related. This means that learning becomes fragmented and tied to contexts, since the overall meaning is missed and not related to other aspects of the child's knowledge or understanding.

Difficulties in this area mean that all forms of play that involve narratives are affected. Bruner and Feldman (1993), for example, have explored these difficulties in autism and shown how even simple games between parent and child depend on this narrative form. They analyse the 'peep-bo!' game showing that it has the narrative form of:

- a steady state—the mother and child gaze at one another
- an event—mother hides her face (or the baby's face)
- a restoration of the steady state—the occluding item is removed
- a 'coda'—the mother marks this by saying 'Boo!'

It is hard to know which is chicken and which is egg in this case, and it may be that a difficulty with seeing the narrative form leads to the difficulty in participating in this interactive game, or that difficulty in interaction makes it difficult for the child to acquire this appreciation of narrative form. In any case it is clear that a problem with understanding and using narrative forms will interfere not only with these early forms of play but all make-believe games with other children in which joint narratives are developed.

Developing creativity

Children with autism may sometimes produce creative works of art (i.e. in visual art or music), but this is very rarely the case where the child has additional sld. Children with autism and sld are seldom creative in art or in everyday life. This lack of creativity is seen in their use of language and in the way in which they go about all activities. If they say or do something that appears to be 'new' or 'inventive', then one needs to check back to sources. Typically, it may be that they are faithfully reproducing chunks of remembered dialogue or actions from a source such as a television programme. Some individuals with autism and sld, however, do 'create' by devising their own patterns, usually within an obsessional interest, although these patterns, once created, may remain rigid. Computer programmes, mathematical manipulations or musical compositions may offer a context in which this is possible.

Play behaviour is a reflection of this lack of creativity. Children with autism and sld will continue to play in exactly the same way with toys for years at a time, unless there is some form of positive intervention. Having found one way of manipulating materials, children with autism and sld do not appear to engage with the materials in a way we would normally identify as 'playful'. They may engage in what appears to be an experimental act but the pleasure for them seems to lie in continual repetition with its consequent predictability, rather than in producing the variations that delight over children. Other children will be inspired by material that allows free expression (such as plain wooden blocks, or an undressed doll) but the child with autism may not be able to work out what to do with such material beyond physical manipulation. They may respond more appropriately to the more rigid toys such as toy train sets or a doll dressed to fulfil one particular role (i.e. a superman doll). Even train sets may not elicit the varied play behaviour seen in other children, but just lining up behaviour or making the trains go round and round the track in a set order.

Developing play

Early lap play

In spite of its name, this does not have to be limited to younger children, nor does it have to take place on a lap. It is a way of describing those games and activities that involve two people in an intimate relationship and are designed primarily to enable the partners to engage emotionally with one another, although, as shown earlier, there are other important learning outcomes. The 'early' really refers to the developmental stage, so it is appropriate play to encourage in anyone, regardless of actual age, who is at a very early stage of this kind of social play (or perhaps has not even started). Nind and Hewett (1994) have used these techniques with some modification to make them appropriate for adults in a professional context in their interactive curriculum, and they are included in the interactions that are supported by music in the work of Wimpory *et al.* (1995) Prevezer (1990) and Christie *et al.*, (1992). Such play is also compatible with the option approach (Kaufman, 1994).

Since the play involved is both interactive and sensitive to the ongoing reactions of the participants, no programme can be predetermined. However, there are principles that should guide the interactions:

- Both partners should be having fun.
- Each partner must take a turn and the play should be structured to allow this to happen, even if the child's response is a minimal one.
- Timing is crucial and exaggerated pauses should allow the child time to take his/her turn.
- Begin with actions which mirror those of the child and develop them into a turn-taking routine.
- Gradually expect more from the child but, if there is any sign of having 'gone too far', retreat immediately to the level the child was enjoying.
- Do not force eye contact or the *'en face'* position; many children with autism can only begin these activities if, for example, they are facing away from the adult, even backed

on to the adult's lap. The child may be able to make eye contact and tolerate the '*en face*' position if this is softened by putting a chiffon scarf between the faces.

- Aim for short periods of successful interaction (as many times a day as is possible or reasonable) rather than prolonging sessions beyond the child's level of tolerance.
- Help the child develop predictive powers by building the tension round the climax (a tickle?) of a familiar routine.

The goals for such activities will vary according to the particular session but will include building a relationship with someone who can then build on that relationship in other learning opportunities. It will also involve more specific goals such as increased toleration of physical contact, ability to take turns (including a reduction in the time it takes the child to take his or her turn), physical and/or verbal imitation, appropriately timed eye contact, and contribution to learnt routines. It can be seen as a preparation for further learning, but it is also a time of shared enjoyment and the value of that should not be underestimated, especially between parents and child.

Exploratory play with toys
This is aimed to help the child move from using toys and other objects purely for sensory stimulation and to adjust what they do to accommodate to the varied properties of the toys. This is in opposition to the current behaviour of the child that may be to use a single 'play' routine, regardless of the toys being played with. One child may lick and chew everything, another tap and bang, another throw, another smell, another flick and twist. The purpose of building up exploratory play is not to eliminate these ways of relating to objects, but to extend their variety and appropriateness, so that the child is beginning to pay attention to the play opportunities offered by different toys.

It is, however, difficult to encourage children with autism and sld to alter their habitual mode of responding. They may concentrate for hours on self-initiated tasks, but they may not perceive the relevance of tasks selected by others. The good teacher will want to adopt the advice to 'broaden out' the child's interests rather than to try to inhibit them in favour of the teacher's agenda, although some obsessive interests or habits are easier to encourage (or even tolerate) than others. However, it is neither necessary nor wise to await the child's spontaneous development of an interest or skill. Natural interests should be capitalised on, but gradual and structured introduction of new activities can enable the child to have new experiences, gain new skills and understanding, and improve the present and future quality of life.

If a routine action is well established, the first step in trying to modify it is to stop it being performed automatically and help the child become aware of performing it. A way of doing this is to imitate the child, in a way that the child notices. The feasibility and/or desirability of doing this will vary and, if the child is doing something dangerous (such as throwing heavy items all round the room), then there may need to be a modification of this behaviour to start with. Often the simplest way to do this is to change the materials—giving the child foam blocks, for example, where it does not matter if they are thrown. If the throwing then stops, it suggests the motivation is the crashing of the objects rather than the actual throwing, so you would need to focus on helping the child throw into a tin, or similar object, before instituting a game of imitation.

Once the child has noticed being imitated and turn-taking in imitation has been established, based on the child's preferred actions, the adult can start modifying the action and getting the child to imitate the modification. If this does not happen, the adult needs to go back to the child's actions, re-establish a turn-taking routine and then reintroduce a modification, but a much reduced one, that the child will copy. Once the child is copying the actions of the adult regularly and these actions are now far from the child's original actions, the adult needs to introduce copying of activities specifically tailored to the properties of particular toys. For example, two drums are presented and the adult models banging the drums. Then two toy windmills are presented and the adult models blowing or even flicking the windmill, depending on which actions are within the child's repertoire. The aim is not to teach new responses, although this may be necessary if the child has only a very limited repertoire. The prime aim, however, is to get the child to pay attention to the kind of toy presented and to adapt his or her responses to that toy accordingly.

Once the child has a range of differentiated responses to objects then a mixture of toys can be provided and the child guided to respond differentially to each one. The final stage of this programme is to get the child to perform more than one action with each toy. This should not be attempted until the child is confidently using different actions with different toys, or the child may revert to doing the same thing (or the same two things) to every object. The child can be said to have usable exploratory play behaviour when s/he is able to respond with differentiated play responses when presented with toys on which s/he has received no training. This play can be further extended by teaching the child to combine objects in play and to develop sequences of actions with toys.

Pretend play
There are two aspects of pretend play: using toy objects as the real objects they represent (functional play) and pretending that one object is something else, or is there when it is not, or is not there when it is (symbolic play). Typical of functional play are play with toy cars, trains, farms, tea sets and all forms of doll play. This is usually the form of pretend play to start with, since it is easier to teach and understand. Clearly, if we follow the model presented above of first teaching the child to imitate, we can model appropriate actions with all these toys. The problem is that it is not clear that the child who is happily copying pushing the cars along and saying 'Beep! Beep!' has any idea that s/he is supposed to be representing a 'real' scenario. We can help the child make the connection, if we use a form of language as a bridge between real-life and play events. Thus we can have symbols for 'feeding' or 'driving' and help the child associate them with real-life examples of these two activities. Once the child is able to do this consistently, then present the symbol to the child in association with the relevant toys. If this does not trigger the appropriate behaviour (which has already been trained in imitated play sessions), then the child can be physically guided or

prompted to engage in the taught routines. Eventually, when the symbol is sufficient to trigger the appropriate play, and is still understood as applying to the real situation, it is likely (although not certain) that the child understands the reference of the play to the real situation.

Once the child has begun to play in a functional way, symbolic pay can be attempted. Sherratt (1999) has developed a way of presenting symbolic play routines in a narrative format to children with autism and sld, that uses structure, repetition, prediction, enthusiasm and directed attention to engage the children. He found that a sustained programme in a school setting was not only successful in engendering imitation of the demonstrated activities but also in producing novel symbolic play acts, at least in some of the children. As long as the child is having fun in such sessions, he or she is likely to be benefiting, even if they do not achieve this ultimate goal, so it is always worth having the highest expectations, as long as the child's learning is supported fully at each stage.

Social play
As has been noted earlier, children with autism and sld will not have intuitive routes to social understanding, so that they will need to use general cognitive capacities to work out the social aspects of a situation. This means they cannot do this at the same time as learning something else, so social play can only be encouraged with play activities that are already very familiar to the child. In other words, children may need to be taught how to do something first (perhaps one-to-one with an adult) before they can be expected to learn how to do it with others. This applies whether one is talking about a traditional work task or the 'task' of playing. Thus, any routinised game with rules (hide-and-seek, table games such as ludo, team games such as basketball) will need to be taught first in the way the child can best learn, and then generalised to situations with other children.

However, this rather artificial process is not necessary to encourage all social play. The child with autism and sld, after all, will already have a repertoire of responses in which he or she happily engages. There have been successful attempts to enrol normally developing children (after some initial training to help them understand autism, but not to teach them exactly what to do) in engaging children with autism in play (Royers, 1995). Many schools where there are children without autism (even if they have sld) will use 'buddy' schemes or specially created 'friendship' groups to help the children with autism and sld play more socially, and these are generally successful, at least to some extent. Siblings have also been helped to play with their brother or sister with autism and once more this can be a very valuable resource. Left to themselves, other children will not understand and may be put off by the lack of responsiveness or the apparently negative reactions of the child with autism and sld. But with some guidance as to the meaning of the child's behaviour (such as explaining that he may be hitting just to get attention or because he doesn't know another way of getting them to play with him) and back-up support for when the children are puzzled or confused, other children can prove to be ingenious and successful 'teachers' of play skills. As with other aspects of learning, it is better that the child with autism and sld has a few moments of successful enjoyable play with others (which can then be built up gradually) than that they are made to tolerate being with others to the point when the interactions become negative and the child with autism retreats further.

Leisure activities:
Although parents of children with autism are usually most concerned that they receive an appropriate education, the issue of occupation during 'free' or 'leisure' times becomes of increasing importance as the child grows older. Just as other children become increasingly independent and able to occupy themselves with their friends, children with autism and sld may become more demanding and may engage in worrying behaviour (such as stereotypies or self-injury) if bored and unoccupied. The more such destructive behaviour is allowed to flourish, the harder it will become to teach more profitable activities. It is thus wise to try to teach the child ways of 'playing' by themselves as early as possible, as well as teaching them to be more social. The more

severe a child's sld, the harder this will be, but the long-term benefits for the child and the family are immense.

Watching favourite videos can provide much useful respite for a family but can also be a source of irritation and upset if the child insists on certain videos (or even bits of videos) being played over and over again. A child's fascination with videos can be used as a teaching device that involves all the family, by using home-produced teaching videos (A to Z video—available from the National Autistic Society.) Interactive video games can be taught on the computer (using the same theme as the favourite video, e.g. *Thomas the Tank* video) so that the child can be learning while engaged in a favourite activity. By moving the interest to a computer, this also allows the opportunity to involve others or to make it a private activity and free the television or video for other family members.

The child may need to fiddle or twiddle objects but parents or others may be distressed to see this apparently bizarre behaviour. It may help if the 'bizarre' behaviour is modified slightly, so that it is still soothing to the child but is seen by others as more acceptable. Thus, a child who likes to hold something in his/her hands and twist it in front of his/her eyes might be given an 'adult' toy which produces visual effects when twisted—this may be meant as an object for a desk or an ornament, but serves the child's purposes well. One adult with autism (without learning difficulties) has a collection of such 'toys', which she refers to as 'auti-toys' because of their particular appeal to people with autism. She uses them to calm herself down when stressed and can spend hours in peaceful contemplation of their effects, whereas, without such aids, she might well become destructive of her environment.

Music can be another soothing and enjoyable pastime. It is worth teaching children with autism and sld to tolerate the use of head phones (introducing them when the child is calm for a few seconds only and then gradually building on this time). This will mean, once more, that they can listen without the rest of the family having to do so at the same time. The head phones also help focus the child's attention on the music and so have a valuable function in improving listening skills.

In school situations, children with autism will usually enjoy situations such as multi-sensory environments. They can also enjoy all forms of physical activity, although they may need help to participate fully. If the child is fit, then walking can be a healthy and relatively stress-free activity for all the family. Many children will also enjoy cycling, although they will probably need to learn to use a tandem, unless a very safe cycling environment can be found. Similarly, under proper instruction and with a full risk assessment, children with autism and sld have learnt to participate in rock climbing, canoeing, sailing and even abseiling, and have derived much pleasure and self-esteem from such activities. Similarly, many children with autism love activities such as snooker (or pool), ice- or roller-skating, trampolining and even skiing, although, as with any other group, this depends on individual taste and ability. It is worth persisting when introducing a child with autism and sld to a new activity, since initial response to a new experience may mask any enjoyment. As the sessions progress, staff and/or parents need to notice whether the child is showing more or less pleasure and more or less distress each time. Clearly if the child enjoys it less each time and shows increasing distress, the activity should be dropped. But if initial distress lessens as the child gets used to the activity and the child's enjoyment is increasing (even by small amounts) it is worth persisting.

Swimming is a common activity in schools for children with autism and is a sport at which many of them excel. However, staff and parent may need to be clear about the purpose of the activity. If it is regarded as primarily a sport and an educational activity, the focus may be on trying to improve the child's performance—either in terms of speed or style or endurance. This may be fine, but may not be understood or tolerated by the child, who then ceases to enjoy the activity, and hence a potentially valuable leisure pursuit is ruined. Allowing the child to enjoy swimming, and just encouraging minor adjustments towards a goal of having more 'fun' at the activity, may in fact be more in the child's (and family's) long-term interest.

It is also useful to try to teach the child with autism and sld some 'table-top' activity that can become a family game. It may be that the game is rather 'young' for brothers and sisters, but they can often get satisfaction from being able to play and have fun with their sibling with autism and good table-top games have an appeal to all ages. Children with autism and sld may in fact excel at certain games involving visual memory (such as 'pairs'— played with picture or symbol cards) or at doing jigsaw puzzles.

Summary
Difficulty in being flexible in thinking and learning is one of the three defining features of autism, so it is not surprising to find that play, which has such flexibility as its essence, is disturbed in autism. It is not just that children with autism miss the 'fun' of playful activities, but that they miss the many opportunities that play presents to learn about their own relationship to the world and to other people.

Play is an activity, then, which needs to be encouraged in its own right and because it provides an excellent context for teaching and learning. Left to themselves, children with autism and sld will play in very stereotypical and repetitive ways that are often primarily concerned with self-stimulation. This may have value in reducing stress, but the child also needs direct teaching to develop more advanced play behaviour. Recent successful attempts to do this have shown that children with autism and sld can learn even symbolic play if they are engaged fully in the learning and the learning is structured in a way that makes it accessible.

Play is also an important leisure pursuit and future and current quality of life of both the child and family can be enhanced if play and leisure skills are developed.

Further reading
BEYER, J. & GAMMELTOFT, L. (1999). *Autism and Play*, London: Jessica Kingsley.
WOLFBURG, P. (1999). *Play and Imagination in Children with Autism*. New York: Teacher's College Press.

7 Supportive Educational Environments

Approaches for working with children with autism and sld

There is little agreement on the 'best' approach for children with autism and ṣld and in any case it is unlikely that a single approach will be 'best' for all such children, for all contexts, at all times (Jordan *et al.*, 1998). In the UK there is a tradition of eclectic approaches, centred round individual needs, as assessed by a statement or record of special educational needs. These needs are seldom specified with precision, however, and there is little guidance on the educational approach to be adopted, apart from general educational principles as laid down in legislation. The forms of support offered to the child and his/her family after diagnosis and at school age is variable across the country (Howlin & Moore, 1997; Jordan & Jones, 1997) but tends to arise from the particular interests, knowledge or pressure of local professionals and parents, rather than any planned policy towards children with autism and sld. This is beginning to change under growing parental demand and the recognition by educational authorities that they have not made adequate provision in the past for this group. In some areas there are multidisciplinary groups at pre-school level that are also developing initiatives, but the integration with later educational practice is not always 'seamless'.

Parents and staff, meanwhile, are becoming increasingly aware (through the Internet and general publicity) of approaches emanating mainly from the USA. These approaches are often in competition with one another and tend to offer a single methodology. Some of these approaches come with claims of significant success (even 'restoration of normal functioning') backed up by some research of varying quality. The American approaches are often very similar to approaches adopted in the UK, but they are usually distinctive in that they are clearly packaged and marketed. There is a value in this 'packaging' in that it often makes complex principles accessible to professional trained and untrained staff and to parents, and this helps them to feel confident in adopting the approach. There are also dangers, however. One is that UK staff may not receive the same quality or intensity of training as the originators of the programme, and short training courses often result in the method being adopted piecemeal without understanding. Then it becomes like a set of recipe cards, used inflexibly and sometimes inappropriately, and vulnerable to distortion.

Approaches should be considered with respect to the extent they support the learning and quality of life of individuals with autism and sld. They should reduce stress and promote learning and development. The features that are most supportive in environments may vary somewhat from one individual to another and an over-arching principle should be flexibility to adapt to individual needs. Nevertheless, there are issues that apply to all cases. Before considering some examples of environments and teaching approaches that support children with autism and sld and their families, the principles for such support need to be considered. These principles derive partly from research on the learning difficulties and learning style of such children, and partly from examples of good practice in the education and care of children and adults with autism and sld.

Issues in providing a supportive educational environment

The medium of instruction

As discussed in earlier chapters, there is likely to be a particular difficulty in understanding and responding to verbal instructions. This is particularly so if long sentences are used, or the pauses between phrases are not long enough for the child to process the language. In all cases, however, speech is more likely to confuse rather than help, yet it is very hard for those caring for, or working with, children to control their natural inclination to 'talk the child through' processes and problems. If there is another system available, this has the double function then of making the instructions more accessible to the child with autism and sld, and

reminding the adult of this need to reduce language when interacting with the child. Below are the 'instructions' for completing
a range of tasks or 'information' about the series of activities to
be undertaken. Within each task or activity, there would need to
be a comparable list of 'instructions' or 'information' unless the
task or activity was one with which the child was already very
familiar.

The medium chosen should be flexible enough to meet individual needs, and teaching goals might include helping the child
move through from the most restrictive forms to the least restrictive ones (in terms of the potential audience for the communication). The range of possibilities (taken largely from Peeters &
Gillberg, 1999) include:

- objects of reference placed on shelves or hung on pegs in an
  order (left to right or top to bottom) that gives the order in
  which the activities will take place or the tasks should be
  tackled.

- picture symbols placed on strips (fixed by velcro or by paper
  clip), placed in see-through pockets or arranged so they can
  be flipped over to the blank side. The order of fixation, as
  above, may be from top to bottom or left to right and will
  reflect the order of the tasks or activities.

- written words describing the tasks and/or activities to be
  undertaken and a similar arrangement for ordering the words
  as used in the first two systems.

- signs used for each of the activities, given as a list. This is
  unlikely to be successful for allowing independent following
  of a sequence of activities, as a sign must be used as a
  way of prompting the next activity in a sequence. However,
  sequences of signs are almost as hard as spoken words to
  memorise, and children with autism and sld are likely to need
  the support of a more tangible system, except for familiar
  sequences.

- spoken instructions. As with the signs, a list at the start of a
  sequence is likely to be forgotten, but spoken words can be

used as verbal prompts for each activity. Single words or short phrases are to be preferred to longer ones, and especially ones that contain irrelevant and confusing matter. Such an example is 'When you've gone to the toilet, I want you to wash your hands and then go into the dining room and set the table for lunch'. It is unlikely that a child with autism and sld, receiving that as an 'instruction', would have any idea of what to do and indeed might just respond to the last part—getting upset when his or her lunch does not appear immediately. This is regardless of whether the child does or does not understand the meaning of each of the short instructions embedded in the longer one.

Vignette

Lee was an eleven-year-old boy with autism and sld in a specialist residential school for children with autism and severely challenging behaviour. Lee had calmed down since entering the school eighteen months earlier but there were certain 'flash points' for him when his behaviour often got out of control once more. One of these was getting ready for school in the morning. Although capable of washing, toileting, cleaning his teeth and dressing (apart from laces) by himself, he would regularly be found wandering around half dressed, perhaps without having washed or cleaned his teeth, and, when asked verbally what he was up to, whether he had done all these things, and told verbally to get a move on, he would sometimes comply but often he became suddenly enraged and lashed out at anyone near him.

Care staff felt they were merely being pleasantly directive and giving Lee verbal prompts for his behaviour. That his behaviour appeared inconsistent led staff to look for explanations of his outbursts in terms of Lee's state of mind that day, rather than their own behaviour. It is not clear how Lee viewed this, but it would seem as if, at best, the verbal behaviour acted as nagging, with which he sometimes co-operated by working to get rid of the nagging, i.e., getting washed and dressed. On other days he seemed totally bemused by the language and at a loss as to where to start and what to do next; frustrated and confused, he would then lash out. It was possible that his mood alone made the difference between these two situations but it was also possible (and more likely) that there was an interaction between his mood (perhaps related to how much sleep he had had) and the confusion and incomprehension of the language used by the staff. In any case, it was the language that staff had most control over, so this was an obvious first step to try.

Lee did not speak but staff felt (an untested assumption) that he understood everything that was said. Even if this were true (and again it was unlikely in this case), that might only apply to language used in short phrases in contexts that made the meaning clear. It might be that the times Lee reacted well were when this happened, and the staff, for example, were telling him to clean his teeth when he was in the bathroom near his toothbrush. The times when he reacted badly might be, for example, when he was asked about cleaning his teeth (already just an indirect implication that he should clean his teeth, not a command) when he was wandering in the corridor and with his toothbrush nowhere in sight. This hypothesis was tested through observation and found to be correct.

As a result, staff agreed that a clear visual timetable in a logical sequence from top to bottom might help Lee keep on task until his daily routine was complete and might prevent him from becoming confused and distressed by 'out of context' speech. The programme was instigated and proved to be a great success. Lee learnt readily to turn over each picture after having completed a step in the routine and to go on to the next without any wandering. An 'activity' that had previously taken up to an hour with much staff stress and nagging, and which often ended in upset and tears, was now usually completed without fuss in fifteen minutes.

Supportive task environments

The same kinds of factors operate as with the medium of instruction. There will be considerable variation according to the abilities and preferences of the child, but common features are likely to be:

- visual presentation of tasks or activities (except where there are additional visual impairments)

- structure (usually visual) that indicates what? when? where? how? with whom? for how long? and what next?
- ready access to computer-assisted learning for suitable learning and leisure opportunities
- tasks that are structured so that the child has only to cope with one dimension at a time, unless more than one dimension has been learnt and the purpose is the integration of the responses to the two dimensions.

The first two of these features are clearly part of the TEACCH methodology (Peeters, 1997; Schopler & Olley, 1982), although seen in other programmes. Signed or written instructions could provide this structure and it is not confined to picture symbols and/or objects of reference. This kind of learning environment should maximise the child's capacity to begin learning. However, it does mean that the child is still dependent on this kind of structure so, wherever possible, staff should look for ways of lessening that dependence as the child gets older, and moves towards adulthood. This might be too high an expectation for those with the most severe learning difficulties and severe autism, but it is the role of education to help the child learn to function in the least restrictive environment as possible. There is always a balance to be drawn between providing the most facilitatory environment for the child's learning to take place and providing an environment so adapted to the child that s/he is in fact not enabled to reach their learning potential.

Jordan *et al.*, (1999) report on a school for children with sld which, like other such schools, has always had a percentage of children with autism. This school, however, has made the decision that all the pupils would benefit from an environment geared to the needs of children with autism. It is an all-age school and at the reception stage, there are two parallel classes, one of which is much more structured than the other. All the children with autism enter this class, as do some of the other children (with forms of brain damage, for example) who need this strict degree of structure. Adaptations to the environment in this room include very low natural light, bare walls with high shelves on which items can be displayed (with a communication board beneath at child height so the children can 'ask' for the item), clearly marked areas for separate activities and for the placement of objects and people (including each child with their own chair with a bottom-shape on the chair to match the child's bottom), carpets to allow for bare feet within the class, large plastic jugs and mugs for drinks time and so on. As the children progress through the school they are taught specifically to cope with less and less structure until, by the leavers' class, they are able to function alongside others with sld and to manage some integration experiences in mainstream settings.

Learning with and from peers

Working in groups is a common approach to learning in most schools. There is an assumption that children will learn effectively through a process of sharing tasks and working through problems together and that this process involves the social negotiation of meanings. For the non-autistic child this may in part be true. Certainly, such children will learn about interpersonal relationships through shared activities. But for the child with autism this process is not automatic, and indeed the social situation may be a barrier to, rather than an enhancer of, learning. Children with autism and sld will need specific help in learning how to learn in groups and even more structured and extensive guidance if they are to learn *from* groups. In autism, much of the learning that takes place will need to be on an individual or one-to-one basis.

As explained in earlier chapters, the difficulties in understanding social situations makes the normal social situation of schools a problematic one for children with autism and sld. Such children will need to be taught directly to act as part of a group, but this may, in some cases, involve an earlier step, of teaching them to tolerate working in proximity to others. This in turn may need to be done in stages, with the child being taught one-to-one with an adult, then learning to perform the same task on their own in ways that are described below and finally learning to do it with others. This latter stage may start with one other child only, but the group can gradually be extended. Other children with autism and sld may not find others so disturbing, but may still need support in knowing how to relate to others and in structuring and timing the interaction.

If the group or class includes children without autism, other children may be able to help in this process of managing the interaction, but this is far more difficult to manage when all classmates have autism. Even so, some children with autism and sld are more socially skilled than others and they may be trained to be supportive of the communicative attempts of others. It is useful to teach the child with autism and sld to imitate others, whenever this is possible, since that is a way to increase their opportunities for acquiring social and other adaptive behaviour, although that depends on them having access to peers whose skills are 'worth' copying. Even in specialist schools and classes, therefore, there should be opportunities for mixing with children who do not share the same social difficulties.

Other children may also be able to give models of classroom behaviour such as holding up one's hand before speaking, lining up and so on and, if specific attention is drawn to these actions, that provides useful learning opportunities for the child. The problem is that the child with autism and sld will not have any sense of what the relevant behaviours are, to copy, and so this cannot be relied upon as the main teaching route. The child will still need specific training to raise a hand before speaking in class, for example, but other more able (or previously trained) children can serve as prompts or cues to the behaviour, once it is established. There are successful teaching methods developed in the USA (Strain & Cordisco, 1994) which use other normally developing peers to cue behaviour in natural teaching situations and, while not specifically tailored for children with autism and sld, they are likely to be helpful for a number of such children and could be adapted to fit a more disabled group.

Therapeutic environments

There are particular environments, common in specialist schools for children with autism and some schools for those with sld, that are claimed to be therapeutic in themselves. Soft play rooms provide a safe comfortable environment, for example, in which a child can learn to relax (perhaps with music, with or without peers, with or without a members of staff). It may also be used to allow a child to 'let off steam' if they are under stress or as a way of pre-empting a behavioural outburst. There have been no studies showing the effectiveness of such usage in schools for children with autism, but most schools themselves view such a room as a valuable resource in behaviour management and encouragement of social interaction.

There is another room (or trolley—since there are now movable trolleys that can be wheeled from room to room to provide these effects) that is anecdotally very effective in helping individuals with autism integrate sensory experiences and gain a sense of themselves as actors in the world. These rooms produce a range of sensory effects with lights, fibre optic displays, music, sound effects, tactile materials, smell dispersal and vibratory stimulation that can all be controlled by the teacher or can be programmed to respond to particular actions of the child. It can encourage interaction between peers or it can encourage the child to interact with his or her environment and learn about cause and effect. There is one school for children with autism and very severe or profound learning difficulties who use this room as a way of enabling memories of events and reflection in their pupils. After a school outing, for example, the children come and lie on the cushions in this room and the teacher arranges for stimuli collected on the outing (or associated with the outing) to be played, to trigger memories of the event. As the children are listening to the street sounds or the sounds of the sea or the woods, they are exposed to appropriate smells and to experiences such as being sprinkled with water if they had been caught in the rain. Simple language is used to tie in these current experiences with the experiences on the outing.

Some schools will use time in the soft play area or sensory stimulation area as a reward for periods of good behaviour and sustained work—clear evidence of their popularity, if not their effectiveness.

Ball ponds or rooms can also be very popular with children with autism and sld and can be used to help them to calm down when stressed. It is not clear how they 'work' but it is thought that they supply the comfort of pressure, which many of us get from physical contact with others, but which most people with autism are denied. Temple Grandin, an able person with autism, has designed a 'squeeze machine' (available in the USA) for holding people with autism in controllable ways and she herself still uses such a device to calm down and relax. Without such specific devices, children (and some adults) with autism and sld often seek this kind of pressure stimulation themselves. They will often try to sleep under rather than on top of mattresses and may pile up mats and rugs and crawl under them. They frequently seek sensory reduction as well as containment by crawling into boxes, under tables and into dark cupboards. It is very common for children and adults with autism and profound learning difficulties to carry objects with them pressed into the palms of their hands, which is another way of reducing levels of arousal.

Remember that it is not stimulation itself that is painful but rather its unpredictability and uncontrollability, although children with autism may be particularly sensitive to some stimulation. Fluorescent lights, for example may flicker in a way that most people to not notice but which drive some people with autism to distraction, preventing them gaining coherent visual stimulation. There are shields for such lights that speed up the flicker to the point that even people with autism are able to ignore, but they are expensive and will not be used if architects and others are unaware of these particular sensitivities. The problem is that some people with autism report such disturbances themselves but there is no scientific evidence for this effect or any real information of how many people with autism are affected and to what degree. Research is needed to examine these environmental variables and to see how attention to such details may improve the learning environment for people with autism and sld, who are not able to voice their own experiences nor act upon the effects (except by closing eyes, squinting, and blocking ears).

The same problems apply to the use of colours. There are people with autism who claim particular disturbances with certain colours or who may suffer from synaesthesia so that stimulation in one sense may have an effect on another. Thus a certain colour may be perceived as a smell or a sound or so on. Some also claim a particular problem with high contrast visual stimulation (such as print) and further claim that Irlen lenses (Irlen, 1995) can help overcome these and other problems with sensory stimulation. Once more, further research is needed both to investigate these therapeutic claims and to see how any such difficulties can be identified in the population (such as those with autism and sld) who are unable to communicate their experiences.

Educational provision for children with autism and sld
Many parents of children with autism and sld think that a specialist school or unit for autism is automatically better for their child than a school for children with sld (Jordan & Jones, 1996). In other cases of dual disability (sensory impairment with autism, for example) it may be accepted that the special school for the other disability may have something valuable to contribute to the education of the child, but a school for children with sld is seldom viewed in that positive light. Yet, just as it is important to have the child's needs that result from autism addressed, so it is important to recognise the effects of sld and the way this will interact with autism in the course of development and learning.

Similarly, 'inclusion' in a mainstream school may be seen as desirable, even when there is no specialist knowledge or understanding within the school and where there has been little or no adaptation to meet the particular needs of the child with autism and sld. Even with children with autism without sld, however, the provision of an untrained support assistant to access a mainstream placement does not result in the child with autism's needs being met nor lead to any real inclusion (Jordan & Powell, 1994). The child with sld in addition to autism, like other children with special needs, will benefit from some integration with normally developing peers, but it may be better for them, and more realistic, if their real inclusion is within a school where the pupils have the same general learning difficulties, but without the characteristics of autism.

This does not mean that children with autism and sld do not need specialist understanding and a curriculum, teaching approach and environmental adaptation to meet their specific needs. Nor does it mean that staff in schools for children with sld do not need additional support and training to understand and meet these special needs, for they do. But the issue of effective education for children with autism is not about location, but about the understanding and skills of the staff and the flexibility of the school in adapting to the individual needs of the children (Jordan & Powell, 1995a). Substantial numbers of children with autism and sld have always been in schools for children with sld, whether or not they have been identified, and this is liable to remain the case for the foreseeable future in spite of moves towards inclusion and the greater provision of specialist schools and classes for children with autism. Some children may benefit from a separate specialist unit within such a school, but there is considerable value in the notion that other children will share some of their special needs and that the whole school will benefit from becoming more autism-friendly, as shown in the case study of Jordan *et al.* (1999). There are also advantages in being with more sociable children with better communication (if not linguistic) skills, provided that specialist needs are recognised and responded to. Aird and Lister (1999) suggest ways in which a school for children with sld can audit their needs and begin the process of adapting to meet this new challenge.

The move to inclusion is, nevertheless, not only an increasing position taken by disability rights groups but is also enshrined in legislation (Department of Education and Employment, 1997). It follows a worldwide movement, adopting the maxim that children should be educated 'in the least restrictive environment'. However, the rhetoric of inclusion may not reflect the reality. It should always be remembered that integration is a process, not a location, and that inclusion involves a system that includes all from its inception to its operation. This is not the case with current educational policies and practices and thus, to produce true inclusion, would involve at least as much change in mainstream educational practice as it would the 'integration' of any group with special needs.

Even in the more limited case of integration, it is not certain whether long-term integration into society is best served by early integrated or segregated provision. For the child with autism, it may be that a period of segregation in which the child is taught skills intensively may enable later more integrated experiences, perhaps bridged by a period of 'reverse integration'. 'Reverse integration' is where mainstream children join the child in a segregated setting and work (or 'play') with the child in that setting. In that way the child with autism and sld needs only get used to the new children and learn how to work or play with them; all other aspects of the situation are familiar to the child. Once children with autism and sld are familiar with playing and working with the mainstream children, it is these same children who can take them with them into the mainstream setting. Now, the children with autism already know how to be with the other children and just have to learn how to play and/or work with them in this new environment.

The comparison with respect to this aspect of policy should be with children with visual impairments rather than learning difficulties alone. There are accepted precursors to fully integrated education for some pupils with visual impairments, which are not seen as the result of 'mere labelling' or as demeaning to the child, but which do not deny the child's real difficulties either. Such provision, in terms of teaching the child to use a system of communication and a way of exploring their environment is seen as a matter of common sense and failure to provide it would be seen, quite rightly, as scandalous and a denial of the child's entitlement to a full education. Nor would it be seen as demeaning, if the child's need for specialist training in the use of aids, or for mobility, or of specialist teaching to make sense of his/her environment were to take place in a specialist setting prior to entry to the mainstream context. In some cases this might be the only viable way to gain access to the required expertise. Blindness is, after all, a rare disorder and such specialist knowledge would be equally rare in most mainstream settings. It is true that peripatetic advise is now the preferred option, but there is no argument in such cases that special expertise is needed, wherever the child is educated.

Yet the equally severe difficulties that are experienced by children with autism and sld in making sense of their world are not accepted in the same way. Although there is now scientific consensus on the biological causation of the disorder, increasing evidence of what the difficulties are in terms of learning and thinking, and considerable agreement about effective methods of education, their problems are often judged at the behavioural level only. Taking the fundamental triad of impairments by which autism is diagnosed (Wing, 1988), we can see the problems of responding at purely the behavioural level. The child has difficulty in relating to others? Give that child lots of opportunities for this by putting him or her with many others in mainstream. The child is not communicating? Again, the answer seems to be to provide the opportunities for communication and the problem will somehow disappear. And what of the difficulties with flexibility in thinking and the dependence on routines? These are often seen as 'settling' the child into the routines of the class and of establishing behavioural control. Seldom is attention paid to the long-term learning implications of such a disability. It is as if exposure to the play and experiences of the other children will somehow automatically be transferred to the experience of the child with autism; sadly, we know that it does not just happen like this (Jordan & Powell, 1995b).

This is not to argue that early integrated or, better still, inclusive education is wrong for pupils with autism, but to recognise that it may be problematic and that the problems need to be addressed on an individual basis. The first question should not be about *where* the child is to be educated; it should be primarily about *how*, with the question of where this 'how' can best be delivered being of secondary concern. There are considerable advantages to mainstream education for all, but not at the expense of denying or ignoring the child's real needs. Each decision will involve a balance of benefits and problems, and both should be considered. Nor should such decisions be 'once and for all' and there should be an expectation that a placement in specialised segregated provision is just a stage in which the child will be taught the skills and coping strategies to enable the move to less segregated provision.

Yet the reluctance to send children to specialist settings in their early years stems not just from the points listed above but also from the philosophy and practice of specialist schools themselves. Since autism has been recognised as a life-long condition, schools rarely claim to offer a 'cure' for autism. That is realistic, but there is no reason that they cannot see themselves as a stepping stone to other less specialist provision for all but the few most severely affected. If the normal expectation was that children entered specialist education first, to develop the skills and understanding they would need to cope with mainstream or other more generic special schools, then funding authorities might be more willing to make a placement that would not be for all the child's school life. However, this would mean specialist schools actually training for integration and considerable adaptation on the part of the 'host' school if this were to be successful.

The 'continuum' of provision

Even within the population of children with autism and sld, there will be enormous individual variation, that should affect the educational provision that is provided. Within the broad 'category' of sld, there can be considerable variation in cognitive ability and it is also true that it may be difficult to give an accurate measurement of cognitive ability when autism is severe and the child lacks language. Children with autism and sld will also vary in their degree of social interest and the extent to which they can tolerate being with others or in noisy or visually distracting environments. All these aspects will need to be considered when deciding on placement. There is no 'best' placement when it comes to children with autism and sld and each case must be decided on an individual basis.

There is, and will likely always be, a need for a continuum of provision to meet this continuum of need in children with autism and sld.

Specialist schools

Although specialist provision has seldom been set up to cater for the specific needs of children with autism and sld, the specialist schools for children with autism are increasingly catering for this group, as more able children with autism are included (with support) in mainstream, or in units attached to mainstream or other schools. Such specialist autism-specific schools were mainly set up by parent-led organisations, as a response to the perceived inadequacy of the provision that was generally available. The inadequacy was seen to result from the lack of specialist expertise in less specialised services and a consequent failure to meet the needs of individuals with autism. However, it is only in the last eight years that any specialised training courses for teachers have been available, apart from narrow training in particular approaches such as TEACCH (Mesibov, 1997) or ABA (Lovaas, 1981). Thus, the staff in such specialist settings may not necessarily have specialist training, and their expertise may depend on the quality of the experience they have gained in that setting. The fact that a school or unit has the word 'autism' in its title does not guarantee any specialised knowledge or expertise, although, of course, many staff will have gained such expertise over time. Parents should ask about how staff have gained their 'expertise' in autism, and whether the school is part of the network of services working towards autism-specific accreditation.

Specialised units/classes/bases

The same caveats about the 'expertise' in such units/classes/bases apply, as in specialist schools. For the group of children with autism and sld, the most obvious location for such units, classes or bases is within a school for children with sld. Yet the most common location, in fact, is within schools for children with moderate learning difficulties, for two reasons. One is the pragmatic one that staff ratios and teaching style in schools for children with sld are often regarded to be sufficient for the education of children with autism, so children with autism and sld in such schools are less likely to be seen as needing something 'special' or additional to the other children in the school. The other is that the first units, classes or bases were often set up to cater for the perceived majority of children with classical autism, those with moderate learning difficulty, and children with autism and sld were included often because it was felt that the model provided by the children in the host school would be more appropriate for integration opportunities, in that it offered a greater linguistic and social level. However, the population of such schools has itself changed, with increasing moves to inclusion, so the children there are no longer such appropriate models either for language development or for social skills, given that many will have additional emotional and behavioural difficulties themselves.

Some areas in the UK have specialised units or classes (less commonly, resource bases) attached to mainstream schools. However, the resource base in a mainstream school is a common situation in the USA and is becoming more common in the UK in response to moves towards inclusion. These are most commonly set up for children with autism without additional sld, but there are reasons why children with autism and sld may be found in such settings. It may be an inclusive policy measure, where full inclusion is the goal but where it is recognised that those with autism and sld will need at least some specialised teaching. It may be a response to parental pressure who want, as they see it, the 'best of both worlds'; they want their child to attend an ordinary local school and yet they want his or her special needs to be met. Such settings may indeed provide this happy outcome, but sometimes it is just a compromise solution that fails to provide for either goal in any meaningful way. It depends to a large extent on the expertise of the individual teacher, who is likely to be isolated in such provision. It is sadly sometimes the case that the child with autism and sld in such settings does not have his or her needs identified, understood or met and because s/he has not learnt the required skills and tolerance, does not have much experience of inclusion with ordinary children either.

The difference between unit', 'class' and 'base' reflects a continuum in itself, of increasing integration into the host school. That is the theory behind these different structures, with units having their own 'head' (and thus being more like 'mini-specialist schools'), classes having their own teachers, and bases having staff attached but most of the work being in integrated settings with the base a source of individual and staff support. In practice, the differences may not be so clear-cut; units are very variable in the amount of integration that occurs, and some classes operate more as units at one extreme or as bases, at the other. In thinking about the suitability for a particular child, therefore, it is worth looking at the characteristics of the host school and the degree of integration that occurs in terms of what is likely to be possible and of benefit to that particular child.

Special (not autism-specific) setting

For children with autism and sld, the most common placement in the UK is a school for children with sld, although in some areas there may be a generic special needs school, or even just a unit in some rural areas. As mentioned above, it is sometimes felt by authorities that the staffing ratio and the expertise and teaching approach within such settings should enable them to meet the needs of children with autism and sld, without further support. As more knowledge is gained of the nature of teaching and learning in autism and the greater potential for improvement that is now known to exist, it is increasingly common, however, for staff to be given further specialised training and even further support. The support may be from outreach professionals with a specialism in autism (educational psychologists, advisory teachers, and language therapists) and/or from dedicated learning support assistants. The latter form of additional support is frequently given, once the child has developed challenging behaviour, although it is not always obvious that another untrained 'body' in the classroom is an actual support either to the child or the teacher.

Full inclusion

This is a rare occurrence and one could argue that it has never yet occurred in the UK, where the onus is primarily on the child to adapt and gain access to a system which has not taken account of that child's needs in its construction. When the child has autism and sld, the chance of the child being able to make such an adaptation, even with the help of a full-time support assistant, is remote. If the child is relatively passive and is not too disturbed by noise, confusion and sensory overload, then it is possible to contain the child within mainstream settings. If staff and children within those settings are trained (or at least 'enabled') and supported, then children with autism and sld can benefit from this setting in many ways. Research shows they are more likely to develop spontaneous and varied behaviour and less likely to become rigid and stereotyped, for example. However, if staff and children are not prepared and supported, then the placement may become mere 'tokenism' without true integration and without the child's needs being addressed. This can happen even when the child with autism has no additional general learning difficulties (Jordan & Powell, 1994) but is even more likely when the additional learning difficulties are severe.

What constitutes a 'special' environment for the child with autism and sld?

The section above showed that merely labelling provision as 'autism-specific' does not guarantee that it is so, and certainly that it represents good practice in the area. Questions of what constitutes 'good' practice in terms of a special provision are problematic and to some extent will vary according to individual factors. However, there are some principles for what might constitute good specialist provision (wherever that specialist education is provided) upon which individualised programmes can be based.

The 'specialness' of special teaching to meet the needs of children with autism and sld should include:

- particular specialist expertise (and not just experience of doing the same thing for many years)
- specific teaching and care approaches that take account of the particular needs arising from autism as well as the individual characteristics of the child, including preferred learning style
- teaching and care environments that reduce stress by providing accessible structure, adapted to the child's needs
- nonsocial methodologies for academic and skill learning, that do not rely on verbal instruction or physical handling (or even contact)
- specific and explicit teaching of early social and communicative behaviour and understanding with some short-term strategies to put in place before full understanding, to enable entry to social situations through which valuable natural learning may occur
- experiences that enable emotional understanding through helping the child understand his/her emotions in real-life potent situations (drawing attention to the relevant emotion through appropriate symbolic cues), rather than as a misleading textbook learning of stereotyped facial expressions (e.g., 'happy' and 'sad' faces)

- appropriate access to social/emotional learning environments, including the development of shared attention and a sense of personal agency; this can be done by joining the child and building on his/her interests and then extending them or it may need additional support from music, aromatherapy or other aids to mutual enjoyment
- teaching to strengths, rather than deficits, to increase the child's self-esteem and enjoyment in learning
- recognising that, within the child's limited cognitive ability, it is likely to be helpful to develop a specific cognitive curriculum that makes learning explicit and helps them become aware of their own learning
- paying attention to present and future quality of life; it is important that skills are taught in functional environments and that they have relevance to the child's future life, while at the same time offering current satisfaction to enable the child to engage in productive learning.

Choosing a placement for a child with autism and sld
Choosing the right educational placement for the child with autism and sld will depend on particular circumstances, including the particular characteristics of the child, the family and the placements that are available. Mostly, the ideal placement will not be available and the choice will be a compromise between competing factors. Even where a placement has been chosen, parents may not always find that others share their perception of what is best for their child and so there may need to be some discussion of the reasons behind the choices they have made. Parents, and professionals, may find it helpful in thinking about what is best for a particular child, and in making the case for a particular choice, to consider some of the following factors.

Social needs
Children with autism and sld will not only have problems in developing social understanding through the normal intuitive routes but, because of the cognitive difficulties, will also have difficulty learning about social skills through specific teaching. A sympathetic environment for the child will recognise these

social difficulties and will not blame children for the results of their lack of understanding. Parents need to ensure that sanctions policies reflect this understanding, to see how staff go about interpreting the child's behaviour, and what procedures there are for flexible responses, related to the individual child's understanding and needs. Children with autism and sld will find it most helpful to be told precisely what to do rather than what *not* to do, so parents should look at how the school rules are phrased and the scope for rephrasing in positive terms.

Children with autism and sld will also need opportunities for learning in ways that do not depend on being able to learn from others, or in groups. A suitable placement will have resources for independent learning in terms of very clear structures, probably using visual (or even object) timetables and instructions for tasks. There may need to be independent work stations and timetables, accessible resources, structured 'plan-do-reflect' sequences and the availability of computers for computer-assisted learning, although this should not be the only learning opportunities available.

At the same time, parents also need to look for the direct teaching of interpersonal skills. This will include ways of teaching the child's peers how to engage with him or her (in class activities and in the playground) and enlisting their help for the difficulties (as in 'circles of friends': Whitaker *et al.*, 1998), rather than leaving the child a potential victim to bullying and abuse. If considering a specialist or special school/unit/class/base, therefore, it is worth looking at the peer group in terms of their potential as supports and models and to look at school policy and practice with respect to integration (in other schools and in the community) and especially 'reverse integration'.

Communication needs

The school should not only recognise and deal with language difficulties but show awareness of the nature of communication and how it is disturbed in autism. They will need to offer teaching about communication, regardless of the child's language ability. Language skills will need to be taught in functional contexts that have meaning for the child and teaching of communication skills, especially, should take account of wider contexts and not just the school environment. The child with autism and sld will need clear simple and practical models of what language is used *for* and not, for example, a situation where a means of communication (often sign) is only used to address particular children or to prompt responses from them. Most children with autism and sld will benefit most from a visual system using pictorial symbols but there should be flexibility to allow for those who will need objects of reference, on the one hand, or who can manage written text, on the other.

Difficulties in understanding spoken instructions need to be taken into account when making sense of the child's behaviour and in providing other (usually visual) ways of issuing instructions. The teacher needs to be aware that children with autism and sld may not yet be communicating intentionally at all and early communication skills (such as sharing attention and holding up objects for inspection, both of which are used extensively in teaching) cannot be assumed to be present.

Above all, the setting needs to be willing to give communication priority over conformity in situations where in fact it is better to teach the child a more acceptable way of communicating (needs, frustrations, protest) than to punish 'bad' behaviour or to insist on completion of a task. (Ways of doing this are discussed in the next chapter.) The child is unlikely to learn to communicate without a sustained programme across all settings, so parents need to look for willingness to involve parents in the communication programme and a genuinely collaborative approach.

Flexibility and the need for routines

Children with autism and sld lack flexibility in thinking and behaviour and need schools not only to recognise the effects of this but to be flexible enough themselves to deal with it. The day should be structured in a way that tells the child where to go, what to do, how long for, when it is finished, what to do next etc. Especially if the school is for all ages, there should also be ways of weaning the child from such a structure, at least in the long term.

As indicated in sections above, it is not sufficient to have a setting that just takes account of the child's problems. Teaching directed at deficits alone is likely to be both depressing and ineffective. Parents need to look for the ways in which the teachers are able to work with the child's strengths as well as compensate for his or her weaknesses. They also need to look for a humane attitude to rituals and obsessions, where the aim is not to just get rid of them but to use them to enrich the child's learning. Teachers should extend those that are capable of being extended and broadened, and understand the underlying reasons behind others that may then need to be replaced by behaviour that serves the same purpose for the child. Furthermore, teachers should be willing to work with the parents in dealing with obsessions, or there is the danger that behaviour that is clamped down on in one setting increases dramatically in the other, making life intolerable for those concerned.

Children with autism and sld, like other children, make most progress when they are actively and emotionally engaged in their own learning and have the opportunity to reflect on their own learning (through symbols, written language or personalised photographs). This would help to develop better memory strategies and to teach fundamental learning processes such as selective attention. Parents should be wary of teachers who are only prepared to operate at the level of behaviour and the products of learning.

Individual characteristics of the child

The child with autism and sld is still a child with an individual personality and particular experiences. No child's educational needs can, therefore, be defined solely in terms of a disability. Parents will want to know that the setting is attending to needs associated with the autism and the sld, but they will also want to know that their child is being responded to as an individual. They need to look for ways in which (and the extent to which) the setting individualises its curriculum and teaching approach.

Apart from paying attention to the child's difficulties in learning, therefore, parents will want to note what the setting offers in the way of developing particular talents or interests. Even when their learning difficulties are severe, children with autism have been known to show remarkable talent for music, art, or working with computers. These need to be developed and celebrated, not only because they aid the child's overall development and self-esteem, but because they may provide a source of income, and therefore independence, in later life. However, it is relatively rare for the child with autism and sld to have such an exceptional talent; it is far more common for them to have preferences for certain activities, and for them to be better at these activities than others. Such activities may not be a source of later job opportunities, but they may serve the almost equally useful purpose of providing for later leisure pursuits. Educational settings, therefore, should provide opportunities for both extending and enriching the child's interests and activities. Parents need to probe further than information about what activities are available in a setting to ensure that some characteristic of their child (epilepsy, for example) does not exclude their child from that 'available' activity.

Parental and family needs/choice
All other things being equal, in terms of meeting the particular needs of their child with autism and sld, parental choice will be affected by all the other considerations that affect school choice for any child. Locality is a prime consideration as is the isolation from the school that might occur if it is far away or difficult to get to, especially if the child is thought to need residential school or if his/her needs could only be met at a particular residential school. This is where the benefits of specialist provision must be weighed against the benefits of local provision where he or she will know and be known by the neighbourhood children. The age range catered for is also important, alongside the likelihood that this particular child will be able to enter the next stage of education and/or care, as expected for those leaving this service. It is difficult to put a ceiling on development, given appropriate education, but if it is unlikely that their child will be ready for that next stage at the appropriate time, parents should think about the likely hassle of finding another suitable placement at that time.

A local school (perhaps with a unit) may suit a family because brothers and sisters also attend it, but equally this may be a reason for rejecting a school. Sometimes it is in the interests of siblings to have a break from their brother or sister with autism and sld, and it may even be best for the child with autism, especially if destructive ways of behaving have become a habit at home. It may sometimes be in the best interests of the family as a whole if the child attends residential school, but then the parents need to ensure that there are ways of involving parents so that they do not become 'deskilled' in looking after their own child. Respite care should be part of any integrated care and education package for a child with autism and sld, but provision of such integrated services is very patchy in the UK.

There will also be very personal likes and dislikes and factors that reflect parental views about education, and how they see their child with autism and sld. For some, the peace and tranquillity of a country-house setting will not only symbolise a peaceful setting in which to leave their child, but may actually provide the scope for a peaceful existence, so that educational aspirations become reality. There is a need to look at the physical environment in relation to each particular child, remembering the child's capacity to adapt, or, as is more likely to be the case, to fail to adapt. Parents need to look at room size with a view to establishing whether there is room for the child not to feel his or her personal space continually invaded and whether there is a well defined area in which the child can feel 'safe'. Most children with autism and sld will (at least from time to time) need room for the child to 'let off steam' when needed and to engage in physical exercise (preferably aerobic) at least once a day. Finally, parents will need to look at the safety of the environment, assessing whether the setting has allowed for the particular features of autism in assessing the risk benefits of its activities and in its siting and care arrangements.

Summary

Children with autism and sld have particular needs for environments that enable optimal functioning and lead to good current and future quality of life. Such children will benefit from environments that offer a consistent and (usually) visual structure to reduce the confusion that comes from trying to interpret socially mediated and spoken instructions. Visual structures should reduce anxiety by helping the child understand what to do, how to do it, with whom, when and what next. Children with autism and sld will need opportunities for learning built-upon strengths and can benefit from peers, as long as such interactions are planned and organised.

There is a range of educational provision available for children with autism and sld, although availability throughout the UK is variable. There is no one placement that is best for all children with autism and sld, but there are principles of a specialised setting that should allow maximum functioning. Parents will need to consider all these factors when considering a suitable placement for their child, while remembering their child's individuality and the needs of the family as a whole.

Further reading
PEETERS, T. (1997). *Autism: From theoretical understanding to educational intervention.* London: Whurr.

8 Understanding and Preventing Challenging Behaviour

Introduction

All those living and working with individuals with autism and sld will have felt, at least at some point, that the main problem in their lives is dealing with the difficult and disturbing behaviour which seems to be so much a part of the condition. Yet such behaviour is not determined by the biology of autism nor the biology of whatever has led to the sld. Children are not born as 'runners' or as 'head-bangers' and, just as environmental factors may lead to such behaviours, so the environment can be used to address them. It is important to remember the message of earlier chapters that there is no such thing as an 'autistic' behaviour and thus that there is nothing that individuals with autism do, that we do not, at least if we are under similar conditions of stress. The most important first step, then, is to reduce the levels of stress. In order to do that effectively, we need to understand the factors that are likely to lead to stress in individuals with autism and sld and we need to understand the causes of particular behaviour in particular individuals.

Remedying challenging behaviour is not a simple or speedy process and does not depend on mere consistency in responding to specific behaviour in isolation. It rests on an understanding of the behaviour concerned, including its causes, and the development of a range of strategies to try. Any behaviour is a result of an individual acting on, or reacting to, the environment and so environmental change is a prime tool in managing or preventing the behaviour. The temptation is to try to get rid of difficult behaviour as a priority, but the danger with that approach is that, unless we first understand about autism and really know that individual, such attempts are at best likely to lead to short-term solutions and at worst may be counter-productive—replacing one behaviour with a more disruptive one. It is a mistake to think that behaviour can be managed or reduced without understanding the causes of that behaviour and without teaching alternative behaviours at the same time. Individuals with autism and sld cannot just inhibit behaviours, so they need to be trained to do something positive instead. As will be shown below, if unwanted behaviour is just punished, people with autism will continue with that behaviour, no matter how much it is 'punished', because it has become habitual in that situation and they do not know what else to do.

We also need to think about current, as well as future, quality of life for the individuals concerned, not just because that is ethical and humane, but because that leads to better long-term consequences. There is a risk in placing behavioural conformity before teaching and learning, in that it can only work by 'breaking the person's spirit', to put it in its most dramatic form; the person must learn to obey others, not because they understand or see a more attractive alternative, but just because someone else has the power to make them. This in turn will increase a dependent style of learning and the individual (child or adult) may become more passive and withdrawn and less able to engage with the environment or with others, spontaneously, or to exercise any meaningful choice. Some degree of conformity is necessary, of course, especially when living or working with children, who are not in a position to make fully informed choices. Everyone has to conform to some extent if they are to live in, and be accepted by, the community. This will not be successful in the long run, however, and will lead to considerable additional stress, if it is not accompanied by some understanding of the world and the meaning behind the 'rules' that must be obeyed.

Staff and carers need to question the long-term educational value of what they are teaching and, in the matter of behavioural control, to ensure that conformity is in the interests of the individual with autism and sld and not just those of the teacher, carer or institution. Behaviour problems and frustrations are likely to be eased if individuals are taught ways of controlling their environment more effectively through communication and social skills, for example, and if they are helped towards an understanding of the world. There may also be behaviour that is so disruptive that the individual concerned cannot be worked with, nor even approached, and then it is clear that that will need to be addressed as a priority.

Parents and staff working with young children do need help in this area of management as early as possible, because it is harder to change well-established patterns of behaviour when many secondary effects will have emerged. The advantage with the early years is not only that behaviours are not so entrenched, but that difficult behaviour is less disturbing and is more easily controlled, because the child is smaller and the behaviour is more acceptable in a young child. The problem with working with problem behaviour in the early years, however, is that the child will not have had the opportunity to learn any of the things (social understanding, cognitive understanding, communication skills) that can be used to help the person deal with the causes of the problem behaviour through alternative behaviours. There is also the danger that we forget that the child with autism and sld is still a child and we cannot expect this child to behave better than other young children. It is sometimes the case that children from well-organised schools for children with autism, for example, are most easily picked out from other school parties at public events because they are the ones who are in fact behaving much better than others! Partly this is the (not unreasonable) fear of staff that, if they allow leeway in behaviour, the child will not understand and will not be able to self-impose boundaries, so behaviour can quickly get out of hand. The trick is to balance the need for enforcement of clear and consistent rules with the need to encourage self-control and spontaneous functioning.

Understanding behaviour in autism and sld
Although it is sad to report that aversive techniques are still used, legally and illegally, in many countries, there is increasing recognition that such techniques amount to abuse and should not be tolerated, whatever the supposed justification. LaVigna and Donnellan (1986) give many examples of the long-term effectiveness of non-aversive strategies in reducing challenging behaviour, and Lovett (1996) makes a strong case against the use of aversive

techniques and gives excellent examples of what a positive approach means in practice. He stresses the need to consider the individual as a whole in his or her functional context and to base treatment within that context. Approaches such as Gentle Teaching (McGhee *et al.*, 1987) are also respectful of the individual and aim to direct and guide behaviour through the development of mutuality and through techniques of nonconfrontation and the 'shadowing' of actions. Above all, in autism, there is a need to consider alternative explanations for behaviour and to try to understand the world from the individual's point of view.

To say that we need to understand the behaviour does not mean that the behaviour should necessarily be tolerated, and it is important to help individuals with autism and sld develop alternative strategies for coping and, where possible, to develop a sense of responsibility for their own actions. There is no point in applying sanctions if the individual just focuses on the behaviour of the staff in applying the sanctions rather than their own behaviour that has led to the sanctions being applied. As in other learning, they may need consequences of behaviour to be given visually, to make it clear, and they need a clear indication of what to do (and to be taught explicitly what to do) rather than relying on inhibiting behaviour.

The setting also needs to be organised to reduce confusion and stress and this will usually mean individual visual timetables, as given in Chapter 6. However, there is no point in relying on this to reduce negative behaviour if what is arranged as the programme is not attractive to the individual. It may not be possible for the person (especially a child in school) to avoid unpleasant activities entirely, but these have to be introduced gradually into an overall positive situation, if there is to be hope of success. Nor must we expect the person with autism and sld to be able to be reasoned out of phobias (none of us can be— that is what makes them phobias) nor to have their (to them) legitimate emotions illegitimised. They may get angry at things which are trivial in our eyes but that is the point of taking an individual approach; we have to learn what it is that upsets each individual and accept that as a starting point. Of course, it may be that the individual cannot avoid that experience and must be helped to tolerate it, but we will not be successful in teaching that until we first recognise and accept the cause for the upset.

Using disruptive behaviour to communicate

One of the most useful ways of looking at disruptive behaviour is to treat it 'as if' it were communication and to try to work out what communicative function the behaviour is serving. Is it intended to indicate that the individual is bored/frustrated/unable to complete the task, or distressed by some noise and so on? The first step is to conduct a functional analysis of the behaviour to suggest some hypotheses about the causes and thus the communicative intent that it is useful to impute. If, for example, a child with autism and sld is head-banging in class, the question the teacher would need to ask is 'What would the child want to tell me, if he or she knew how?' This would apply whether or not the child had spoken language because, as was seen in earlier chapters, in autism, speech does not necessarily imply the ability to use it to communicate.

Once the potential communicative function of the head-banging has been determined, then he or she can be taught an alternative form of communication to achieve the same ends. However, it must be remembered that the child who is engaging in disruptive, aggressive or self-injurious behaviour is likely to be upset and so not necessarily amenable to producing high-level behaviours. The aim should be to find an alternative behaviour which is at the same kind of developmental level as the one you are seeking to replace.

Vignette

Sean is a six-year-old child with autism and sld who regularly bangs his head on any available surface, but mostly on hard edges. This is a behaviour that is dangerous now, in that it could lead to immediate damage, but is also likely to lead to damage in later life when it may be responsible for detached retinas and consequent blindness. It is clearly a matter of concern that needs to be addressed. Observation of the behaviour in a classroom situation suggests the function of the behaviour for Sean in that situation is that it enables him to escape from work demands, when faced with a task set by someone else (not self-chosen). He displays the behaviour over a range of tasks and situations but always when there are demands made in the context of an unfamiliar task.

In such situations, there is a choice. The child can be made to do the task, regardless of the self-injurious behaviour, but that is not feasible here, given the effects of head-banging. The more useful approach is to teach Sean an alternative way of indicating that he does not want to do a task. Sean has no speech nor any signs and he has additional physical problems that make controlled gestures problematic. He was, therefore, given a small communication device that was programmed to say 'No!' when a prominent red button was depressed. The aim was to present an unfamiliar task to Sean and immediately (before he could head-bang) physically prompt him to depress the button and, just as immediately, remove the task, ready for another presentation in a few minutes.

Timing is important in such cases, in that removing the task should not follow the head-bang, or it would reward the bang and thus increase its likelihood, rather than reduce it. After a short interval (one minute perhaps), the task is re-presented and the same procedure of prompting the button depression and removing the task is gone through. This may be repeated many times until eventually Sean comes to trust the fact that he has another way of getting the task removed and is spontaneously pushing the button each time the task is presented.

Once this communication is performed regularly and calmly, the teacher might try to get Sean to perform some of the rejected task, before it is removed. The teacher must indicate that saying 'No!' is still effective (or his trust will go and Sean may begin to head-bang again as a more reliable way of getting his own way) but now must negotiate a compromise. The teacher might say something like: 'I know you don't want to do this Sean, but I want you to do just this one bit (or to do it for just a minute until this timer pings, as appropriate) and then I will remove the task' (drawing the child's attention to his visual schedule, which shows him performing the task and then shows him having access to a favourite activity).

At this point, Sean was able to communicate with his recorded 'No!' but was accepting that he could try unfamiliar tasks. However, his head-banging had not ceased altogether, because the programme had been directed at replacing the head-banging for the one function alone. It was necessary to take each functional use of head-banging and teach an alternative for that. One other function readily identified, was that Sean used head-banging as a way of attracting attention when understimulated. A new behaviour was needed, because a recorded 'No!' was not appropriate for this situation. However, the same communicator could be used, this time with it programmed to say 'Hi!'

In a situation where staff were normally busy (although freed for the operation of this programme) and the head-banging for attention had occurred, Sean was physically guided to press for 'Hi!' which then resulted in others coming to see him to play exclusively with him for a few minutes. Once this had been trained successfully, a more sophisticated device was chosen with two switches and Sean was taught to discriminate situations where the different messages (via the different buttons) were appropriate. Thus a programme to get rid of head-banging, had a wider educational outcome in teaching Sean to discriminate his own actions and the appropriateness of situations to which they should be applied.

The 'last straw' phenomenon

A problem in applying those principles, above, is that there may, on some occasions at least, be no clear function for the unwanted behaviour. No 'trigger' for the behaviour can be identified, with the child reacting badly to something or some situation which had been well tolerated on other occasions. It is hard, in those cases, to see what function the behaviour is serving. The common feature of such situations is usually that the child's stress levels have reached such a pitch that the smallest extra pressure is too much, leading to the challenging behaviour. When stress is high, any one of a number of things can be sufficient to provoke the behaviour. In such cases, the priority for any programme should be stress reduction and alternative ways of managing the stress.

What is challenging behaviour and what kinds are there?
The use of the term 'challenging' reflects a change from thinking of behaviour as 'unwanted' or 'undesirable' in itself to a more interactive concept that implies that there is variation in the type of behaviour that will be seen as challenging, according to the viewer and to the situation. 'Challenging behaviour' should not be a euphemism for 'difficult' or 'unwanted' but should include a notion of severity and some consideration of the situation.

As was mentioned above, one cannot predict from the behaviour alone, what any individual will consider to be challenging. Below, however, are kinds of behaviour that are frequently chosen by parents and professionals, working with individuals with autism and sld, as challenging to them.

Running away
There are two kinds of running 'away' in autism, one of which might be better characterised as 'running towards'. In the latter case the person may have seen something of great interest to them (e.g. a lawnmower, a swimming pool in a garden, chocolate in a shop window) and at the first opportunity s/he 'escapes' to find that object, albeit that it may be miles away. The person with autism may have very little sense of danger, so even such 'purposeful' running can be a severe problem, especially as the behaviour may be very determined and hard to deflect. However, this kind of running is easier to manage in that the cause is clear cut and the person usually gives some warning when they have seen the desired object, at least to a carer who knows him or her well. Thus, even when the person has escaped, it may be a simple matter to find him/her again. If the person is at risk from this behaviour (through road accidents, or getting lost or getting distracted by even greater dangers) then it will have to be addressed and prevented, if possible.

The best approach is to note the person's source of interest as it occurs, and to indicate to the person that you have done so (preferably by showing a picture—although this implies that you have been able to predict what you will see). This is a step towards getting the person to share interests and maybe to have a 'comment' book of pictures which s/he can point things out to you as they see them. Having 'discussed' this interesting object with the person as they see it, the next step is to make a 'controlled' visit to it (if that is feasible) or to a nearby and more accessible alternative. The purpose is to get the individual with autism and sld to change from following his/her own interest on their own (the source of the running 'away') to communicating interest and pursing it with someone else. In time, this is usually effective in reducing instances of running off and has the extra benefit of improving social and communicative skills.

When it comes to 'running away' proper, the sources are usually very different. It has its roots in biology, in that the young child with autism does not seem to exhibit the same kind of attachment behaviour as other young children. When they begin to be mobile, young children go off from the base of a securely attached mother to explore their surroundings, but they go only so far before returning to their base. This pattern is repeated so that they are performing as spokes of a wheel emanating from the mother at the centre. In relatively safe environments (and it is not certain how recent anxieties about safety in young children will affect this pattern) mothers do not need to call after, let alone fetch, their offspring, but can happily allow them to explore with only supervisory attention, knowing they will be repeatedly 'reporting back' to base.

Children with autism may not have this instinctual urge to return in this regular way, or they may wander beyond the perimeter that the mother regards as safe. She will then be alerted to call after her child and, if that does not work, will keep running to fetch him or her back. Children with autism can understand very few social games, but one of the few is the simple clear one of chasing. They may not yet be able to respond to their name being called and, when mother starts to chase after them, this may be the trigger for the game they so much enjoy—chasing. They are unable to pick up the social and postural signals that indicate that mother is not in fact 'playing' and so they continue to run with great glee. If mother does catch him or her, the predictable anger may further reward this exciting game of chasing. The person does not understand the social significance of the anger, but just sees the predictable and enjoyable effects in terms of blazing eyes, red face, and shouting.

In similar situations, then, when bored or when in the same environment, the child is more likely to run off again. When they go to school, such children are often delighted to find amid all the change and confusion, that these new people also play this game. Other children may need to be hit before they will chase after you, but teachers will often do so, perhaps when other children are lining up or when going out as a group. It does not take long for a very strong behaviour pattern of running away to become established. Once established, it is difficult to change and yet can have a devastating effect on quality of life as opportunities are restricted and the person may end up living behind locked doors.

This running away behaviour, then, is largely the result of 'training', albeit the training has been unintentional. In order to remedy the situation, therefore, training of an alternative behaviour will be needed. The longer the person has practised the running-away behaviour, the longer the alternative training is likely to need. It will also need to be done intensively, so that the person is not being trained in the alternative while at the same time practising, and further reinforcing, the running away. For a primary-aged child, a period of three weeks, three or four times a day (including weekends) is usually sufficient, but it depends in part on the severity of the learning difficulties that accompany the autism. For these reasons, such a programme is best set up for a period in the school holidays (when clinical psychology students may be glad of a project to become involved in) rather than in school time.

The actual training involves two trainers, one of whom acts as a stooge at the single 'exit' or end point of a cul de sac, or stands at the only other gate in a field. The other trainer takes the individual with autism and sld to this venue (the safe cul de sac, or the field with one entrance and exit) and lets him or her go, without any attempt to restrain, call after or chase after him/ her. Once the individual has reached within grabbing distance of the other trainer, the first trainer then shouts the name and an instruction to 'Come here!' The stooge, again without saying anything, then turns the person around and leads him/her back to the first trainer, who has in his/her pocket some very appealing reward (or token of a reward). In other words, the individual with autism and sld is systematically retrained to show the behaviour that is wanted (coming when called) rather than the behaviour that has become a problem. Nevertheless, there is still more to be done if the behaviour is not to recur. It is clear that the individual enjoys chasing, so we must introduce a new acceptable form of playing chase or it will be difficult to replace the behaviour permanently and the individual's quality of life will be diminished.

Fears, anxiety, panic and phobias
Mere existence of fears, anxieties and phobias just expresses the human condition but such fears, anxieties and phobias have different qualities in autism and are more pervasive; they are triggered by 'everyday' stimuli and not those that give rise to such phenomena more commonly. In autism, also, these emotions are more likely to be expressed in an extreme and uninhibited way, because of the lack of social control and because they have not been helped to develop coping strategies. Cognitive behaviour therapy may be used with the more able to help them overcome such fears, or to modify their expression, but with individuals with autism and sld, another approach is needed. Carers will need to identify the source of these fears, which may be very particular to that individual, and then attempt to prevent or avoid these sources. Where that is impossible, and the individual's life (or the life of those who live and work with that individual) is being affected by continual exposure to these sources of fear, then a process of desensitisation may be needed. Even where the main thrust has been to avoid situations that produce such stresses, it is wise also to train coping strategies for when the unexpected happens and there is unplanned exposure.

For example, a common fear in individuals with autism is a fear of dogs. All animals may be feared to a degree, because they leave dirt and disorderliness and because they are difficult to predict and control, but a dog usually represents an extreme form of this. Dogs will suddenly jump up or bark without warning and it is this, rather than any rational fear that they may cause harm, which is the root of the fear in autism. Thus, even if the child with such a fear were able to understand the language, it will have little effect to reassure the child continually that 'It's only a dog; it won't hurt you!' That kind of reasoning is irrelevant to the fear of a phobia, which is, of its essence, irrational. We have to accept that the fear is both irrational and real, just like other people's phobias. However, what we do not have to accept is the behaviour the person may exhibit as a reaction to his or her fear.

A fifteen-year-old young man with autism and sld (Brian) had a very severe fear of dogs. Teachers had coped with this by trying to pre-empt the appearance of dogs and getting him to sit down, close his eyes, and sing (or rather babble, since he had no speech) loudly, whenever he encountered a dog. This was done to try to stop his normal reactions of banging himself and others wildly, fleeing at top speed and even jumping on top of cars to avoid a dog. If the dog was little and quiet, it still produced a reaction but this time it was a pre-emptive strike by Brian, who would kick the dog with full force. As one might imagine, this had led to many difficult situations in the past, especially for Brian's family, and eventually they found it impossible to take him out at all, further restricting his life and doing nothing to help him overcome his fears or to deal with them in more acceptable ways. The pattern of behaviours trained by Brian's teachers did help him manage more situations and his successful 'coping' may over time have helped lessen his fear, as is often the case as the person grows up. Yet there were still many situations that were not managed, when staff attention was distracted so that it was Brian who first saw a dog on the horizon. In such cases, Brian would show some of his more unacceptable behaviours and it was too late then to prompt the alternative repertoire. As Brian got older and stronger, the damage such outbursts caused was greater and even these occasional outbursts were judged unacceptable; Brian was in danger of becoming restricted to a few 'safe' environments.

It was decided that Brian needed some desensitisation so that he could tolerate at least milder situations (the dog on the horizon, the quiet little dog near him) and he needed a programme to help him self-prompt his pattern of coping behaviour. The desensitisation chosen started in the sensory room where he could be made relaxed and comfortable with lavender scent, gentle music and comfortable soft cushions. In this relaxed state, slides depicting very small dogs very far away were projected on to the ceiling. Once he was able to tolerate these without getting disturbed, the size of the dog was increased and dogs in close-up were projected. The next step was to introduce video of dogs, with sound. Once more this started with small dogs a long way away and with the sound turned very low. When Brian could tolerate these videos, he was shown other videos where dogs were more centre stage and the volume was gradually increased. Brian was able eventually to manage to stay calm with all these familiar videos, but strange videos, where dogs would suddenly appear and bark, provoked almost the same fear reaction as real-life situations.

It was not expected that Brian could easily become totally desensitised to these videos or that, even if he could, that would generalise to real-life situations. What was hoped was that the prior desensitisation programme would enable him to tolerate these videos sufficiently to enable him to use these as training to self-prompt his coping behaviours. Just before the dogs appeared on the video Brian was taught to prepare for their appearance by following his coping strategies. To begin with this was prompted, but the prompts were faded until he was producing the coping behaviour himself on sight of the dogs. This success was 'overlearned' to new videos and then to real-life but controlled situations. Thus situations were engineered within the school grounds where he could be warned that a dog would appear and could go into his coping strategies before the actual appearance of the dog triggered the fear. Once he was doing this easily and without stress, the warning was faded and Brian was given a gentle physical prompt (if needed) to trigger the coping behaviour as the dog appeared. Once Brian was able to manage these engineered situations he was taken back into real-life situations where he was able to generalise. The whole programme had taken twelve months but had made a great difference to his life and that of his family. After several more years, when Brian was in an adult establishment, he was given more desensitisation treatment, but this time at a higher level. He was introduced to quiet well-behaved dogs and taught gradually to manage without his coping behaviour. This was successful and Brian can now tolerate dogs as long as they do not directly touch him.

Problems with transitions

In autism and sld there is likely to be great difficulty in changing set behaviour or moving from one situation to another. It may result from not having cues in the new situation to trigger the right behaviour or from not being able to predict what is coming. Pictures or objects of reference can help, as can warnings of change. Where the change is predictable, and permanent (such as moving class or moving to a new school or to an adult placement) it helps to have a programme to ease the transition. Wherever possible, the individual should be taken to visit the new situation. This will not of itself have much impact on the acceptance of the new situation, but it can be the opportunity to start a programme that will help. If the individual is photographed in the new situation, this can be used prior to the move to 'talk' about it and what the individual will do there. Once the move arrives, the individual can take the picture with him or her to help him/her accept and understand the new situation.

In general, carrying something that tells individuals where they are going can be very helpful in coping with transitions, and these may be pictures, or objects of reference, such as a toilet roll to signify being taken to the toilet, or a toy car (or car seat-belt buckle—whichever carries the appropriate meaning for the individual) to signify going out in the car. It should be remembered that for individuals with autism and sld, speech may not work as an effective bridge to understand what is going on, so to them it often appears that they are whisked off without any idea of where they are going or why. Not surprisingly, without any clue in the form of a picture or object, they are liable to protest.

Indiscriminate arousal

Whatever the fundamental cause, it seems true that many individuals with autism and sld have problems in managing their levels of arousal. Levels of arousal may shoot up, resulting in the person being overwhelmed by stimulation and reacting with extreme irritation or withdrawal. Alternatively, the person may be under-aroused and appear completely unresponsive and therefore unable to learn. For individuals with autism and sld, there may be difficulties in discriminating relevant from irrelevant stimuli in any of the senses (e.g. pain versus touch) and some stimuli may be reacted to in an oversensitive way, resulting in phobias, or aversions. In eating this may result in either extreme, oversensitivity resulting in anorexia-type behaviour where very little is eaten, and undersensitivity resulting in pica (where inedible substances are eaten).

Although it is hard to alter fundamental perceptions, it may be, as some believe, that forms of sensory integration therapy can help with this problem; however, there is no research-based evidence of such effects. One thing that can certainly help, is to use careful and sensitive observation of the individual to determine when they are over or under aroused and to respect their own ways of coping with the situation. As discussed in earlier chapters, children with autism and sld may not, for example, be able to hear someone if they are required to look into their eyes at the same time, because of the very high levels of arousal that result from direct eye contact. They may deal with this themselves by closing their eyes when someone is talking to them or looking at bland stimuli like the ceiling, rather than directly at the person. If teachers ignore these coping mechanisms, however, because they do not understand the problem, and insist that children look at them when being addressed, they are making it impossible for the children to listen at the same time.

Lack of motivation
Apparent lack of interest in anything can seriously affect access to education and quality of life. Some of this may be a reaction to difficulties with levels of arousal, as discussed above. Other problems arise from inability to see the point or goal of the activity or to understand intentions and goal-directed behaviour. Failures to attribute meaning or to see the meaning perceived by others adds to these difficulties. Solutions to this problem involve ways of extending and developing tasks and activities in which the person is already involved, and structuring other tasks to

make the 'meaning' clear, that is, what the final result will be, and how to achieve it. A clear picture of a goal may help the person understand when it has been achieved or the steps that need to be taken to achieve it. Sometimes, however, it is not possible to broaden out the individual's interests to cover all the learning tasks, for example, that will be necessary in schools. In such cases, motivation may be achieved by a picture or symbol timetable showing the preferred activity to follow the less preferred one. Whole series of activities can be built up by using the fact that individuals with autism like to do familiar tasks so that, once a task is familiar, it can be used to 'reward' less familiar ones in such a series.

Sleep problems

These problems are clearly most potent for parents and carers although the effects of a child or adult who is chronically sleep-deprived may be felt by all those who live and work with him/her. Traditional sleep medication tends to have paradoxical effects in autism, often making the child (in particular) more hyperactive, and side-effects may occur. Some adults with autism have been given melatonin to good effect but the long-term side-effects are not known (especially for children) and it seems to be effective at getting the person to sleep, but is not so effective at keeping them asleep. There is currently some experimentation with slow-release melatonin to try to overcome this problem. However, as with other drug 'remedies' in autism, they tend to be most effective when used in tandem with behavioural methods. Something like melatonin may be useful in breaking a habit of staying up or wrecking a bedroom, but behavioural remedies should be set in place to deal with the situation, should the effects of medication wear off, or the side-effects require that the medication be stopped.

It is very difficult to make someone sleep, so the first step is to set goals that can be achieved and that may help lead to sleep. For example, it would be appropriate to set the goal of a young child with autism and sld retiring to bed at a reasonable time and staying there quietly so that parents can have an evening to 'recover' and later can get some sleep themselves. This may still be difficult to achieve, especially when the child turns to other disruptive behaviours such as smearing, destroying the bedding, or screaming, but it is easier than making the child actually sleep. There are principles that can be applied that will make it more likely that both the family and (eventually) the child can get some rest:

● Make sure the child is tired, by instituting a period of strenuous activity in the day.

● Make sure the child is relaxed at bedtime by appropriate bedtime rituals. This may involve use of a warm bath with a calming essence, spraying calming oils in the room and on the bed, making sure the child has a full, but not overfull, stomach, having low lights in the bedroom, playing gentle relaxing music and not allowing TV or video or anything too stimulating within an hour of bedtime.

● Make sure there is nothing in the room that is likely to stimulate any behaviour that might compete with staying in bed and going to sleep. One parent of a child with autism and sld, for example, complained that the child spent hours at night and in the early hours of the morning (preventing others from sleeping as well as not sleeping himself) banging loudly on books and shouting as he did so. This was such a particular behaviour, in that he only shouted when he was banging his books, that the solution was obvious. Removing the books from his bedroom stopped the behaviour and allowed the opportunity to train him to lie and listen to music through earphones, which was successful in both keeping him quietly in bed and eventually getting him to sleep earlier.

● Particular problems of the child staying in his/her own bed should be tackled firmly, once it has been decided that this is not something the child will 'grow out of' and that it is a real problem for the parents' quality of life and the child's future development. If the child is joining the parents in their bed, the first step is to insist on the child staying in his/her own bed, but having one of the parents 'sleep' alongside the child, making sure the child stays there and giving the child the security and continuity he or she needs. Once this is working, in that the child has accepted it (although the parent may be getting little sleep—it might make sense if parents alternate in this role, because of that), the parent can gradually move to sleeping a little away from the child and gradually increase the distance until the parent is back in his/her own bed.

Depression and other mental health problems

Dual diagnoses are difficult to obtain and an adolescent or adult who develops mental health problems may not have these problems taken seriously, but instead have the behaviours attributed to the autism. Individuals with autism and sld will need as much help, both medical and in terms of social support, as anyone else with such a problem, but the difficulty will be in finding doctors and other professionals who will understand the interactions between the mental illness, the autism and the sld. It is very important not to provide chemical straitjackets for behaviour problems or to attribute all problem behaviour to mental illness, but the possibility of depression should be recognised.

Rituals/Obsessions

Rituals may help the individual make sense of the world and make it more predictable. Thus, they may be serving a useful function for the person, in dealing with stress, and they should not be removed unless there are alternative ways of coping. Repetitive stereotypic behaviours may be a forerunner to challenging behaviour and may start as a need to shut off from over-stimulation or conversely to compensate for under-stimulation. They may also, like the rituals, be used as a way of coping with stress. It only makes sense, therefore, to try to reduce or eliminate rituals or obsessions if they are seriously interfering with the person's life or the lives of others and if they can be replaced with alternative behaviours that serve the same function.

Andy was a man with autism and sld who spent his days in a social education centre, as they were then called. He had always had a number of rituals, but these were fairly constant in number and did not seriously interfere with his functioning. However, the social education centre underwent some rebuilding and the noise and confusion of the building works seriously upset Andy whose ritualistic behaviour greatly increased. He had often needed to give a twirl before going through a door but now he began to twirl and twirl and had to be physically guided to stop and get himself through the door. At first this was tolerated, because it was seen as a temporary reaction to the disruption of the building works, but it continued after the rebuilding was complete and the centre had returned to normal. Not only did Andy not stop twirling, but he became even more frantic and his parents reported that he had started to twirl at home and when out shopping. Clearly, the ritualistic behaviour, which had started as a clear reaction to a certain situation, was now self-generating and was getting out of hand.

Since one twirl seemed to lead to another, and the twirling no longer seemed to have a clear function in stress reduction, it was decided that the best approach would be to replace rather than reduce the behaviour. The behaviour appeared to be triggered by going through doorways so it was decided to prompt and reinforce going straight through doorways without twirling. This was done by giving Andy a lot of concentrated practice of walking through doorways with a member of staff on either side, preventing Andy deviating or twirling, and modelling and prompting walking through while chanting 'one two three four, let's go through the door'—the rhythm helping with the purposeful actions. After a few weeks and hundreds of opportunities of practising this in a range of doorways, one member of staff dropped out, so that only one supported Andy with his actions. This meant that Andy might have tried to re-introduce a twirl, but he did not. Then the second member of staff dropped out while staying nearby and using the same chant to prompt Andy's behaviour. It took a further two months before Andy was walking through doorways (with the same eight steps as in the training) unaided and with no attempt to twirl. That is not to say that twirling might not re-appear should Andy become stressed once more, but it was not the aim of the programme to eliminate all rituals, rather simply to stop one ritual that had ceased to have a useful function and was interfering with Andy's quality of life.

Total withdrawal

A child or adult with autism and sld who has been more sociable but returns to being very withdrawn, or anyone who becomes totally withdrawn, signals that something is wrong. Such reactions may be a reaction to trauma, or the result of depression, and the child or adult will need specific programmes to help them overcome their difficulties. It is important that the causes are addressed but, as with Andy above, the withdrawn behaviour may persist as a habit, even when the original cause has been resolved. In that case, there may need to be a programme of desensitisation to others, to help reduce the withdrawal.

Aggression

It is true to say that it is rare for children or adults with autism to be truly aggressive, in the sense that they target someone for a violent attack. Of course, they may learn to attack certain people, but that is usually because they react in interesting and predictable ways, not really aggression. Most of what is labelled as aggression in dealing with children or adults with autism and sld is more likely to be panic, when things do not happen as expected, or when routines are disrupted. Nevertheless, violent behaviour directed at others, whether or not it is really aggression, has severe social consequences and is likely to restrict life chances. It is, therefore, usually something that needs to be addressed. Sometimes biological factors may be involved, as when it is related to temporal lobe epilepsy, but may simply be a learned behaviour, producing a desired effect. Violence, after all, can be very effective in controlling the environment and it is a challenge to the intervention to provide an equally effective way of exerting control. Whether or not it is intended as such, it is worth treating such behaviour as if it were a form of communication, so that will guide the behaviour chosen to replace the violent one. Similarly, it is important to know if the behaviour is a defence reaction to fear or anger. In such cases, calming techniques may be a better way of managing the behaviour than mere attempts at restriction.

Self-injurious behaviour

Although we are all liable to show some form of self-injurious behaviour from time to time, the kinds that are associated with children and adults with autism and sld are usually more serious. They have the potential for extreme and irreversible damage, and, for that reason alone, should not be ignored. Such behaviours also affect the possibilities for independence because of the reluctance of carers and teachers to persist with unwelcome demands. In that way, threatening or performing self-injury (such as head-banging) can become a very effective, but ultimately destructive, way of controlling others. As with violent acts directed at others, self-directed violent acts need their causes and functions determined, if they are to be replaced with equally as effective, but less damaging, alternative behaviours.

One of the problems in trying to replace these behaviours is that a single such behaviour may serve more than one function for the child or adult (especially if behaviour is limited); a different alternative behaviour may have to be taught for each of these functional substitutions. Related to that is the problem that reducing one self-injurious behaviour may result in the reappearance of another self-injurious behaviour that serves that same function.

Self-injurious behaviour may be a form of stereotyped behaviour that reflects the fact that the child with autism and sld is performing at a very low developmental level. Just as a young baby may suck and bite objects including the self, the child with autism and sld may do the same, and for the same self-stimulatory reasons but, because they are bigger and stronger, the results may be more serious. Head-banging, for example, may arise from the rhythmic banging that babies often exhibit, but may get out of hand and may then come to be used for other functions. Head-banging may start as a comfort and self-stimulatory behaviour but reaction to it may mean that it is then used to gain attention, or to get out of doing something, or as a reaction to frustration and so on. Self-injurious behaviour may also be used to 'shut out' painful stimuli. It may become learned behaviour to meet needs directly or to communicate needs. Thus, it will not be possible to deal with any self-injurious behaviour by teaching a single alternative response; there will need to be a separate alternative taught for each identified function.

Destructive behaviour

This resembles both aggression and self-injurious behaviour except that it is directed at objects rather than people. Many of the same problems and possibilities will apply here as to these other categories of challenging behaviour.

Bizarre behaviours

These are not of themselves challenging behaviours, but some authorities and teachers may regard them as such and they may easily become challenging, if not understood. Individuals with autism often behave in ways which seem bizarre to others, but which make sense to the person in question. Such behaviours may not directly harm the person with autism and sld, not anyone else, but they can have indirect harmful effects in that they restrict the lives of the person exhibiting them and of families and others.

Everyone feels anxious at times and may then produce behaviour that others judge as bizarre. What distinguishes people with autism and sld from others are the kinds of events that lead to their anxiety and the fact that they do not inhibit their responses in the light of other people's reactions. It is this that makes the behaviour of those with autism appear unpredictable and abnormal, when in fact they are reacting in typical ways in response to extreme anxiety. The unwanted behaviour needs to be tackled on a number of fronts, but long-lasting effects can only be gained by tackling root causes, not symptoms; symptom suppression will only provide a short-term solution and in the long term may make the problem worse.

Understanding causes and reasons for behaviour is part of the solution. The child with autism and sld, for example, may sniff people because information from olfactory senses is easier for the child to interpret than that from vision or auditory channels. If this is understood, the behaviour may no longer seem so bizarre. This may need to be addressed through teaching. It is not fair to block a child's main way of making sense of the world and force him/her to use information from senses that s/he may find distorted and confusing. Thus, rather than just forbidding the child or preventing the child from licking or sniffing others, the teacher might develop a programme whereby the child is taught to pay attention to the visual and auditory features by which people can be distinguished, and which will give the child plenty of practice in making those distinctions through those senses. Only then, should the licking or smelling be tackled directly.

Setting priorities for changing behaviour
Most behaviour has a function and it is a serious matter to decide that someone else should not be permitted to behave in certain ways. Where the person has no disability, it may be more reasonable to set the rules for what behaviour can be allowed in certain situations. That is because people can make judgements about whether they are going to accept these particular rules and how much they wish to conform. When dealing with children the situation is somewhat different since we assume rights to control behaviour in the interests of teaching conformity and in passing on cultural norms, although, even then, we assume that children will grow to make their own independent judgements on the rules to be kept or rejected.

The situation is more complex ethically, however, when dealing with any disabled group and even more so when, like autism, the disability is such that the person does not understand the rules, nor their cultural context and may have so few behaviours with which to influence the world. There are also more severe practical difficulties in changing behaviours with such groups, since they will have no desire to change and no concept of the purpose of changing.

The teacher or parent might consider the following reasons for deciding to try to change a child's or adult's behaviour.

The behaviour is dangerous
This is the clearest reason for deciding to change a behaviour, where it is a danger to the child or others. This will include severe forms of self-injury (including extremely restricted diets and anorexia) and violent outbursts such as biting, hitting and

kicking. It may also include running away or climbing in dangerous places, such as onto roofs.

Interference and restriction
The behaviour itself may not be so bad, but the rate at which it
is produced and its inappropriateness to certain situations (loud
swearing in church, for example) may make the behaviour a
priority for reduction. If the behaviour is engaged in obsessively,
to the extent that it interferes with the child learning anything
else, then this suggests that it needs to be controlled or changed.
However, it is important to use attractive alternatives as a way
of modifying this behaviour and not just try to suppress obsessions. It is not just restriction of educational opportunities through
obsessions that needs to be addressed but also behaviour that
itself leads to restricted opportunities. Parents or teachers may
keep the child away from situations in which the child behaves
embarrassingly or in a way that hurts others, and so the life of
the child (and often of the family as well) becomes very restricted.
A boy with autism and sld was a terrible 'hair-plucker'. He had
pulled out all his own hair (from head, eyebrows, eye-lashes,
under-arm and the pubic hair) and had been put on a programme
to prevent him pulling out other people's hair. However, this
programme could not be maintained in the face of severe temptation and so, in spite of him loving them, his horse-riding sessions
had to be cancelled.

Effects on others
This goes beyond inconvenience, to the point where the quality
of life of the person is affected. It might include a child who
continually plays with saliva, draping it round surfaces and over
other people's possessions as well as his/her own. This is not
only highly unpleasant but, when the child has a cold, it can
spread infection. It also includes behaviour that might cause
others to lose control, such as continual flicking of paper or the
banging of the window frame to make a piece of paper, placed
on the sill, flutter.

Destruction
The hair-plucker's activities might be considered a form of destruction, although the main reason for wanting to reduce it was its restriction on the child's life. There may be other behaviour, however, which is not really restrictive, nor dangerous but, in its severity and relentlessness, deserves to be a priority for reduction. This includes continual destruction of clothes and/or furniture or continual sweeping of items in the classroom or workshop on to the floor.

Criminal or socially unacceptable behaviour
Unless the child or adult is to end up in prison or in a secure unit, any behaviour that might be considered criminal needs to be addressed. The actual behaviour in this category will vary from one society to another, but will include immodest behaviour (e.g., stripping in public, touching genitals or masturbating in public), unhygienic behaviour (e.g., picking one's nose, urinating, defecating, or spitting in inappropriate places such as shops or restaurants) or grossly insulting behaviour (e.g., sniffing someone's armpit or bottom, commenting aloud on someone's appearance in a derogatory way).

Ways of changing behaviour
Some examples of programmes to change behaviour have been given above. Children and adults with autism and sld will have very limited way of learning, and most techniques will be forms of behaviour modification, but taking account of the autism and the characteristics of the individual. The three broad approaches that follow can be tried.

Change the setting conditions
If one can identify the features that are cueing the unwanted behaviour, changing these should prevent the behaviour's occurrence. This is usually the best course of action in that it can be very difficult to change behaviour, especially if it is well established. It is easiest to do this when the behaviour is limited to one particular setting. For example, if a boy only scratches the person sitting next to him in assemblies, it would be sensible to

look for the features in that particular situation that were provoking the scratching. Some of the questions one would need to ask would be very particular to that situation, while others recognise more general factors that may have a role in the behaviour. They could, for example, include

- Is the boy stressed by the noise and crowding in assembly?
- Is the enforced sitting in the hall frustrating?
- Is the victim doing something to irritate the boy?

Training an incompatible alternative

The alternative behaviour chosen should fulfil the same function as the behaviour it is to replace, and should be incompatible (in terms of its ability to be performed) with the unwanted behaviour. The incompatible behaviour will have to be consistently rewarded in the same situation, until it too becomes a habit. In the example above, such a behaviour might include something to do with his hands, that would prevent the scratching. However, exactly what behaviour would depend on the function that had been identified by the questions on the setting conditions. If it appeared to be the noise and confusion that is stressing the boy, then it might be appropriate to teach him to cover his ears with his hands, although this is not a good behaviour to encourage (in that it shuts the child off from learning) and it should only be a temporary measure to deal with the scratching. It might be better, in fact, to reduce the time spent in assembly to a very short tolerable length that would not provoke any disturbing behaviour. This short positive experience of the assembly could then be gradually extended.

Changing the consequences

Consequences are most sensibly used in changing behaviour by rewarding other incompatible behaviours that are being trained in the same situation. In the example above, merely closing ears to the noise should be rewarding, without the need for additional reward (if the noise is punishing) and that is an advantage. It is also important to recognise that the unwanted behaviour may be being rewarded itself (usually unintentionally). In the example used above, it may be that the reaction of the scratched child, or the reaction of the teacher, is more interesting than the assembly. Many children with autism and sld will perform actions deliberately just to get the predicable effect of someone displaying anger.

It may also happen that scratching his neighbour leads to the child being removed from the situation, so that scratching becomes a learnt way of escaping from assembly. If this were the reason for scratching, then, the boy might be taught to make a sign that would indicate that he had had enough—in effect a request to leave. Note that it would be impossible to teach an alternative way of asking to escape, at the same time as making the child sit through the assembly. If that were the route taken, then there would have to be a separate programme to help the child tolerate the assembly.

Summary

Challenging behaviour can arise in autism and sld for a number of reasons and often has high priority as a teaching target for both parents and professionals, living and working with individuals with autism and sld. Such behaviour, however, must be recognised as deriving from the interaction between the individual and the environment and it cannot be tackled effectively without an understanding of its causes and the functions it serves for that individual in that setting. In autism and sld, the individual will have a limited repertoire of behaviours, so it is likely that a single behaviour may serve a range of functions and each function will have to be tackled separately.

Positive approaches are most effective in the long run, as well as being more ethical. The most useful positive approach is to treat the unwanted behaviour as a form of communication, whether or not it was intended as such. Then the task becomes one of teaching the individual a more acceptable way of communicating whatever it is that has been identified as the function of the behaviour.

Further reading

CLEMENTS, J. & ZARKOWSKA, E. (2000) *Behavioural Concerns and Autistic Spectrum Disorders*. London: Jessica Kingsley.

9 Approaches to Planning and Management of Behaviour

Particular reasons for challenging behaviour

As has been said, and will be illustrated below, there are no uniform causes of challenging behaviour and each individual in each situation may have a different reason for the same kind of behaviour. Nevertheless, there are reasons why certain kinds of challenging behaviour may be common in people with autism and sld and certain underlying reasons for such behaviour. One reason is that individuals with autism and sld will have fewer adaptive behaviours than normally developing peers, and so are more likely to resort to maladaptive ones.

Biology

Biological causation does not mean that nothing can be done, but it may be reassuring to carers to know it is not all due to mismanagement, and it may alert them to periods when the individual may be 'irritable' and where s/he will need to be watched more closely or put in a safe environment, or have demands reduced. There is a much increased incidence of epilepsy in this population (sld and autism) and Gedye (1989) has associated an increased risk of aggression with frontal lobe seizures. There may be perceptual problems in autism that result in over- and/or under-stimulation and both situations may lead to challenging behaviour. Extreme forms of stimulation may cause pain or may release endomorphins and so become addictive (e.g., physical struggling), whereas sensory deprivation may lead to self-injurious behaviour. Hormonal imbalance (especially allied to a lack of understanding about what is happening (e.g., in pre-menstrual tension)) may lead to challenging behaviour also. There may also be side-effects of any medication the person is on.

Failing to understand others' intentions

Many of the problem behaviours seen in autism and sld stem from difficulties in making sense of the social world and other people.

Having little understanding of one's own or others' intentions means that many actions appear random and that it is hard to see the pattern or to understand what is required in any situation. This in turn makes it hard to see the point in activities or to follow any but the most explicit of instructions. Thus, instructions should always be clear and precise (and possibly visual) and not reliant on the person with autism and sld making any implications. Many apparently challenging behaviours arise just because the person has simply misunderstood instructions or rules and extreme naïveté is translated as obstinacy or rudeness.

Predicting and being aware of consequences

If one is unable to appreciate intentional actions, then one is also unable to predict future behaviour and the consequences of current behaviour. This makes other people somewhat frightening and also means that it is impossible to trust others or to judge how they will react. In respect to one's own actions, it means that children with autism and sld (and possibly many such adults) are not fully responsible for their behaviours, in that they are not fully aware of the consequences of behaving in certain ways, especially the effects on other people's emotions. It also means that it is very difficult for them to learn from their mistakes, even when supposedly punished, since their focus will be on not getting caught (the behaviour that led directly to the sanction) rather than on not performing the original act itself.

Reacting to others

Reactions to 'normal' frustrations are likely to be expressed in a pre-socialised manner in that they are not tempered by a sense of embarrassment or awareness of the effect on others, beyond any behavioural consequences. Individuals with autism and sld are not susceptible to social control, and their poor understanding of social situations makes other people frightening; this may then lead to panic and consequent challenging behaviour. Nor will

individuals with autism and sld have developed subtle or sophisticated ways of controlling others and so will often attempt to meet
their own needs directly, ignoring or demolishing any obstacles
to this. Proximal sensations (like touching, smelling and licking)
may be used more and may lead to challenging behaviour if
others react unfavourably to this.

Difficulties in communicating

Apart from the significant failures in understanding, another main
reason for challenging behaviour in autism and sld is that people
with autism and sld have so few ways of influencing the world
and making their needs known.

Frustration: When things go wrong and the child's (or adult's)
normal routine or habitual modes of responding do not work, the
child with autism and sld is simply at a loss as to how to proceed.
This can lead to frustration and, in the absence of problem-solving
strategies, challenging behaviour is likely to emerge.

Communication failure: Regardless of language ability (and that
is likely to be limited in children with autism and sld) people,
especially children, with autism and sld will have very few ways
of asking for help or other ways of expressing frustration. In such
circumstances, therefore, challenging behaviour may come to
serve this communicative function. Challenging behaviour may
start as a primitive reaction to aversive stimuli, or to stress, but
it may develop a communicative function from the way that
people have responded to it.

Lack of self-awareness

Much of the behaviour of those with autism and sld is triggered
by environmental stimuli and is not under conscious control.
Language difficulties may also mean that there is no 'inner language' for controlling one's own actions. Individuals with autism
and sld may be at a primitive developmental level, where words
simply trigger actions regardless of whether or not they are
intended as prohibitions. Thus there are people with autism going
around saying 'Don't spit!' to themselves as they spit; the prohib-
ition does nothing to stop the spitting but is now the context for
that spitting. Problems with waiting arise from these difficulties

also, as do inabilities in dealing with failed strategies and both may lead to challenging behaviours. Individuals with autism and sld often show a lack of discrimination in their dealings with the world, and in its severest form this may result in pica, where all manner of inedible substances are ingested.

Finally, it may be that unsociable and difficult behaviour may lead to a vicious circle whereby individuals with autism and sld are placed in specialist settings with others with similar behaviours, and where there are therefore few better models to imitate. In such settings, the more violent behaviours may be more noticeable and therefore are more likely to be copied.

Managing challenging behaviour—basic analysis

Defining the behaviour

In order to make sure that everyone is behaving consistently, there needs to be a clear, and shared, understanding of the nature of the behaviour that is considered 'challenging'. This will also help when it comes to assessing whether we are being successful in controlling it. Behaviour needs to be described in terms of:

- *Topography*—What the individual does, given as explicitly as possible. For example, if we say he is spitting, is the spit forceful or more of a dribble, directed at others or at particular things (dark surfaces, windows?) or random?

- *Cycle*—How often? When? This helps us see the pattern and provides a baseline for evaluating treatment. We need to note the context (is it only with specific people, at specific times, in specific environments?) and individual factors such as only when the person has a cold or when a period is due.

- *Course*—Duration and changes over the time of one episode. For example, does the child start screaming loudly for ten minutes or so and then tail off to a whimper, or perhaps start with a whine and build up into a full-bodied scream? This might help us when thinking of the function it is serving and the treatment that might be effective.

- *Strength*—This is useful even as a rough estimate for some behaviours. Thus, it makes a difference if the child is hitting in a controlled way or if it is a 'no holds barred' flaying around.

A *functional analysis*

This is a systematic way of collecting information about the individual, the environment, the individual's life history, behaviour, abilities, current opportunities and reinforcers. These may be described simply by an ABC chart, although this is likely to miss important parts of the analysis:

A: *Antecedents*
B: *Behaviour*
C: *Consequences*: Note absence or removal of stimulation as well as what is present

A more complex and useful form of functional analysis is the STAR Model (Zarkowska & Clements, 1989)

S: *Settings*: Stable aspects of the environment. This can include places, times and occasions when the behaviour occurs and the particular state of the person at the time.
T: *Triggers*: Particular occurrences or sets of stimuli that appear to trigger the challenging behaviour directly, i.e., act as signals to start or stop behaviour. Failure of a known trigger to lead to an expected desired outcome can also lead to challenging behaviour. An example of this is when a child is used to eating dinner at the dining table and then the parent tries to work with the child at that table. The child may come to the table willingly but then display difficult behaviour when, instead of the expected meal, the child is presented with a task.
A: *Actions*: This is a more precise and detailed term than 'behaviour'. It includes not only the challenging behaviour but also an analysis of the actions that are missing, in that they are needed to be taught, in order to prevent challenging behaviour.
R: *Results*: Events that follow an action. This includes unconscious

as well as conscious reactions. People with autism may be more sensitive to bodily tension and to body smells (such as the smell of fear, from hormonal reactions) so that they may not notice your pretend indifference when you are trying to ignore something like spitting, but instead be aware of your true feelings of disgust.

Consequences of challenging behaviour available to the teacher/carer

There are different kinds of consequences (provided or taken away, following the challenging behaviour) that are available to the teacher/carer. There are four options in two categories:

Reinforcement

This may be positive or negative, but the effect of both is to start or increase behaviour. Positive reinforcements or rewards involve the addition of something the individual wants, following the behaviour. Negative reinforcement is the taking away of something the individual does not like, following the behaviour. The problem with negative reinforcement is that behaviour is also controlled by setting conditions, so that the negative reinforcement not only strengthens the behaviour it follows, but the stimulus that is taken away also acts as a cue for the behaviour. Nagging is the clearest example of this. It is a negative stimulus and works by stopping nagging (i.e. removing the negative stimulus) the moment the person performs the task he or she is being nagged to perform. Unfortunately, the removal of the nagging may strengthen the behaviour, but the nagging is also the cue for that behaviour, and so the behaviour may become dependent on the nagging.

Parents often complain (and not just about children with autism and sld!) that their child comes in each day from school and drops his coat on the floor until nagged to pick it up and hang it up. 'Why does he never learn to hang it up?' they say. If we analyse the situation, we can see from the child's point of view that the nagging does nothing to affect the habit of taking off his coat and dropping it on the floor. What the nagging does is reinforce (by its stopping) the boy picking up his coat from the floor and hanging it up on the peg. It also provides the cue for the boy to pick up his coat from the floor, and so the boy never learns to pick it up without this cue. Even worse, it does nothing to influence the real behaviour the parents want to encourage— hanging up his coat when he takes it off instead of letting it drop to the floor. In order to do that, the parents must catch him before he has removed his coat and prompt him (silently, or the instruction will become the cue) to take it off and hang it up in one movement sequence. The physical prompts for this are gradually reduced, until the boy has developed the habit of hanging up his coat. It is better not to add a separate 'reward' at the end, because we want to keep to natural situations as far as possible; nor is an external reward usually necessary. However, praise can be used, as appropriate.

Punishment

This refers to two processes designed to reduce or eliminate behaviour. It covers the addition of a negative stimulus (punishment 'proper') following the behaviour and the removal of a positive one following the behaviour (time out). Evidence (Donnellan *et al.*, 1988) is that it does not teach anyone not to do the act *per se*, but just suppresses it. Problems with punishment are given below.

The use and abuse of punishment

There are ethical and practical problems in aiming to reduce or eliminate any behaviours, especially as individuals with autism and sld have a very small repertoire of behaviours in the first place. There are also very practical problems to do with the operation of a system of punishment.

Practical objections to punishment

- It is ineffective in the long run.
- It causes unwanted side-effects, such as fear.
- It indicates what *not* to do rather than what to *do*.
- It justifies inflicting pain (especially if it involves aversives).
- It relates only to the particular situation of the punishment

(so that, for example, the small boy may learn not to jump on the sofa when Daddy is around, but will jump even more when he is not, to 'make up for it').

- It may elicit aggression towards the punisher or others.
- It may replace one undesirable behaviour with another, which it is hoped is less severe, but there are no guarantees that will be so.

Alternatives to punishment

- Changing the circumstances leading up to the difficult behaviour, so that it is not triggered or cued.

- Satiation of the undesirable behaviour—This is a risky strategy in autism where the person may never seem to tire of a 'favourite' activity, if the response is an habitual one. If the response is a sudden reaction, on the other hand, being made to do it without the trigger may be irrelevant or even aversive and have no effect on the behaviour occurring again once the trigger is there.

- Waiting for development to eliminate it—It is sometimes the case in an individual with autism and sld that failure to achieve a milestone (like being toilet-trained, or sleeping in one's own bed) is regarded as a trigger for teaching, forgetting that the child's development is not yet at the stage when such a milestone could be expected.

- Extinction—A positive stimulus is no longer available. This is different from 'time out' in that it is not removal of the positive stimulus for a while but permanent absence of that stimulus.

- Time out—This presupposes the existence of a positive reinforcer. Thus, it is not 'time out' if the child, who does not like the noisy classroom nor the activities within it, is sent outside to calm down. Social exclusion only works as punishment if the person wants to be socially included.

- Token economy—This is where convenience or practicality

makes it better for the person to be given tokens for good behaviour (or for periods of time without engaging in bad behaviour) which they can 'save' and exchange later for a greater range of rewards. This can be very effective and has a normalisation function, given that most people work for tangible tokens called money. However, such token economies can get out of control, especially if things which are in effect that person's entitlement are used as rewards and consequently as punishments as well. Token economies must be monitored to make sure they do not become punitive.

● Reinforcing incompatible behaviour—This is usually the most effective technique in the long term, but there may need to be appropriate support to get it established.

Plan to manage behaviour positively

As was seen in Chapter 8, challenging behaviour is best dealt with through the same processes of understanding, reducing stress, and teaching, that underpin all good practice in working with individuals with autism and sld. As was illustrated in earlier chapters, however, autism is a disorder that affects those who live and work with the person with autism almost as much as that person him or herself. Just as people with autism seek control of others, because of their fear and lack of understanding, so those surrounding that person may similarly experience fear and a consequent need for control. Two 'control freaks' together is a situation likely to lead to friction. It is hoped that it would be adults without the disorder who would have the greater understanding and skill to enable them to retreat from such a confrontation, but, alas, that is not always so. It is important, therefore, to cultivate ways of developing positive interventions and to examine some of the factors in parents and carers that may lead to less positive interactions.

Develop long-term positive interventions

Developing a supportive environment can promote learning and prevent disruption. Individual factors will partly determine what is positive and supportive in each case, and there are ways of determining what this will be.

Consider the needs of the person with autism and sld in each of four dimensions:

Places

Here, the factors that need to be monitored as likely sources of stress or triggers for challenging behaviour include the size of the living and working space, especially in relation to room occupancy. People with autism may have a sense of their personal space being invaded if someone comes within a few metres of them, while they may themselves have no recognition of others' personal space. When a group of individuals with autism and sld are put together, therefore, there are potential problems with the mutual invasion of one another's space and the reactions that may evoke. Sounds, too, need to be monitored, both in terms of overall level of noise as a distraction and in terms of certain sounds being painful for the person with autism. Staff need to be aware of those who are over-sensitive to all or certain sounds and the need to help toleration by providing shields (in the form of sound-absorbing curtains, for example, or earphones at an individual level) or developing a programme of desensitisation.

For some individuals at some times, certain colours may be disturbing and the fact that someone is wearing a bright yellow T-shirt may be the explanation for the fact that the person with autism, who has been passive, or even friendly, with that person before, suddenly attacks them today. At the same time, it has been argued that certain colours are soothing and that judicious use of colour can help produce calming environments. That remains to be proven, but it would be a useful, and easily accomplished, way of managing the behaviour of people with autism and sld.

Some places act as triggers for challenging behaviour in individuals with autism and sld, not because of any particular aspect of that setting, but because it has been associated with something upsetting in the past. Anxiety about what has happened in a place, or indeed what happens there now, can provoke extremely resistant behaviour in people with autism and sld. Unfortunately, while such behaviour in anyone else might provoke staff to look for such a reason for the person's resistance to the place, in autism it is often attributed to the autism itself, as if this were an explanation for a particular behaviour.

People

In the first chapter we examined some of the reasons why people with autism might see other people as problematic. Except for a very few, most people with autism and sld do not, however, continue to avoid others throughout their life, nor to resist when others approach them. In fact, most individuals with autism and sld eventually become very attached to their parents and other familiar adults. However, there remain some particular features associated with other people, which continue to present problems to most people with autism. The most common disturbing feature is lack of familiarity. Challenging behaviour may arise as people with autism try to adapt to the new, but find it too stressful. In some cases it is not the newness of staff that is the problem but the way they behave. This may just be that they have a very different teaching style or way of interacting, that either makes them hard to understand, and therefore obey, or is a confrontational style, which people with autism tend to resist. Of course, it may not be a particular member of staff that is upsetting the person with autism by their particular behaviour, but just that there is inconsistency in the ways in which different staff treat the person with autism.

Objects

Although objects are usually more comforting and attractive to people with autism, there still may be particular triggers for anxiety and consequent challenging behaviour with some features of some objects. As with people, one disturbing feature is likely to be newness, especially where there has been a change. Thus new furniture at home may provoke extreme reactions and one young man with autism and sld insisted on demolishing his parents' new three-piece suite in spite of considerable efforts to distract him and to get him to accept an alternative behaviour. It is seldom the newness of itself that is the problem, but rather that something that was expected to stay the same had changed. This can apply to furnishing and décor, but this can at least be planned for and the person prepared for the change.

Sometimes, however, the 'change' may only be apparent to the person with autism and so the challenging behaviour may be seen as 'coming right out of the blue'. A young man with autism and sld, for example, lived in an adult community and came home infrequently. He had settled well into this routine, so it was rather frightening and sad to see him suddenly revert to all manner of challenging behaviour. It was his mother who realised that it was that week she had finally got round to giving his room a thorough cleaning, removing piles of 'rubbish' he had collected there. Once she had thought of that, his behaviour made it obvious that that was in fact the case; his piles may have represented 'rubbish' to his mother, but they represented well known and well loved objects to him, all of which he knew, including where they 'should' be.

Time

Time itself is unlikely to be a factor in determining challenging behaviour, but it may be a kind of shorthand for other factors that vary with time. A child with autism and sld, for example, is liable to have very little sleep at night in the pre-school years especially. This may make such a child highly irritable in the mornings and very tired at night, both of which might make challenging behaviour more likely. Equally, the adult with autism and sld may behave very differently at the start of the week, from the end of the week; some children will start the weekends worn-out from the week's work and yet at the same time they (or others) may be looking forward to the weekend. Monthly cycles of challenging behaviour are not common, except for the particular case of pre-menstrual tension. It is even harder to find any good evidence of a seasonal effect in autism except for factors that affect us all, such as less daylight. Even if factors are not general to all with autism, they need to be examined for particular effects on certain individuals.

Control by certain environmental features

This identifies the more specific setting conditions for the behaviour. It may be necessary to teach the appropriate settings, for example, for masturbation, where the person may have to be taught to restrict this to his or her own bed. There is also a need to teach the child the conditions that distinguish whether the behaviour is appropriate or not. For example, it is not the child's fault if she has been taught to use a toilet and then uses the dummy toilet set up in a DIY store; someone should have pointed out to her during toilet-training that the toilet must be functioning and in a private place, in a way that she could understand.

Positive programming

There is a need for twenty-four-hour continuity, to fit in with the individual's learning style and a whole environment that respects the dignity of the child or adult. Whatever treatment or approach is used, it should relate to the person as a whole, rather than concentrating on isolated behaviour. The emphasis should always be on teaching new alternative behaviours, rather than on the elimination of unwanted ones. Sometimes teachers interpret a twenty-four-hour curriculum as meaning that parents should be persuaded to continue to work on school-based programmes at home, but that is not the case. It might as well be argued that teachers should see themselves as working with their pupils in school, according to the dictates of a domestic programme. What is needed is genuine collaboration, so that there are shared attitudes and values with respect to education, across home and school, but also a recognition that children need different things at different times and that a broad approach is valuable.

Steps to take in a positive behavioural programme

The overall behavioural assessment

Assessment should help understanding of:

- why the behaviour occurs,
- what we can do about it and

- how we can build on the positive behaviours the person already has.

  Teachers, parents and carers should all be involved.
  In managing behaviours in class or adult work groups, attention needs to be paid to how positive behaviour can be supported by the way the environment can be used.

Assessing the setting conditions
Information about all of the following factors will help determine which factors are relevant in predicting (and therefore preventing) challenging behaviour.

- *History and background of the individual and his/her environment*—It is useful to know whether this is a new behaviour, whether it has been happened before and under what circumstances, how it was dealt with then and with what result, and whether this current bout of challenging behaviour had a precursor or not.

- *Functional analysis of the challenging behaviour*—As discussed in Chapter 7 and below, the best and most educational way of dealing with challenging behaviour is to find out what function it is serving for the person in this situation, and then to teach a better way of achieving the same function.

- *Changes in lifestyle and environment that will be needed to help the individual change*—We all find it difficult to change our behaviour, especially if it is well established and habitual. If we want to go on a diet, most of us would try to ensure that the house was not full of biscuits, or if we wanted to give up smoking we might avoid going out with smoking friends, at least for a while; we recognise that we need to have supportive environments to help us change our behaviour. This is even truer of people with autism and sld, who are not able to imagine their own goals to spur them on, and whose behaviour is much more habitual and much less capable of being monitored and controlled. Thus we need to identify those aspects of the environment that either need to be removed, because they are supporting the challenging behaviour, or which can be used to support alternative behaviours.

Note that assessing the setting conditions is the first step, because it does not rely on the individual him/herself being able to change, but concentrates on changes that the parent, carer or teacher can make to support behaviour change.

Adapting the behaviour
The following are the steps that need to be taken to help the individual change his/her behaviour.

- *Teach a functionally related skill to replace the challenging behaviour:* You may need to act 'as if' the behaviour were serving a particular function. If, for example, you judge that the girl is throwing the dinner plate to communicate that she does not want her dinner, that does not have to mean that she intends to communicate that. She may just be reacting to the fact that she does not want it, but we make the decision that, if she could communicate, that is what she would want to convey. Thus, we teach her a way of communicating that and in the process we not only replace the challenging behaviour but also teach her something about how to communicate.

- *Add to the individual's repertoire so that the challenging behaviour is no longer needed*: This might include social skills training, for example, if the child was thumping others in order to play chase and did not know how else to attract attention and to negotiate a game. As with the example above it will also commonly involve teaching communicative gestures to replace challenging behaviour, because it is the lack of such skills that has led to frustration and hence the challenging behaviour.

- *Focus on socially acceptable alternatives and ways of communicating confusion (e.g. through using symbols)*: One way of avoiding challenging behaviour is by reducing confusion and, therefore, stress. Picture timetables (Peeters, 1997; Watson *et al.*, 1989) can help the person stop worrying about what is to happen next, or when something is going to happen. More problematic with people with autism and sld is to teach them how to ask for help when they are confused, perhaps by using a symbol that you teach them means 'I don't understand'.

- *Indicate that requests have been understood, even when not immediately granted, or teach (as in PECS) that choices are limited to items on the 'menu'*: When teachers or parents first teach a child with autism and sld to communicate, they commonly start with request, since this is the easiest to demonstrate. Once the child has learnt the word (or sign, or symbol) for something like a sweet, though, there is often a problem. The child will ask for it continually and you do not want the child to have so much access to it. Yet, if you refuse the desired object at this stage (even if you use words like 'later' and 'not now'), the child's grasp of communication is so slender, that it is likely to evaporate. The child may well see the sign or symbols as 'not working' any longer, and revert to the former way of 'communicating', which may have been through challenging behaviour.

- *Teach the individual some coping strategies for dealing with stressful situations*: These will include actual stress management techniques of relaxation, counting to ten before acting (or three, if ten is too high) and deep breathing exercises. It may also include desensitisation exercises, to increase tolerance of whatever, or whoever, they fear.

- *Teach relaxation, exercise and escape training*: This involves recognising when one is getting 'worked up', which means that staff or parents have first to recognise these signals in the person, in order to teach him or her to react to them in a positive way, before they trigger challenging behaviour. As with other groups, people with autism and sld need to 'let off steam' in a safe way when faced with situations that they too find challenging. They need to be taught a routine of daily vigorous exercise to bring down anxiety and reduce the incidents of challenging behaviour and they need to have ways of recognising and responding to their signs of increasing distress by 'escaping' from the situation they are finding so difficult.

Working on the consequences of behaviour
Although it is preferable to help individuals with autism and sld through supportive environments and the teaching of self-management skills, it has to be recognised that people with autism and sld are not able to inhibit habitual behaviours and may need more direct and specific training of substitute behaviours. Straightforward behavioural techniques can be used for this, as long as you are always trying to take account of how that individual is responding and what sense he or she is making of the procedure.

• Use reinforcers as part of the strategy; at the beginning the alternative behaviour will need a high rate of reinforcement and strong reinforcers, but later the reinforcement rate and the kind of reinforcement used should be more like that found in natural situations. Thus, to begin with, you might praise and give a small edible reward to a child every time he tapped someone gently on the arm (in a set situation, where this was being prompted) to gain their attention, instead of hitting them hard in the back, as had been his former habit. Note, one should praise just before giving the edible reward, so that the praise becomes a signal that a reward is on its way and thus comes to function as a reward itself. If you praise the child after giving the edible, the praise will never be noticed. Once the boy is tapping successfully most of the time, the edible reinforcer can be gradually faded and then eventually the praise can be faded, while always keeping to a level of reward that is maintaining the child's best level of performance. Eventually you hope that by prompting the behaviour in natural situations without these rewards, the natural satisfaction of playing chase will compensate for the loss of more tangible rewards, and will help the child generalise and maintain the behaviour in natural environments.

- A direct way of training the person to drop a challenging behaviour, is to target that behaviour as the only one to be missed out of general reinforcement to all other behaviours in a targeted context. This 'blunderbus' approach is usually only adopted when the challenging behaviour has no clear function but seems to be being performed for internal (perhaps, self-stimulatory) or unfathomable reasons. The procedure is to reinforce anything and everything except for the behaviour you wish to stop, and to do so with a strong reinforcer.

- This is similar to the above, but is a much more common approach in which the trainer reinforces a specific alternative behaviour that serves the same function, and is one the individual cannot do at the same time as the unwanted one.

- People with autism and sld tend not to pay attention to the consequences of their actions and, if they are ever to become self-autonomous in the monitoring and control of their own behaviour, they need to be helped to see the consequences of their own actions and to be able to make a choice of a behaviour for themselves. If the person is able to follow picture sequences, then flow charts can be used to help the child literally 'see' the choice point and the consequent pathways. More able individuals may be able to cope with alternative pathways here, but the individual with autism and sld will need to see the correct path to follow only.

Managing challenging behaviour in schools—issues

Short-term strategies produce long-term problems
Oliver (1986) has produced a model of how short-term strategies, intended to prevent or shop challenging behaviour, may in fact exacerbate it. The teacher may respond to difficult behaviour (e.g. by taking away the task, sending the child outside, soothing the child who is self-injuring) in ways that 'work' in the short term, in that the challenging behaviour stops. The teacher is, therefore, reinforced in using this strategy, which is now regarded as 'successful'. However, such actions are in fact rewarding the

challenging behaviour (either positively because the teacher is giving the child something desirable, such as attention, or negatively in that something unwanted is being taken away) so, on future occasions, that same challenging behaviour is likely to recur. Over time, unless the teacher learns to change, the challenging behaviour gets worse.

How to avoid making things worse
Most of the discussion so far has concerned how to prevent challenging behaviour occurring or how to minimise its future occurrences. In reality, there will be times when such strategies are hard to implement and the parent or teacher is faced with a person who is already beginning to act in a challenging way. The issue then is: how do we monitor, modify, and evaluate such responses, and how do we make sure things do not get worse?

● Take charge of the situation; like a young normally developing child, people with autism and sld may be disturbed by their own lack of control and are often calmed when someone else sets the boundaries.

● Where it is not possible, nor perhaps necessary, to change the challenging behaviour directly, it is best to divert the pupil's attention; re-directing to a familiar work routine can be very effective in calming a pupil and getting him/her back on task.

● Reduce the background stimulation; even when children can cope normally, being upset is likely to reduce their tolerance to stimulation.

● Encourage the child to calm down, using techniques that have been taught when the child was calmer. These might include deep breathing, sitting or lying down, folding arms and so on.

● Find relaxing things to do, such as visiting the soft-play area or the sensory room, or listening to music. One has to be careful, however, not to reward the challenging behaviour, so this is best done at the first signs that the person is getting upset, rather than waiting until the challenging behaviour has occurred.

- Talk the individual down, in a soft calm voice, but avoid nagging or using complicated language. Short repetitive phrases are best, such as 'It's all right now; let's go and sit down'.

- Avoid eye-to-eye gaze, approaching too fast, standing too close, leaning forward, gesticulating with arms, raising volume and pitch of voice, giving orders and making threats.

Strategies for causes and effects

Although we have concentrated on environmental causes of challenging behaviour, because these are more within our control, there may also be internal contributory factors. Challenging behaviour may start as a reaction to pain, for example, although it may then come to serve other functions as the person realises that this is a good way to get attention, control others and so on. Thus, if our focus is on preventing challenging behaviour, or at least in preventing these secondary causes, we should try to screen for these internal factors as a first step.

Medical treatment

The first step is to eliminate possible medical causes such as ear-ache, toothache, excema, and so on; the purpose is to identify any such causes and treat them. People with autism and sld often cannot identify the source of their own pain, even if they are able to communicate, and so challenging behaviour may be seen as their way of expressing that pain.

Physical intervention

There are legislative reasons why most professionals will not want to use physical restraint as a way of managing behaviour. Even in the home, however, physical restraint easily becomes punitive or leads to further outbursts of frustration, so it should be used, if at all, only as a last resort. If there is a need to use physical restraint, all schools and centres should have a clear policy with guidelines available to all, including parents and/or advocates and staff should have training, regularly updated and rehearsed. It is important that methods are chosen that keep everyone safe, including the people exhibiting the challenging behaviour themselves. Restraint methods should be seen as short term and should be performed in the least restrictive way.

Whole service approach
As mentioned above, there is a need for fully developed policies in relation to behaviour management and this applies to all approaches, not just physical restraint. Whenever there is an incident, that should trigger a review by all care or teaching staff. Challenging behaviour in an individual with autism and sld indicates a failure in our ability to help and support him or her. That is not to say that we can manage to eliminate all challenging behaviour, no matter how good our care, but we should never accept that challenging behaviour is 'inevitable'. Each occurrence should be looked at for what can be learnt in terms of how to manage the situation better in the future. However, we must also recognise the extreme stress staff suffer when exposed to challenging behaviour on a regular basis. Just as the person with autism and sld may need stress reduction measures as a matter of priority, so also do staff, and there should be supportive debriefing sessions following all incidents in which a member of staff is hurt.

Possible causes of violence in the treatment and care of individuals with autism

Sadly, in spite of legislation, there remain cases of abuse towards children and adults with autism and sld and it is important to recognise the reasons why this may happen, if it is to be prevented. Just as it is necessary to understand autism if we are to treat individuals with autism effectively and with respect, so it is necessary to understand the causes of violence in the carers and educators of those with autism, if we are to deal effectively with that. There are special factors in autism which may lead to such violence in addition to the normal pressures of family or institutional life that sometimes result in violence.

The transactional nature of autism

This leads to the frustration and de-skilling of both parents and professionals. Autism is essentially a disturbance of the relationship with others (Kanner, 1943; Hobson, 1993). This has two important results. One is the effect on the individual with autism and sld who, contrary to all other groups of individuals, will be disturbed and confused rather than consoled and comforted by the proximity and social overtures of others. What is intended as a gesture of affection or comfort, or a placatory attempt following conflict, will not be perceived as such by the individual (Attwood *et al.*, 1988) and indeed may be experienced as, at best, further confusion and, at worst, intrusion and aggression. The person with autism and sld may then react in turn with distress and panic and this too may be perceived as aggression by others.

The second result is the effect on the person who is caring for, or working with, the person with autism and sld. Even when they understand the condition at a theoretical level, but especially if they do not, they will experience the reactions of the person with autism as rejection and even aggression. This will make them feel helpless and angry. Their natural instinctive reactions do not work, nor do their previously successful professional strategies—they feel demoralised and de-skilled. The natural consequence of those feelings is frustration and anger.

Reading behaviour literally

As mentioned above, even when autism is understood at a theoretical level, our normal intuitive 'reading' of the behaviour we see in autism is liable to mislead. In particular, the attempts that the person with autism and sld does make to communicate are not recognised or understood and we naturally impute an intentionality (such as aggression) to the behaviour we see, which may not in fact be the case.

It is natural that the behaviour of others is processed unthinkingly. We do not 'work out' the motivations of others as a kind of theory (as the 'theory of mind' theorists—e.g., Baron-Cohen, 1995—would have us believe); real-time processing is too short for that. We reserve such conscious analysis for written and dramatic texts or for a *post-hoc* analysis of events. At the time, we respond instinctively to the emotional subjective 'meaning' of events as conveyed through the behaviour of others. We can discipline ourselves to recognise that what we see in autism and sld does not mean what our subjective reading of events tells us, but this is something we need to be trained to do. If we respond intuitively, we will misinterpret the behaviour we see, reading it literally according to our subjective experience and our understanding of normal development and motivation. Thus, behaviour will be misinterpreted to mean just what it would mean if we were doing it and we will assume a kind and level of intentionality that is not really there.

There may, for example, be an incident such as the one in which a person with autism was asked to do something quite unexceptional, to get into the back seat of the car, and reacted with apparent unprovoked aggression, screaming and throwing the things she was holding at the person making the request. Yet, if we analyse the situation from the point of view of the young lady with autism, a different picture emerges. When asked later, she cannot remember what she did and reports being in a panic and reacting blindly to that. The cause of the panic? She has been told that she will be picked up from the station by one person but now, when she goes to enter the car, she is confronted unexpectedly by someone else sitting there and, even more disturbing because even less predictable, it is a child. It is no good punishing people with autism because they have reacted in panic, since the behaviour is not under conscious control at the time. We need to prevent the behaviour (as far as possible) by our prediction of the likely reactions of someone with autism to such events.

Fear
Just as it is difficult for the person with autism and sld to understand and predict our behaviour, so it is difficult for us to understand and predict what they will do. They are following a different developmental path and show many very idiosyncratic behaviours, which can lead to fear of loss of control in those who are living and/or working with them.

Thus, it is not always the behaviour itself of someone with

autism and sld that can provoke an angry and violent reaction, but the fact that the different developmental path and the consequent different and idiosyncratic behaviour make it hard for others to predict that behaviour. Just as people with autism and sld are confused and fearful of us because it is hard for them to predict and understand our behaviour, so we experience fear and confusion when faced with behaviour that we can neither understand nor predict. A common response to such feelings is the desire to inhibit and control the behaviour and so our demands on the person with autism may become coercive and even violent. It must be remembered that the person with autism will be experiencing the same need for control for much the same reasons, so there is then a clash, whereby both participants in an interaction are seeking control of the other. The experience of this conflict may increase the fear in the carer or professional and the extremity of the measures used to re-establish control.

Short-term success reinforces long-term exacerbation of problems
As we saw above in relation to the use of short-term reactive strategies in school, using violence may bring about short-term success for the carer or professional in terms of stopping unwanted behaviour or coercing the individual with autism and sld to do something. The immediate effect will be to reward the person for using this violent act as a strategy in similar situations in the future. The unease the person may feel about using violence may be counterbalanced by self-justifications such as, 'It's the only thing that works' or 'It allows him/her access to a better learning situation or environment'. Such positions may even be taken in textbooks or in approaches meant to guide professionals (Kraijer, 1997; Lovaas, 1981). In such a way, such people are able to feel vindicated for the use of violence and even to gain in self-esteem because they feel they have a strategy that 'works'.

Over time, of course, the short-term 'solution' leads to longer-term problems, but the pathway to this is seldom recognised unless it is pointed out in training. To begin with, for example, the professional may slap the child for pinching as they sit together to do a task. This appears to work; the child is upset but stops pinching and can be redirected to the task in hand. The adult is relieved and feels successful overall, in spite of some initial feelings of discomfort at slapping the child. But what has the child learned? In a situation that the child finds disturbing (perhaps because of the confusing nature of the task or the way it is presented, perhaps because of the proximity of the adult at the table), the child performs an action (pinching) that in the past has led to others leaving him in peace. This is not the effect this time; instead, the adult slaps the child, there is a pause in the activity as the child is distressed and then the adult gives the child something concrete to do by positive redirection to the task.

This works for a while because the child's pattern of behaving has been disrupted. But now the uncomfortable situation re-asserts itself; the task may still not be clear (maybe the adult has reduced his or her level of guidance at this stage) and the adult is still uncomfortably close. So the child tries pinching again and this too is followed by a slap. Gradually, a new pattern is established. It is true that pinching now no longer leads to being left alone, but now it leads to the even more clearly predictable reaction of being hit. This may be intended as a punishment, but in a confusing world any predicted response is preferable to unpredictability, so the child comes to seek the predictable pattern of the pinch followed by the slap. For the adult this is infuriating and frightening. The hitting becomes harder in an attempt to re-establish control and a vicious (metaphorical and actual) circle is established.

Some approaches based on control and reward/punishment
The short-term effectiveness of some measures have meant that some programmes have incorporated them as part of the training advocated. In spite of Skinner's (1957) own strictures against punishment, they have, for example, often been advocated as part of behavioural training techniques.

A very influential book in the UK in the 1970s (Copeland, 1973) had parents in particular hitting their children with autism regularly, in the hope that this would bring about the 'cure' promised by the author. Lovaas and his colleagues (Lovaas, 1981; 1987; Lovaas *et al.*, 1965; Lovaas & Simmons, 1969) were regularly using aversive techniques to eliminate all manner of unwanted behaviour and even, it was claimed, to train pro-social behaviour. Although the current educational and ethical climate means that aversives are no longer promoted as part of the Lovaas treatment, the home-training programme (Lovaas, 1987) was not only based on the use of aversives but Lovaas saw these as an essential part of the programme.

> . . . In the within-subjects studies that were reported, contingent aversives were isolated as one significant variable. It is therefore unlikely that treatment effects could be replicated without this component. (p. 8)

Even without specific advocacy of aversive techniques, however, it is likely that methodologies that stress control and manipulation of behaviour without an understanding of the underlying causes, and thus meaning, of that behaviour, will be more likely to lead to forceful (and ultimately, aversive and punitive) ways of establishing and maintaining control. On a more positive note, however, current versions of ABA home-based treatments include play periods, and stress positive reinforcers. Giving the parents hope and something positive to do may well reduce stress and allow a much more relaxed atmosphere to develop.

Vulnerability of people with autism

The lack of speech and/or communicative ability makes people with autism and sld vulnerable, and perpetrators of violence can 'get away with it'. Sadly, the most basic (and base) reason why violence may occur in the treatment of those with autism and sld is simply that it can. In many cases the individual with autism and sld will have little or no speech and perhaps even no alternative form of communication. Even where there is speech, the person with autism and sld will not understand about communication and will not be able to communicate what has happened to others or even to themselves, especially if the perpetrator of the violence is giving an alternative account.

Violence has been shown to increase in situations where there is less chance of detection (Blunden & Allen, 1987). The short-term success of violence, as indicated above, may encourage its use and, if undetected, the cycle of abuse may continue.

With the possible exception of this last reason for violence, it should be emphasised that violence does not usually come from evil intent or from a perverted pleasure from other people's pain. I accept the helpful and hopeful doctrine of the Option philosophy (Kaufman, 1994) that everyone is doing the best they can with the resources available to them. This implies that carers and professionals resort to violence because of fear, misunderstanding and lack of knowledge about autism and alternative effective strategies to achieve the same ends (Harris *et al.*, 1996). If that is the case, then these are all aspects that can respond to education and they provide the rationale for an effective and necessary training programme.

Summary

Adults and children with autism and sld have very few ways of understanding and managing their environment so, if we want to change their behaviour, we need to think positively. They will need help from the environments in supporting more adaptive behaviour, help in developing a repertoire of more useful skills and in substituting these for those that are regarded as challenging. Behavioural methods may be used to prompt and reward appropriate behaviours, but this should all be based on understanding the person with autism and sld and a careful analysis of all the factors underpinning the behaviour.

Individuals with autism and sld will find it difficult to inhibit behaviour so it is more likely to be successful if the individual is taught what to *do* rather than what *not* to do. Settings may be easier to change than behaviour. Individuals with autism and sld have few skills for interpreting and controlling their world, so it is not surprising if they act in ways that produce predictable responses, regardless of the nature of those responses. Parents and teachers need to try to understand how the individual is perceiving the situation in order to understand the causes of the behaviour and the approach to modification that is likely to work best.

It is recognised that autism and sld do not just affect the individuals who have them, but also those living and working with them. Carers may suffer some of the same pressures as experienced by people with autism and sld and may be led into punitive or aversive methods, in an attempt to do their best for their children. It is important that carers as well as people with autism and sld, have good support structures.

10 Daily Living Skills, Leisure and Support for Families

Introduction

As was mentioned in earlier chapters, people with autism and sld remain people and have the same rights to a good quality of life as anyone else. When they are children, their own quality of life is closely bound up with the quality of life of their families and the support that they receive. Education to enhance development and improve life and leisure skills is not only important to the individual with autism and sld, but also acts as a support to the family, reducing anxiety in the parents and improving the opportunities of the family to engage in daily living and leisure pursuits together. Such effective education can also, of course, make a big difference to the quality of life of the individuals as adults, and life-long educational opportunities make sure they continue to develop and gain as much as possible from opportunities to contribute to life and to benefit from it. This is a group who are unlikely to achieve full independence, but, with suitable support, they should be able to enjoy life and be able to live with dignity and in the least restrictive way.

How each individual with autism and sld develops will depend on many factors, including the severity of their autism, the severity and complexity of their additional learning difficulties and, most importantly, the quality of education and support they receive. Education is not just about what happens in schools, but also about daily living support in the home and continued development throughout life. The dual disability will create challenges to individuals, their families and their carers, but a certain degree of optimism is warranted, as early diagnosis, early intervention and more effective educational techniques lead to far better outcomes. However, we should not value anyone just for what they can achieve in absolute terms, for then these individuals are always going to be at a disadvantage. We should look at their achievements in coping with life, in spite of the difficulties they may have to overcome, and set goals that show high, but achievable, expectations. Educational goals, then, should be directed at those life-long objectives, rather than at getting them to jump through particular curriculum hoops in pale imitation of others with very different developmental paths.

Parents' role

The value of hope
Parents have an extraordinary battle to face in getting the best help for their children, providing the bulk of the education they receive in the 'twenty-four-hour curriculum', making sure brothers and sisters are not squeezed out of their rights to attention, and planning for life-long care and/or support. It is always humbling for professionals to recognise this parental contribution and the fortitude and amazing good humour with which many of them rise to the challenge (Rankin, 2000). One mother complained once that she could cope with anything except being told that she was the 'expert', that she was wonderful and 'special'; 'I am just as I was before I had this child with autism', she said; 'I am not particularly wonderful, or brave or patient and I am not an expert. There was no training for this "job" and I did not choose it; nor can I walk away from it when I feel I can no longer cope. I have to cope because there is no one else and I love him, but it does me no good to be called a heroine; it just allows others "off the hook", because then they can pretend I am coping, and leave me to it.'

Peeters and Jordan (1999) support this in their description of the qualities needed by professionals in autism. Parents are doing the most important job but with the least training and support. There are increasing opportunities for parent-training (see below) and a lot of mutually supportive parental organisations, yet, much of the time, many parents feel fundamentally alone. There are occasions, especially in the early days after diagnosis, when the child's current difficulties and a sense of the long (and unending) road ahead can lead to despair. Parents need practical help at these times but they may also need help in recognising the value of their children and the joy they can represent (Gilpin, 1993).

They cannot do this when they are exhausted through coping, or trying to cope, or when the only way they are offered of managing their child is to change him or her. That is not to say that they should not believe in their child's capacity to achieve and develop, because that is realistic, and parental expectations themselves affect development. A very interesting finding, for example, in one of the controlled trials of the effects of secretin on the development of children with autism was the importance of this parental expectation. The trial did not support the benefits of secretin, since the control group did no better than those who received a placebo (a dummy injection), but the truly remarkable finding was how much both groups of children improved, compared to a baseline period. Parents did not know whether their child was receiving the drug or the placebo, so both groups felt that something was being done; they had hope and looked for (and so noticed, and built on) their child's progress. We all need hope to survive, even if it does make it difficult to decide on the real value of certain approaches. It is true that advocates of some approaches are unscrupulous in the way that they promote them to vulnerable parents, yet there is a balance needed between that and the offer of hope. Raul Kaufman, in the foreword to a new edition of his father's book (Kaufman, 1994) talks about how his parents were castigated for offering parents 'false hopes'; he argues that there is no such thing as 'false' hope, just hope.

Proper support for families, then, is part of proper support for the child. Parents will always seek the best they can for their child and that is to be expected and applauded. If they are some-times misled in the process by people trading on their vulner-ability, that is sad, but it should be remembered that parents seek out 'cures', mostly because they are offered little or insufficient help for themselves or their children. It is a waste of time and effort, when there is so much to be done, to fight over 'best' methods. We need to look for evidence, but there is sufficient cumulative evidence on what can help, for us to get started. If we are working positively with the child, and the child is making progress, nothing will be wasted.

Parents' particular problems

Parents of those with autism and sld face some of the same problems as parents of other children with special needs. There are, however, some particular problems and challenges associated with having a child with autism and sld.

Parents' lack of expertise

The first, and most significant, of these is that it is very hard for them to understand their child or to help him or her. As was discussed in earlier chapters, autism is the cruellest of conditions, in that it deprives parents of the one consolation of having a child with a disability—the opportunity for helping your child overcome their difficulties. Not only do parents not know what to do, but their attempts to help their child are often rejected by the child or appear to make things worse. When they turn to others, including the professionals who have made the diagnosis, or whose role is one of support, they often find that they too are at a loss, and parents are left to work things out for themselves or pursue the often elusive sources of expertise and guidance. The additional sld make it harder to work with the child and may make the child seem different to the people with autism who appear in the media, or even from other children with autism whose parents may attend the support group. Although language is seldom of much help in working out your child's problems if s/he has autism, there is still yet another barrier to communication when there is no speech, as in many cases of autism and sld.

Parents' self-esteem

Clearly, the role of being a mother or father may be central to a person's sense of self-worth, and therefore any implications of inadequacy in this respect will be particularly damaging. If, for any reason, the parent already has a low sense of self-esteem, then all the feelings of inadequacy engendered by being unable to make contact with their child are likely to add justification to these existing feelings and fears. An important concern for the professional, therefore, should be to guide the parents to a greater understanding of the nature of autism and of the positive part that parents can play in their child's social and intellectual development. If there has been a late diagnosis, this needs much sensitivity in order to help the parents feel positive about their future role, without feeling guilt and despair about past 'failures'. Parents may need to be reminded that, although early intervention is best, it really is never too late to make a difference, and it is likely that they have already done much that is good and helpful, even if more can now be done, with increased understanding of where the difficulties lie. Whatever the state of the parents' self-esteem, it is clear that anxiety and inadequacy are likely to be two initial reactions on their part, and professionals must expect and allow for the expressions of pain and anger that are liable to come as a result.

Life-long condition
A third issue is the life-long nature of the condition, especially as many approaches are marketed on the idea that this may not need to be the case. Parents are not sure what to believe or expect, especially in relation to the future of their own child. The problem is often one of terminology. Current research shows that early effective education is making a tremendous difference in the development, and thus the life chances, of people with autism (Jordan *et al.*, 1998). Yet even the approach with some of the best documented evidence of its effectiveness (Lovaas, 1987) was only able to make significant differences to fewer than half of the group, who received forty hours of treatment for at least two years. The group with autism and sld are likely to be among those who do less well in absolute terms, whatever approach is used, although they may make significant gains when compared to their functioning before treatment. Parents, therefore, have to face the likely 'fact' that their child will need support throughout life, and current decisions about schooling are often influenced by parental perceptions of what will provide the most security in terms of life-long provision. They may, for example, press for a school at secondary level that is run by an organisation that also makes provision for adults with autism, regardless of its relative merits as a school (Jordan & Jones, 1996).

Multiple effects

Another area of particular concern for parents of children with autism and sld is that the additional problems the child may have (from the sld or from other conditions such as sensory impairments, specific language impairments, physical disability) are not just additional in their effects but interact with the autism, so that their effect is multiplied. If we take the case, for example, of a child with autism, sld and a visual impairment, there will be significant problems for parents in obtaining advice and help in working with their child. Most guides on autism for professionals and/or parents stress the value of using visual methods rather than verbal, to promote learning and communication. The child's visual impairment may make such methods inappropriate, especially as the techniques for adapting them easily for a blind child (e.g. the use of Braille) will not be appropriate because of the learning difficulties. There are increasing solutions to such problems from advances in information and communication technology, yet the point remains that very little addresses the problems of dual or multiple disability, and trying to read up on each and add them together simply does not work. This is a problem shared by professionals, of course, and is increasing in specialist schools for particular disabilities where the children who are not mainstreamed tend to be those with multiple problems, quite often including autism.

Socio-emotional effects

As discussed in earlier chapters, difficulty in relating to others is the core of the condition and failure (or extreme delay) in bonding is common in autism, especially when there are additional sld. Once autism is diagnosed, parents at least have some explanation for this, but diagnosis of autism may be delayed when there are additional sld, because of problems with differential diagnosis or because people think (erroneously) that a placement in a school for children with sld will meet all needs, and the autism, therefore, does not need to be picked out. This means that parents have had a long time of trying unsuccessfully to relate with their very special baby without any guidance on how to do so and without any understanding of why this might be so. The sld may cause some problems in interaction, because reaction times are slower and it is harder to get and sustain attention but, unless they also have autism, social games (as opposed to developmental milestones) proceed normally. Failure to get this responsiveness from their baby and to establish a sense of mutuality when there is autism, however, is usually experienced by the parents as self-inadequacy and they become frustrated or depressed, according to personality. A diagnosis can help resolve some of this, but not immediately. If it has built up over a number of years, parents have a residue of guilt and feelings of inadequacy that may continue to affect their ability to function with their child and make positive progress. This may be exacerbated by others who also 'blame' the parents, as discussed below.

Explanations and social support
There are often difficulties faced by parents in telling other people about their child's problems. This is true for all disabilities and there is a need for support at the point of diagnosis, to help parents with this problem. When the diagnosis occurs at, or soon after, birth this is bad enough, having to accept congratulations but then listen to the embarrassed mutterings when the other person is told that the baby has certain problems. Parents of Down's syndrome babies, for example, have reported being sent sympathy instead of congratulatory cards and have had neighbours cross the street, soon after the birth of the baby, to avoid talking to the parents, no doubt through embarrassment and not knowing what to say. In time, however, the shock passes, family and friends (with a few exceptions) get used to the baby who begins to be loved and accepted for him or herself and not as a category.

When the baby's problems are not recognised at birth, however, and when, as in autism, they are not understood just from the label, all these problems become much worse. Sometimes, whatever has led to the sld results in visual signs that something is wrong (late motor milestones, dribbling, rolling eyes, stiffness in the fingers) but autism itself leaves no visible sign. When a child with perfectly normal appearance exhibits problems with social behaviour, emotional expression and discipline, explaining this to family and visitors, and resisting their spoken or unspoken assumption that it is your fault, can be both upsetting and exhausting. The very people one would expect to turn to for extra support—both practical and emotional—may not only turn away but add to the parents' distress by thoughtless and ignorant comments. There is just beginning to be literature on explaining autism to brothers and sisters and children at school but this needs to be extended to grandparents, friends and neighbours.

Parent workshops and training

The need for, and value of, early education in autism, and the problems, outlined above, faced by parents in understanding their child with autism mean that there is a need for parent-training programmes in the pre-school years. This may be training in a particular approach such as Applied Behaviour Analysis (ABA, e.g., Keenan *et al.*, 2000) the Son Rise programme (Kaufman, 1994), TEACCH (Watson *et al.*, 1989), PECS (Bondy & Frost, 1994) the revised Hanen approach (Sinssman, 2000) or a UK-developed approach such as music-supported communication (Wimpory *et al.*, 1995). Some of these have good evidence that they work, at least for many children, although none have been shown to work for all children and there is as yet no good evidence proving that one is better than another. It is likely that some will suit some children and some families better than others and that what is best at one time may change with changes in circumstances,or as the child develops in particular ways. There are more general workshops available in the UK which do not train in any particular approach but help parents understand their child and develop a way of working that suits them and their child. Unfortunately, these are not available everywhere, but there are packages that have been developed, such as the EarlyBird project (Shields, in press) which is offering training for other professionals to make the scheme available in their area. EarlyBird is generalist in that it works through a ten-week workshop (one day a week) with parents alone plus two home visits where videotaped sessions with parents and their children are analysed and discussed. The approach is one of helping the parents understand their child and develop approaches successfully for themselves, but it does provide specific training in techniques developed from TEACCH, from PECS and from the interactive programme supported in Hanen.

Developing a programme for a particular situation

There is no one right approach, and parents may need help initially in deciding which approach is likely to be more helpful in their situation. They may also need the support provided by programmes such as EarlyBird or parent support groups in developing their own eclectic programme, taking what suits them and their child from a range of approaches. Some parents, for example, may start with an interactive method in order to start building a relationship with their child, through which further learning may be possible. They may then introduce some aspects of PECS to get their child to begin to communicate and some aspects of TEACCH to help their child understand what is happening and what s/he is to do. They may then want to use a positive version of an ABA programme for teaching some basic skills, especially those that can be performed habitually, and for helping to manage any difficult behaviour. In truth, most approaches are no longer 'pure' in that they too incorporate ideas gained from others; that is sensible and hopeful, although it is not always acknowledged. Researchers may wish parents to follow one approach only, so they can see which the successful approaches are, but in terms of an ethical approach to a child, an eclectic mix may offer the best opportunity.

Comparison of some pre-school approaches

The table below (Table 9:1) gives some idea of the type of methods used in some common approaches, and shows whether scientific evaluative data are available, as well as some of the demands made on the family. These are given to provide an initial guide to parents on the approach they may want to pursue. Parents are usually involved in these, at least to some extent, but the extent is variable. Some involve intensive one-to-one work with the child, but this may be done by the parents, by volunteers or by paid professionals. The professional status of these workers is also variable: some are full professionals, such as speech and language therapists or teachers, others have minimal training only in the particular approach being adopted and may know little of general child development or of autism. Parents will need to ask about the professional status and expertise of the 'specialists' whom they are often employing. The approaches below are all marketed or developed as special approaches, although some may be available through local educational or health authority initiatives and may even use their own personnel to deliver the service. This is by no means an exclusive list and there are many visiting teacher schemes and suchlike that develop their own professional approach from an informed electric mix of these (and other) approaches. Some of these approaches, especially those originating in the USA, may insist that their approach needs to be adopted in its entirety and should not be mixed with others. There is no evidence that a 'pure' approach is better than an eclectic one, although eclecticism does make it much harder to know which part of the programme is working, or not working.

All the approaches in the table below are given as named programmes, but that does not mean that these are in any way superior to a programme that may have been worked out individually by a professional. Pre-school children with autism and sld are likely to be given some help from professionals such as speech and language therapists and/or educational psychologists and either may devise a programme involving parents and some additional support. Nor does this allow for many other very valuable resources such as toy libraries, parent support groups, and local and national autistic societies, all of whom may provide training of a general kind, or directed to the particular needs of the child.

The 'twenty-four hour' curriculum

The need for a twenty-four-hour curricular approach
As for all children, one of the most important determiners of educational success is parental involvement. Children with autism and sld, in particular, need education that is not confined to the classroom, that provides a consistent teaching approach, and that uses daily opportunities to teach and generalise skills in everyday

Table 9.1: Summary guidelines for popular pre-school approaches

Approach	Kind	Evaluation	Most used for	Parents involved	Provider
MUSIC INTERACTION	Live music supports interaction	Case studies— comparison under way	Mother/child or key worker/ child relationship	In home programmes —1+ hour a week, plus support	Specialist centre. Speech & language therapist
PECS	Symbol exchange	Extensive but no controls	Developing communication	Usually as management	Specialist training
TEACCH	Visual mediation, assessment & targets	Extensive, but no controls	Reducing stress— developing understanding & work habits	Targets and hours variable. Co-therapist with professionals	From specially trained professional
LOVAAS (ABA)	Applied Behaviour Analysis	Controlled study showed 47% mainstream performance, but used aversives	Building skills and modifying behaviour	Most intensive home-based programme, but may involve 'therapists'	Specially trained professional —usually supervised by psychologist
OPTION (SON-RISE PROGRAMME)	Social interaction	Single case studies only	Motivating interest in others	Intensive home-based with parents & volunteers	Parents trained at Option institute and train others
PORTAGE HOME VISITING PROGRAMME	Adapted behavioural approach to developmental curriculum	No evaluation with this group	Supporting parents to work with their child	Parents work according to ability— visited once a week	Trained portage workers visit and train parents
EARLYBIRD	Facilitation of parenting using eclecticism	Evaluated from parental reports	Supporting parents to work with their child	Parents, daily plus parent training/1 day week for 10 weeks	Trained professional & parent pack as resource

functional contexts. When the child is in residential schooling, this means that care staff are as much involved in curriculum planning and the operation of individual educational programmes, as classroom staff. When the child is a day pupil, parents need support and encouragement to take on this role, as far as is appropriate. The home or care situation is often the most natural and meaningful context for the education of daily living skills and even for the initiation of communication programmes such as PECS (Bondy & Frost, 1994).

Partnership with parents

It is especially important, therefore, to find ways of involving parents of children with autism and sld in their education. This is not, or should not be, just a matter of trying to get parents to behave in ways that schools have deemed appropriate, or to reinforce and help generalise the skills the child has learnt in school. Partnership should be just that, with both parties to the partnership (parents and school staff) making different but equally valuable, and valued, contributions to an agreed twenty-four-hour curriculum. School staff would be expected to know more about autism and sld, although this is far from always the case (especially in autism), and here too there may need to be genuine sharing of resources and expertise, rather than teachers being the only ones to offer advice and support in managing the child. What staff may have, in addition to professional skills in observation and enabling learning, is a broader knowledge about these conditions, gained from their experience of many different children. What parents bring, of course, is knowledge of their particular child and the kind of interest and commitment which can never be equalled by professionals. Teachers need to learn about the child, but they also need to learn about the family, about home and cultural values, and about parental expectations of the school. Parents vary in their ability to offer support in the form of specific 'teaching' towards joint curricular goals, and the generalisation opportunities for skills learnt in school. They also vary in how much they will seek support and guidance from professionals about care and management issues.

The history of development of services in autism is a history of collaboration between parents and professionals, dating from the time when parents ceased being regarded as the problem in autism, and started to be seen as the solution. The TEACCH programme in North Carolina (with influence world-wide:

Mesibov, 1997) introduced the idea of parents as co-therapists and this idea is common to a range of successful programmes for children with autism. In the TEACCH approach, parental concerns are given high (though not sole) priority in setting the goals for the child's individual education programme and parents are as involved as they want, or are able, to be across home and school settings. Legislation in the UK (Department for Education, 1994) also enshrines a parental role in establishing and monitoring individual educational programmes, and parents have to be consulted in the assessment for special needs and in the annual review of those needs statements. It is parents who will have a life-long perspective on the child's difficulties and progress and who will have the continued involvement with the individual with autism and sld well into adulthood. Teachers and other professionals need to be sensitive to that perspective and the fact that parents must balance competing needs, of brothers and sisters, of job or career, of the need for adequate rest just to keep going. A teacher should be a support to parents, not someone who adds to their pressures and who makes them feel guilty if they are unable to do the agreed 'work' at home that week. The ideal home programme is one that enables any 'work' to be an accompaniment to activities and routines that would be happening anyway, so that extra work is not required.

Daily living skills and their social aspects

Given that gross and fine motor skills are relatively intact in autism (unless the learning difficulties are very severe), problems in certain everyday living skills sometimes come as a surprise to parents, carers and teachers. When the child is able to perform some tasks with apparent ease, yet fails at others that seemingly involve similar levels of skill and knowledge, difficulties are often put down to motivational problems or problems in compliance. There are many possible reasons for this patchy and uneven development of skills, some of which are discussed below, but one possible source of difficulty is the social element in a task, and it is this that can lead to some of the differential ability across tasks. Some daily living skills are clearly social, such as greeting people or saying 'thank you' when someone has done something for you, whereas in others the social element is subtle and/or hidden.

Crossing the road
Teaching a child with autism and sld to cross the road, for example, even at a pedestrian crossing, can proceed well for a while but often seems to fall down once the child has to manage him or herself. As long as the learning difficulties are not too severe, the children may be able to learn the actual procedures associated with certain cues, whereby the red man means stop, the green man means 'go', and flashing signals mean that the signal is about to change. Yet the child or adult with autism and sld may master these skills but still be unable to cross the road unaided. Children and adults with autism and sld either respond rigidly to the signals (and are then vulnerable to drivers who try to get through as lights are changing, or who anticipate the lights changing), or they dither at the kerb, in literal terror of crossing.

The prime reason for this is that crossing a road also involves using eye contact to judge intention (in the drivers) or to make one's own intentions clear. It is noticeable, for example, that if a pedestrian intends to jay-walk (e.g., walk across a crossing in front of the car, when the red man is on), they will studiously avoid making eye contact with the drivers, thus avoiding having to admit recognition of the driver's rights. Without that facility to signal their own intentions clearly through eye contact and body posture or recognise the signals of others, people with autism and sld are at a loss to understand what is going on. They may be aware that drivers and pedestrians do not always follow the rules, but this may just upset them without them being able to anticipate or control how they will behave.

There is no simple answer to this, of course, since people with autism appear to have no intuitive way of interpreting social intention, and sld make it very difficult to overcome this problem by working things out cognitively. However, understanding the real root of the child's problems in tackling such tasks at least means we can direct teaching to the right area, and not just assume that we are dealing with a motivational or behavioural problem. We can model and prompt the giving of the correct social signals of intent to cross, for example, and, through successful crossing using these signals the child or adult gains increasing confidence in their use. Interpretation of subtle social signals will always be a problem, but we can at least teach children to respond to gross indicators (such as eye position) to note whether the driver has noticed them, and how this should affect their own actions. The person with autism and sld is unlikely to be able to infer or understand any implications of behaviour, so everything must be taught explicitly and directly.

Intimate care

For those with the most severe difficulties in tolerating the presence of others, even basic aspects of life, such as personal care, become a problem. As indicated earlier, this is a priority for teaching, since it has such severe implications for a basic quality of life. Carers will often focus on the context of the problem (the fact that the child bites, scratches, kicks those who try to help wash or dress him/her) rather than the core problem: the child does not know how to be comfortable with others, and especially with intimate situations of touch. The goal of getting the child to wash or dress him or herself, in such situations, needs to be put on hold. The first priority is to identify the source of the child's distress. It may be that there is something particular about the task (problems with over-sensitivity to clothing, for example) but a common problem in such situations is that the child is made uncomfortable with close contact with others.

This problem can be addressed by a programme of desensitisation. Choose something that enables the child to relax, probably warm comfortable seating, dim light and gentle music. Then approach the child up to the point where your presence has been noticed but you are at sufficient distance not to disturb the child. Leave after a few minutes and then re-enter after an interval, approaching a very little nearer each time, but never to the point where the child ceases to be relaxed. If the boundary is crossed and the child becomes upset, you should withdraw immediately and then re-enter but at a step further away. When the child has gradually got used to the encroaching adult, you can come next to the child and you can gradually extend the time you spend near the child. Once this is accepted, you can begin to touch the child. This is almost certain to be rejected at first, but if you gently persist (i.e., withdraw the touch immediately, but then re-touch), the child will eventually come to accept the overtures of the adult, and even to seek them. Children with autism and sld seek regularity and predictability, and touching that provides those two features will usually come to be acceptable even if this takes some time. Once children can tolerate nearness and touching, it becomes easier to help them manage care tasks such as getting dressed or washed.

Problem areas in self-care skills

although autism and sld may give rise to problems in any area of functioning, there are some very common areas of concern for all parents, that have a marked effect on the quality of life for all the family. Helping parents and carers resolve some of these difficulties, therefore, is a priority for professionals, whether the programme is started at home or at school; eventually, of course, it will need to be a shared programme across all settings. Autism and sld are both *pervasive* developmental disorders and this pervasiveness means that success is more likely if work is carried out across the range of the child's experiences. Also, difficulty in generalising is central to autism, so there is a need to deal with issues (such as toilet training) in consistent ways across the child's learning environments. And learning environments are not neatly circumscribed by the school syllabus or even by the school day.

Toileting

Children with sld will naturally be delayed in their use of the toilet and, if there are additional physical difficulties, full control may never be achieved. Autism, on the other hand, does not directly affect the ability to gain control of toileting needs, but it may interact with the sld to make the process of learning to gain control more difficult. Children with autism and sld may have feelings that they need to go to the toilet but may not be consciously aware of those feelings. They can then still be trained to use the toilet, but that will only be by associating going to the toilet with that feeling—still not at a conscious level. That is all right so long as the action of going to the toilet can be triggered by the feeling but, if the action is blocked in some way (the child does not know where the toilet is, the toilet has been changed, there are difficulties in getting undressed, and so on), the child will then be at a loss and may well then wet and soil him or herself. Even if the child has some form of communication, they may not use it in such a situation because they are not aware of the problem, and, thus, of their need to communicate. Teaching the child to use the toilet, then, is the first, but not the only step in a toileting programme for a child with autism and sld (see Table 9:2).

The child with autism may have particular fears or difficult problems in using a toilet and these need to be dealt with if a toileting programme is to succeed. The following are a list of possible fears and problems with solutions, but there may be other ones in any particular case. Each situation should be treated as an individual one and local help sought (from a clinical psychologist, or special teacher, perhaps) to determine what might work best in any particular case.

- Fear of the noise of flushing the toilet or of listening to the cistern fill up—let the child flush the toilet and give symbols to explain the sequence; if necessary, let the child block his/ her ears.

- Fear of sitting over the 'void' of the toilet—let the child use a potty with the nappy still in place, then take off the nappy but place it over the pot, then remove nappy and finally transfer to seat on toilet and then the normal toilet seat.

- Aversion to the smell of faeces—use masking smells with aromatherapy oils and allow child to use these diluted in a room spray to spray the toilet. If all else fails, it may be necessary gradually to desensitise the child to the smell.

- Pain through constipation—adjust diet (check with dietician but the child may need more fibre, or may have a particular food intolerance—not allergy), and visit an encopresis clinic

Table 9.2: Steps in a toileting programme for a child with autism and sld

Pre-step	Check that child is at correct developmental level for toilet control
STEP 1	Make a record of the times the child wets and soils and the relation of this to food and drink intake. From this, draw up a timetable of when there is most chance of 'catching' the child just before s/he needs to go to the toilet
STEP 2	Ten minutes before each designated time, take the child to the toilet or the potty to the child—whichever is the most appropriate
STEP 3	Make the toileting situation comfortable for the child. This means reducing all fears and adding calming effects such as music to help the child remain on the potty until s/he has produced
STEP 4	Draw attention to the child's success with a reward that is as natural as possible—for some, for example, flushing the toilet may be a reward
STEP 6	Allow the child to leave the toilet after having been successful, but not before, unless keeping the child there is punitive
STEP 7	Once all (or most) visits to the toilet are successful, start work on getting the child to become aware of the trigger for going to the toilet by noticing how the child behaves just before s/he goes and drawing child's attention to that behaviour
STEP 8	If the child is not using the toilet in spite of these frequent visits, optimise success by increasing fluid intake and frequency of visits to toilet

to get ideas about helping the child with massage to express him/herself. Check with GP whether child needs to see a gastroenterologist if problems persist.

- Smearing—dress child in way that allows no access to faeces. Give child other similar tactile experiences to compensate and direct to these. Check that there is no constipation, piles or worms that might start the child poking around in that area.

- Eating faeces—this is a form of pica, albeit a particularly difficult and unpleasant form, especially if the child eats others' faeces from toilets. This should be addressed as soon as it appears and not let become a habit. Treat as pica but with more emphasis on pleasant things to eat and just denying access to faeces by extreme vigilance over a period when toileting is being trained.

Feeding

Children with autism often have very definite views on what they will or will not eat and may have a very restrictive diet as a result. There are some suggestions that food intolerances may make people themselves more faddy about what they will eat, so consultation with a dietician is a sensible precaution when the child's diet appears restrictive. The reasons for refusing food may be various, and the parent or carer will have to do some detective work to see what is happening in each case (see Table 9:3).

A common reason is to do with texture. The child may not be able to tolerate lumps or (more commonly) not be able to adjust to two textures in the same dish—lumps within a smooth texture. They may like something like baked beans on their own, and toast on its own, but not be able to stand baked beans on toast because of the way the beans soak into the toast and distort its texture. They may not like any sauce or gravy at all, often because it touches their lips, where they are supersensitive. This class of problems should be dealt with by being aware of textural preferences and (in a young child at least) instituting a programme to reduce lip sensitivity, such as brushing the lips daily with a clean paintbrush.

Often there will be problems with physical control of the muscles involved in chewing and swallowing and the co-ordination between them. This may make certain foods difficult to eat because they need to be chewed, and may have an effect on eating everything. Typical of these problems is the child who continually adds food to his/her mouth, in spite of being told repeatedly to 'finish what you are eating before adding more!' The problem is that the child is unable to swallow without the stimulus which comes from putting food into the mouth and so, until the child can be taught to swallow without this primitive reflexive action (through physiotherapy exercises), the child will be unable to obey these commands for more polite ways of eating. Other children try to resolve the issue by drinking to 'force' down the food but, once more, they may be told off for impolite behaviour. Recognising that these are actual feeding problems, rather than behaviour problems, will be the first step in getting children the help they need to improve their feeding skills.

There may be perceptual problems which interfere with the enjoyment of food. Often taste is disturbed so that the child can only seem to taste foodstuff with very strong tastes, such as Marmite, Piccalilli, and raw onion. In other cases, certain colours may be disturbing to the child, who may then seek to restrict his/ her diet to one or two bland colours. As with anything else in autism, once a behaviour or a preference is established, for whatever reason, it becomes very difficult to shift.

Dressing

If the child has profound and multiple learning difficulty as well as autism, and especially if there are additional physical impairments, the goal for dressing programmes might be to cooperate in being dressed, rather than to dress independently. As with intimate care, above, the problem may be intolerance of contact and a desensitisation programme may be needed. An individual who is always going to need help to get dressed is more likely to benefit from such a programme, where s/he is happy to be dressed than, for example, a programme of pulling up the last two inches on his/her pants while struggling to avoid the contact entailed.

Where the individual is more able, but still struggles with dressing, the solution may lie in better structuring of the task. Giving the individual a heap of clothes (even if they are piled up in the correct order) will often result in the clothes getting out of order, the wrong way round and so on. Thus, even if the individual has mastered how to put on each item on its own, the totality of the dressing task may defeat him/her. In such cases a TEACCH-style visual display of symbols (from top to bottom or left to right) will help the individual structure the task, putting on each item in turn and turning over the symbol at the same time. Some individuals may not be able to manage this symbol sequence and may need the actual clothes hung up on hangers in the correct sequence for dressing. The secret is to train the individual to follow the sequence without stopping, for it is when the individual pauses that the sequence may be forgotten and the dressing programme as a whole falls apart.

Problems in actual dressing usually centre round fastenings. Teaching buttoning is best done with something on the person's

Table 9.3: Steps in a programme to change a very restrictive diet

STEP 1	Check that diet really is unhealthy and not just faddy
STEP 2	Check for (and remove) problems due to the perception of the food or physical problems in eating
STEP 3	Set up a system whereby the individual learns to swap a picture of his/her favourite food for a small portion of that food. Do this for each of the foodstuffs the individual will eat
STEP 4	Set up a visual sequence with a picture symbol representing each small portion of food that will constitute the individual's meal. If there are two or more foodstuffs the individual will accept, and which are appropriate to eat as part of the same dish, alternate these symbols in the sequence
STEP 5	Teach the individual to swap the symbols in the sequence for the portions of food so that mealtimes change from situations where the individual is being coerced to eat 'new' foods to one where that individual has to ask for each small portion of food
STEP 6	Once the number of favoured food portions the individual will normally eat and the habit of 'asking' for each of these portions has been established, arrange a symbol system with one or two portions less than this 'normal' amount and then put a symbol for a very small portion of a 'new' food (one pea?) and then two more symbols of favourite food
STEP 7	As the individual reaches the last of the familiar food symbols, point out that the next symbol is for the new food. Do not force this choice but be firm that this symbol (and therefore the food it represents) has to come before more of the favourite food. If the individual refuses to 'ask' for the new food, the meal is at an end. The individual has already had a reasonable portion of the favourite food so is not being deprived of nourishment
STEP 8	If the resistance to asking for the new food continues for longer than a week, substitute the new food for another new food that might be more acceptable, but do not give up on the principle that, after a reasonable amount of food, further favourite food is only available after trying a new food
STEP 9	When the very small portion of the new food had been taken, allow the favourite food until more is refused. Next day increase the new food by a very small amount (e.g. 2 peas?). Do this gradually until the symbol represents a reasonable portion
STEP 10	Once a reasonable portion of the new food has been taken, add a second symbol for another portion before the first new food symbol and reduce the number of favourite food symbols by one to accommodate this
STEP 11	Gradually (one step at a time, waiting until each step is accepted) mix up the 'new' and 'favourite' food symbols
STEP 12	Once a mixture of favourite and new foods are being eaten in this way, add another 'new' food as before. Continue until an acceptable range of foods is being taken, remembering to allow for some choice

own body (so the body position is the same as the natural one) rather than a 'dressing doll' or some such. Choose a very loose waistcoat with enormous buttons and buttonholes and prompt the person through the movements from behind. The same principle is true of other fastenings such as tying shoelaces. This can be helped, not only by physical guidance through the movements needed but with practising the correct sequence of movements without the shoelaces present—as a kind of mime.

Leisure skills

The pressure of 'free' time

As the child with autism and sld grows, so parental priorities may alter. The early years are dominated by the need to secure and support the best education for the child. Once this has been achieved, the problem that seems to take over is that of how to occupy leisure time. Children with autism and sld badly need time to relax, away from the constant pressure to achieve, in a largely incomprehensible world, but they do not necessarily know how to relax, at least not in ways that are acceptable to others. Far from being a chance to recharge batteries, leisure times often become a source of additional stress and distress, and it is usually in 'free' times that most challenging behaviour occurs.

Just as such times are stressful for the child, so they are for the parents. In addition, the parents have a large number of associated problems. There may be other children in the family whose needs for leisure, or time to pursue studies uninterrupted, are being affected by the inability of their brother or sister either to join them in a leisure pursuit (and so allow family interests), or to occupy him or herself while others are busy. Just at a time when children are increasingly seeking leisure activities outside the home, with friends, the adolescent with autism and sld will become more dependent on parents for occupation and entertainment. Parents feel guilty about their neglect of other things (the rest of the family, their job, their home) if they devote their time to their child with autism and sld, and they feel guilty if they do not, fearing that the child is missing out, and suffering the consequences of any challenging behaviour that may result.

Making leisure 'work'

It often feels wrong to parents or carers when it is suggested that
they may need to organise leisure pursuits for the child or adult
with autism and sld, in the same way as they would organise a
work activity. Yet we can accept that young children are much
happier when a playground or outing is organised so that they
know what to do and so that everyone has fair shares of resources
and time. People with autism and sld have very similar needs,
but are even less able to organise their own time without that
structure and support. We can still leave them time to indulge in
activities of their own choosing, but they will need help in making
that choice and will need the security of knowing when that
permitted activity is to start and end.

Structuring leisure time

As in class or workrooms, children or adults with autism and sld
will need to know (preferably through visual means) exactly what
they are supposed to do, where, when, with whom, for how long
and what next. Pictures or symbols (or, where necessary, objects
which 'stand for' the activities) should be displayed in some way
left to right or top to bottom to give this general time structure
to leisure sessions. Space structure means that areas where certain
activities are to occur should be clearly marked. Many problems
in leisure time arise because people are expected to 'play' or
'relax' in the same place that has previously been associated with
a work activity or having a meal. If it is not possible to separate
off areas in this way (at home, for example) then use other means
to clearly indicate the change in expectations. If, for example a
parent expects a child with autism and sld to sit at the dining
table to do some leisure activity (a puzzle, perhaps or just to
fiddle with some pegs), they should cover the table with a special
tablecloth reserved for this leisure time and never used when
eating.

When the individual has severe autism and/or very severe
learning difficulties, they may need ongoing support to provide
a structure as the leisure activity proceeds. The individual may
be given a symbol 'timetable' of an outing but they may not be
able to make sense of it in terms of what is happening without

one to one support to do so. The supporter will need to point out the stage in the timetable that has been reached and help the individual mark the passage through the outing by removing or crossing through activities or experiences as they occur. Many outings, also, are not entirely predictable and the supporter may have to show the individual how an unscheduled event fits in with a broad category of activities (such as seeing the animals) that have been programmed on the timetable. Supporters may come from family members, from entitlement to social service support or from a volunteer befriender. All will need training in autism and time to get to know the individual as an individual before they can be left to accompany that person on their own. It is sometimes the case that students begin befriending a young person with autism and sld while at school but retain an interest while at college and beyond, perhaps not seeing the person as regularly as they once did, but being available for special outings or short holidays.

Hobbies

It is often difficult in this group to see their natural interests as hobbies, or potential hobbies. Someone's interest in flicking a rubber band or tapping a block is more likely to be viewed as an annoying habit than a hobby. It is here we have to make judgements about 'informed choices' and the relative needs and rights of the person with autism and sld and those who are living with him or her. As was seen in earlier chapters on play, we should be working on developing play skills, for it is only when someone knows other things to do with pegs or rubber bands and has had some pleasurable experience in engaging in that more productive activity, that we can be sure that the 'choice' to flick or twiddle is really a choice at all. On the other hand, if this is meant to be leisure time, then it is not the time either to teach or insist on that 'more productive' activity. Thus we should distinguish between teaching the individual to have a hobby (preferably developed from something that person is already doing, or showing an interest in) and allowing them space and time to indulge in whatever they find relaxing at the time. As the hobby becomes more familiar to them and they can perform it with increasing ease, so it should also become more relaxing for them to perform and the more likely it is that they will choose to do it in leisure time. But this process should be a natural one and the 'work' of learning the skills to participate in a hobby should be clearly separated from this leisure-time choice.

All this suggests, therefore, that personal choice is an important aspect of leisure time activities that separate them from those that would be considered work. Problems may arise, however, if indulgence in a chosen activity interferes with the rights of others (to peace, to freedom from attack, to some space of their own) or works the individual up into a highly excitable state, or where the individual does not want to stop the activity at the end of the leisure time. In other words, there may be problems in limiting the activity to acceptable boundaries. As with work activities, there should be a clear way of marking when an activity is going to end, when it has ended, and what is to happen next. If it is a favourite activity, there will also need to be some warning that it is to end to ease that transition to the new activity. Thus the person will be told (by words or symbol) that it will end in two minutes, then one minute, and finally, that it is to end now.

Some adults with autism and sld may develop interests and skills in an area sufficient to constitute a recognisable hobby. This might be a hobby that can be indulged in alone; good examples of these are puzzles, listening to music and stamp collecting. Other hobbies could be solitary but will need a companion/supervisor to make sure the person remains safe; such hobbies might be trampolining, fell-walking or canoeing. Yet others need other people and a certain level of social skills; these would include hobbies such as line-dancing, ten-pin bowling and draughts. All the hobbies mentioned above have been enjoyed by people with autism and sld and clearly there are many more. When encouraging the development of a particular hobby, to the extent that the person is open to guidance, one should consider the social classification system as part of the process of choosing a hobby. If there is no one to be with the individual for most of the time, it would be most sensible to opt for an activity that can be done on one's own. Activities that involve social skills should only be encouraged where the person already has those skills or it seems feasible to teach them. Other factors to consider are the interests of the individual (the most important factor) and the availability of others with the same interest, for activities that will involve others.

Academic skills

There is little point in teaching academic skills for the sake of it, but academic skills can be needed to engage in some leisure pursuits and some teaching of academic skills might itself be a leisure activity. To take the latter point first, it would not really be leisure if the person were getting no pleasure or relaxation from the activity. Yet many people with autism and sld, for example, may not learn to read or tell the time or deal with money while at school and get a real sense of achievement and pleasure from learning these skills later. This is especially so if the learning can be presented in an attractive format, such as via a computer programme. They may also enjoy learning such skills if they can clearly see that they are an entry to a particular hobby they wish to pursue. A young man who wants to go and watch football, and does not want to depend on someone being available to take him, for example, may be happy to learn how to read bus timetables and how to work out change for fares. It is important, therefore, to continue to teach socially useful academic skills well into adulthood so that the individual learns to cope with money and time, to read messages and programmes and so on.

Physical activity/sports

There is value in physical activity, especially if it is aerobic, as was discussed in earlier chapters. This is not only effective in reducing challenging behaviour, but has positive effects in increasing fitness and perhaps providing a hobby for the individual. However, the very features that make such activity useful in reducing unwanted behaviour also mean that it may become addictive. This is particularly so in autism, where there is already a love of routine and habit. Of course, an addiction to running is far less of a problem than an addiction to self-injury or attacking others, but everyone need to be aware of the danger and teach limits to the behaviour at the same time as it is being encouraged.

Activities like jogging, running, swimming, riding, and aerobics, all provide healthy leisure opportunities and are commonly enjoyed by people with autism and sld. If the person is not interested in such physical activity, but parents and/or carers feel such activities would be of benefit to them physically and emotionally, there is something of a dilemma. If we are talking of a child, it is a legitimate educational goal to help pupils enjoy and participate in, physical activities. For children, then, it is worth pursuing the teaching of these activities, whether or not the child currently enjoys them, on the assumption that it is doing them good and they might come to enjoy it, given enough experience and time. When they are adult, this is more problematic. It might be argued that 'encouragement' of such activities might need to involve some training in that the person may not be able to understand the benefits of something s/he has not experienced. In that case, rewarding the person with something positive (even chocolate) for completing participation may motivate them to engage and from there it would be hoped that successful engagement would become rewarding in itself. For example, a child with autism and sld (Susie) hated hill-walking and would moan repeatedly if required to do it. By offering a bar of chocolate at the top of the hill (a reasonably common reward for climbing a hill—even a good self-reward) she was encouraged to climb to the top (and not give up half way as she was wont to do) and not only took pleasure in the view, but also in her achievement in reaching so far.

Learning such activities can also increase social skills and self-esteem, especially if it is a sport or activity indulged in by people without autism. Water sports provide opportunities for people with autism and sld to develop leisure pursuits and to engage with others, both with and without autism. The majority of people with autism and sld will enjoy swimming or at least playing in warm water. Some can be very adept and for many it will be a useful way of exercising with enjoyment. Others can participate in canoeing or sailing, although they will generally need the participation of 'helpers' to keep them safe and provide advanced skills. Whenever it is planned that the child or adult should engage in such activities, of course, there will need to be a full risk assessment to determine any risks and to develop strategies to avoid or deal with them.

Summary

In the fifty-seven years since autism was first identified, the view of parents has changed from seeing them as the cause of their child's condition to seeing them as the prime therapists and educators. At the same time services for children with autism and sld are still insufficient, following diagnosis, and so parents, unsure of how to help their child, become vulnerable to proponents of a variety of approaches. Regardless of the merits of particular approaches, professionals need to remember the value of hope and a positive approach in furthering the development of children with autism and sld.

Parents of children with autism and sld will not only share the problems of parents of all children with special needs but will have specific additional problems. These relate to the problem of finding appropriate and knowledgeable professional help, the uncertainty of the future for their child, the complexity of the interactions between the features of the dual disability, the devastating effect on their own sense of self-worth and competence and the difficulties in gaining understanding and support from family and friends. Parents need both emotional and practical support in handling their child and obtaining the best educational option as early as possible. No one approach has been proven to be superior to others and it is likely that individual needs and situations will determine suitability.

Even when the child with autism and sld is in full-time education, parents and carers will enhance the child's development and provide a better quality of life for the family, if they are involved in the education of life and leisure skills. They also have an important role to play in supporting, generalising and extending the education in the school to provide a 'twenty-four-hour' curriculum. The role of parents should be seen as equal to, and complementary to that of professionals.

Education in daily living skills will form an important part of the education of children with autism and sld, both at home and at school and continues to be needed throughout adult life. One of the difficulties experienced by people with autism and sld in acquiring daily living skills comes from the fact that many of these skills contain social aspects. The goals of some skills such as dressing may need to be changed for those with the most severe autism and learning difficulties from independence to co-operation, at least as an initial step. There are common problem areas in self-care skills in people with autism and sld around issues in toileting, feeding and dressing which need to be tackled systematically as early as is relevant, taking account of the level of development.

Occupying children, and later adults, with autism and sld becomes an increasing problem as they grow up. Leisure skills need to be developed and supported by taking the same structured approach as might be applied to work tasks, while remembering to retain the elements of fun and choice. There needs to be a balance in each case between providing structure and allowing freedom to relax from pressure to perform.

11 Transition to Adult Life

Independence

Independence as a mark of adult status

As mentioned in earlier chapters, the majority of individuals with autism and sld will not achieve complete independence in adulthood, no matter how early or how effective their educational experience. They are likely to need some support throughout life, but this no longer implies the institutional or semi-institutional life it once did. There are now many different models of support that vary both in degree of support and in how that support is arranged. The most able of this group might manage with individual support in the community, whereas those with the most complex needs may need twenty-four-hour care, probably in some form of group home or supported living environment.

Yet even within these more sheltered environments, the degree of independence and choice that the individual is able to show will play a large part in determining the quality of life of that individual. As the child with autism and sld approaches adulthood, therefore, independent skills begin to have an urgency that may not have been there before, and the child will need particular forms of educational facilitation to develop those skills. Clearly this should start in childhood, but such education can be of benefit to all adolescents and adults with autism and sld, as long as current needs are also remembered.

The child may need to learn first about dependence, before true independence can be shown. Many children with autism (even those with additional sld) appear very independent, but this may be a kind of premature independence. For example, parents may feel proud that the child can help him or herself to drinks from the fridge, food from the larder, and so on, without needing to ask. It is only later that they realise that this is a sign of a difficulty (with communication) rather than a strength. True independence comes from having the ability to mobilise all forms of help (including other people) as needed and not just depending on what is readily available. Independence includes independence from one's immediate desires as well, so one is able to control, or delay the impulse to gratification in order to obtain a more worthwhile objective. This implies a degree of control of one's impulses and the ability to plan and monitor one's own actions. It is this kind of thoughtful independence that we associate with an adult and behaviour that is controlled by the environment entirely is generally seen as immature rather than independent.

Training for independence

In order to achieve this level of independent action, it is not sufficient to be taught skills alone; the individual needs to be aware of his or her own skills so s/he can transfer them to new situations and be flexible in their use. This may be difficult to achieve with this group, but it is, nevertheless, a worthwhile aim. This means that children and adults with autism and sld will require help to plan activities explicitly, perhaps with the use of picture symbols, and to become aware of the execution of the plan. Wherever possible, this should involve the emotional appraisal of the task. Thus, the person can be helped to think about whether they are enjoying the activity, whether they are finding it hard or easy to do, and so on. After the task is over, that should not be the end of the teaching. That is the time for reflection on the task, using the same symbols or words as were used during the task. This time, also, the individual's attention will need to be drawn to the relevant cues that can be used in the future, when the skill may need to be used again. For those with less severe learning difficulties, teachers and carers may practise 'what if' scenarios to help the individual prepare for less predictable situations and to adopt problem solving approaches rather than reliance on set routines.

Example

Paul was a nineteen-year-old young man with autism and sld who had developed a good range of practical self-help and domestic skills, as well as the ability to communicate through single-word speech. He could attend to his daily needs with minimum supervision and he could ask for things that were not in the immediate environment. However, each of these skills was the result of rote learning and, while he was able to function with seeming independence in a familiar environment, he was not able to cope with changes to the cues in that environment or to generalise his skills beyond the context in which they had been trained.

Paul had been assessed as suitable for a supported employment scheme and a living environment of a small group home with low levels of staff support. This assessment had been based on his current functioning in his residential specialist further education college, and there was concern that he would not be able to demonstrate that level of skill in a new environment, and that failure would have a detrimental effect on his self-esteem. To avoid these difficulties, and to develop his capacity further for independent functioning, it was decided to try to teach him to become more aware of his learning strategies and to develop his problem-solving strategies.

Tasks were chosen where Paul had learnt to perform them one step at a time, and where he always performed them in the same way. Such a task was cleaning his bedroom. In the past, the cleaning materials had always been provided for Paul and he had been supervised in the task, with occasional verbal prompts or 'nags' if he faltered or missed a dirty patch. The first step was to withdraw that supervision, to test how far Paul could actually complete the task unaided. On being presented with the cleaning materials, Paul started off well, but would become distracted by getting the lead of the vacuum cleaner tangled round the furniture, or by finding something on the floor (like a pair of shoes) that had not been put away. These were just the kind of situations where he had received a verbal prompt in the past to keep him on task. Without that, he would just stop, often remaining motionless for several minutes and then might become distressed (flapping distractedly) or start to fiddle with something else.

It was clear that Paul was still very dependent on cueing for completing a task. It was decided, therefore, to change the cues from those given by a member of staff (who would not be there in the new setting) to picture symbol cues, that could either be faded out for full independence, or could be taken with him to the unfamiliar environment. To start with, Paul was given a picture list of the materials he would need and taught to obtain these for himself. Then he was given a picture sequence of all the steps involved in cleaning his room. Each step, of course, needed further training. The first part of cleaning the floor, for example, was removal of any small objects from the floor, but Paul needed training to discriminate what was 'small' in this context, and how to put away things like shoes, while leaving things like standard lamps to clean round.

The next task was to divide the floor visually into small sections (approximately one foot square) that Paul could readily 'finish' without getting distracted. At first these were marked with tape, but then he moved to having a foot square wooden frame which he was taught to move himself as he cleaned from top to bottom and left to right, until all the floor was covered. Once Paul was cleaning the floor automatically in this way, without supervision, the square size was altered to a three-foot square until eventually the whole floor could be tackled in one go. Each cleaning task was gradually tackled in this way, replacing Paul's dependence on adults to prompt and cue him with an ability to follow through a pictorial sequence on his own.

The final step was to help him become aware of the goal of all these activities, and to know when he had reached it. For this, a photograph was taken of Paul's room in a clean and tidy state. At each step in his progress through the cleaning routine, he was encouraged to consult this photograph, and identify the cleaning tasks he had already undertaken, and those still left to achieve. At the end, he was led to identify the fact that he had achieved his goal, and to reward himself with a tick in his daily chart. At the end of the month these ticks were tallied to see what 'treats' or outings he had earned. Once this was all securely learned, Paul was taught (with the aid of picture symbols representing the tasks) to vary the sequence of the tasks needed to complete the cleaning of his room. He did this prior to starting the cleaning, so that there was not the usual panic about getting him to make changes in a set routine. In this way he planned the order before-hand and then just followed the picture sequence. This was accepted, because he had already learned to identify goal completion with a number of separate tasks, and he saw (literally) that these tasks all led to the same outcome. This process needed to be undertaken for all the daily living tasks, and there were some tasks that were more difficult to represent clearly in this pictorial way, but it was possible overall to decrease Paul's dependence on others and to give him some control of his tasks through the use of these symbol sequences.

Managing self-care

As the person with autism and sld moves into adulthood, responsibility for self-care and maintaining a healthy lifestyle moves towards an expectation of independence in these areas. Clearly, this depends to some extent on the severity of the individual's learning difficulties and the degree of autism, but the training of staff who work with adults in care will emphasise the rights of the individual to make his or her own decisions, and sometimes there is insufficient recognition that this may conflict with the overriding duty of care. This is especially so where the emphasis of the service is on 'normalisation', and that has been misinterpreted as getting people to behave in 'normal' ways rather than equal valuing of all ways of being.

Thus, a parent may find that their son or daughter, who has been carefully nurtured and supported throughout school years and taught to perform daily hygiene rituals of cleaning teeth at least twice a day, may stop cleaning their teeth at all when they enter an adult service. It may be that the disruption to the normal daily routine has led to the person not cleaning his/her teeth as usual, and to some resistance to doing so when asked. Instead of taking this as a sign that more teaching is needed to re-establish this healthy and necessary routine, however, staff have been known to argue that lots of normal young men do not clean their teeth much, if at all, and that the person with autism and sld is only exercising choice in a lifestyle matter. When parents complain at what to them appears a lack of care, they may be told that they are fussing and refusing to accept the adult status of their son or daughter. The problem is one of informed choice; the person cannot be said to be exercising informed choice until and unless s/he understands the consequences of, in this case, not cleaning her/his teeth. This is very unlikely to be the case in individuals with autism and sld.

One way of dealing with such problems is to try to increase understanding among staff who work with these adults, but a surer strategy is to help establish relatively independent routines of self-care that can withstand changes of environment and personnel. Just as with Paul above, there is a need to establish self-monitoring routines, using picture symbols. There is also a need to make sure these are well generalised before entering adult care services. This means they will need to have been used with many different people giving overall supervision in many different situations. One can never be certain that routines, even when supported by symbols, will not break down, but they are less likely to when they have been generalised in this way. Also, having the picture sequences may act as a prompt to staff who may then at least offer the person the opportunity to engage in the activity (e.g., cleaning teeth) and are more likely to get compliance with these familiar symbols. Staff may also need to work on self-care routines being done within a fixed period of time (perhaps by having a rewarding activity to follow) or to a fixed rhythm, since, if they just allow routines at the individual's own pace, they can become increasingly drawn out and occupy most of the day.

Transition to adulthood and markers of adult status

Moving into adult life may herald a whole succession of changes and the effects of these on the individual with autism and sld can be catastrophic, if the changes are not recognised and coping strategies taught. It will also be best if changes can be staggered.

The adult role has social and cultural markers. It may be that the child with autism and sld cannot achieve adult status, because these markers are unobtainable as, for example, when open employment or a sexual partner are not realistic goals. There is also the parallel danger that these markers will be seen by the child with autism and sld as automatic once one has reached the age of an adult, and there may then be considerable depression or even anger when, for example, reaching eighteen does not automatically bring a job, a girlfriend or a driver's licence.

Possibility of employment?

Work has social and status benefits and occupies time in a structured way. However, work must be 'real' if it is to have any meaning or dignity, and people with autism and sld are better learning to look after themselves and developing their leisure interests than doing boring repetitive tasks that serve no useful function. Some workshop environments also represent difficulties in coping with large numbers of people, or a noisy or brightly lit environment, and work should not be seen as the only meaningful lifestyle. Farm communities are now out of fashion in the long-term adult care of adults with autism and sld, although the ones that do exist appear to have great success in providing a work environment that is productive, meaningful and allows opportunities for personal development. Where paid work is not possible, voluntary work may help the individual gain in confidence and self-esteem, and may be a precursor to later paid employment.

Independent living?

Even if parents are able and willing to continue to care for their adult son or daughter with autism and sld at home, there is value for all concerned in the adult moving out of his/her family, but very few (if any) of this group can be expected to live entirely unsupported. There are growing numbers of small group homes that support adults with autism and sld, usually supplying residential care, but using community facilities for daytime occupation. Some larger facilities include both residential care and daytime opportunities, including further education, vocational and leisure training, training in basic life and domestic skills. As the adult prepares to move from the family home to a community service, there needs to be as careful planning to manage the transition as in earlier transitions from home to school or school to adult life. A more or less rigid structure (depending on the adult's needs)

needs to be in place in the new setting, before the move takes place, or there may be a danger of the placement failing.

Family or adult relationships?

There may be problems with sexual relations as detailed below. It may also be the case that the person with autism and sld has an unrealistic view of what it means to be married or to have children, and simply asks to do these things because 'that is what people do'. Depending on the level of ability of the adult with autism and sld, it may be best to present several lifestyle alternatives, so that marriage is not seen as the only option. There are also problems in working out how much is understood by the person with autism and sld, and one should continue to be aware of them being misled by literal interpretations. One should always ensure that choices are informed choices, and take a positive attitude to voiced choice. Rather than suggesting to the person that a certain goal is unrealistic, however, it is more fruitful to approach a person with autism's expressed desire with the attitude of 'what support will be needed to effect those choices?' Sometimes just working through all the steps the person will need to take to achieve a certain goal can make the goal itself seem less attractive, and the person can then be more realistic in settling for an alternative.

Managing transitions

From school to the world

School may have had problems, but it is likely to have provided a more structured environment than post-school life. Good schooling will have been preparing for this change from fourteen at least, but it is often difficult to train independence from the structures on which the individual has come to rely, and some of these may not even be appreciated. Working towards transportable structures (as in visual schedules) can ease this problem.

Home

At the same time as the individual with autism and sld is moving into the adult world, there are liable to be concomitant changes in the home situation. Older siblings may move from the family home, go to college, get married, have children and so on. Grand-parents or even parents might die and there may then be problems with bereavement. Attitudes of younger siblings may change to an adult, especially if they are now vulnerable adolescents with their own problems and wanting to bring friends home. There are no set answers to each of these potential problems, but there needs to be sensitivity to the effects of these changes and the need for support in adjusting to them.

Cues for skills

These cues may have been established within the school environ-ment and so removal from that environment may mean that the individual may appear to lose skills and lack motivation or com-petence. These may, therefore, need to be reinstated and the role of transportable cues, such as visual prompts, is very important in that respect.

Sexual identify and function

Sex education

Some twenty-five years ago a voluntary organisation providing services for children and adults with autism commissioned one of its staff to write a guidance document on sex education. After some months of deliberation, a document was produced whose message could be summed up as 'Don't!' Clearly that is not an adequate response, but one has some sympathy for its conclusions when one starts to think about this area, especially in relation to the group with autism and sld. Yet this is also the most vulnerable of groups, and guidance is needed to help protect them and keep them safe. This vulnerability is the most pressing imperative for sex education, but there is also an issue in protecting others against sexual harassment (whether or not it is intended), and protecting the individual with autism and sld against being arrested or sent into psychiatric care for inappropriate sexual activity, or activity that might be regarded as sexual or provocative, even if it is not intended as such. Thus, education about body changes, gender differences and sexual development is important in autism and sld. Yet some of the ways this might normally be done with normally developing children, by parents and/or teachers will not be appropriate with this group. Any talk about the 'birds and the bees', or couching the discussion in overtechnical scientific terms, may make it more comfortable for the teacher or parent, but is likely to be of little benefit to the child with autism and sld. This group will have little or no generalisation from sex education, delivered 'out of context', so it is up to carers (parents and others) to help them understand the body changes as they happen, to deal with the results of emotional turmoil, as well as providing general sex education to make these changes more predictable and so more acceptable.

Body changes
Like others going through adolescence, youngsters with autism and sld have to be prepared for changes in their body that will otherwise seem terrifying and open to misinterpretation. It must also be remembered that people with autism and sld will not have friends with whom to talk things through, or with whom to compare notes, and the absence of these normal mechanisms for anxiety reduction will have to be compensated for by support from parents and caring professionals. Common misunderstandings are that periods represent an injury, and that 'wet dreams' represent a toileting accident leading to a wet bed. Both situations are, of course, likely to cause distress and even fear (especially with the blood and pain that may accompany periods). As with all other such instances of fear and distress, the person with autism and sld is unlikely to recognise the cause of their emotional reaction themselves, and they will certainly not be able to communicate the cause. Parents and carers will need both to try to pre-empt these responses by education about the body changes beforehand, but also to look for signs of fear or distress (which are just as likely to be behavioural as a communicative or emotional expression) regardless of this training.

There are some texts available, sometimes developed for children with speech and language difficulties, which help the child understand about the different bodily changes to be expected in adolescence. Even when they appear to have understood that this is going to happen to them, however, it may still come as a shock when it actually does. The problem is that one cannot predict the changes that will occur, either in their size or relative or absolute timing. It is also desirable that they understand about changes to others as well as themselves, so that they learn not to embarrass brothers or sisters (or classmates) by trying to investigate these signs of growing breasts or testicles. Unfortunately, education may sometimes exacerbate these problems rather than resolve them. The young person may be alerted to these interesting changes, which otherwise may have passed them by, and may begin commenting on people's body shapes in public, or want to investigate in a more direct physical way.

There is no magic way of balancing these risks, but it is important that education about sexual changes is backed up with education about appropriate ways of behaving in relation to these bodily changes. Teenagers have to be taught to be even more meticulous about personal hygiene and how, when, and how often to use deodorants. Boys will need to be taught to shave or to tolerate being shaved, as appropriate. Girls, too, may need to know about under-arm hair removal, if this is judged to be in her best interests in maintaining hygiene and meeting the wishes of her family in terms of aesthetics. Girls will also need to be taught all the relevant rituals surrounding menstruation, and the benefits and risks of different forms of protection will need to be discussed in relation to the particular needs and difficulties of the individual. For example, a girl's problems in disposing of her sanitary towel appropriately and changing it when necessary may be solved by the use of tampons, but only as long as there is no danger of the girl continually fiddling with the tampon, introducing infection into the womb and leading to other forms of inappropriate masturbation. It may also lead to the girl seeing this as the 'red light' to inserting all manner of other items into the vagina, with similar distressing consequences.

For all these activities, the notion of privacy, first introduced into toilet training and then into changing for PE, becomes very important. We may need to have clear rules, but once more we must be careful that they are not too rigid. A young girl, for example, was taught by her mother that she must never undress in front of a strange man, even if he told her to. This was clearly done with the best intentions of keeping the girl safe from molestation. However, a problem arose when she became ill and refused to undress in front of the male doctor, even when her mother told her it was all right to do so. In one establishment the way round this difficulty was to teach the children first the narrow range of people it *was* all right to undress in front of, rather than specify the reverse, and then they were taught that they should seek permission from one of that number if asked to undress by anyone else. This was never a system they could learn to operate for themselves, but it did provide a useful framework for teaching about these rules of privacy and the particular exceptions that might arise (being examined by a doctor, being fitted for clothes, undressing after swimming in communal changing rooms and so on).

Feelings

All adolescents find the see-sawing of emotions that accompany sexual development a trial, as of course do all those who have to live with them at the time. Autism is no shield against these mood swings and indeed may even make them worse. Even if they are not in actuality any more severe than in other adolescents, the effects may be worse because they have no way of mitigating the effects. Most adolescents have friends to hang around with, to share in, and support them through, these difficult times and with whom they can identify as a beleaguered group whom no one else apparently understands. Others, too, may at least have some understanding of what is happening to them and may be able to mitigate at least some of the worst effects of depression or manic elation by recognising its cause and the fact that it may soon pass. Young people with autism and sld do not have this consolation and the feelings may come upon them without warning and with no support from the knowledge, for example, that this is just premenstrual tension and will be eased once her period has come.

As well as these general mood swings, sexual development is also accompanied by more specific feelings related to desire and the need for sexual gratification. It is true that a number of people with autism do not seem to have a very strong sexual urge and for them it would be foolish (and rather cruel) to try to introduce them to an area which is as likely to be a source of difficulty and distress as of joy. Unfortunately, a complete lack of interest in sex is by no means typical in autism. It may be that their sexual interest is not in people (in line with a lack of interest in people in general), but this can give rise to different, but equally challenging behaviours. As will be seen in the section on masturbation, below, it may lead to almost as much sexual frustration, as fetishes develop but are difficult to indulge, or it may lead to behavioural challenges as the person desperately seeks their particular fetishistic object. Yet the feelings that accompany sexual interest are not just another source of problems in autism; they can have positive effects. It has been known, for example, for this to be the first time that the individual with autism and sld has ever taken any interest in others. The sexual element may not be so important as the fact that they are now more willing to be engaged with others, or to modify their behaviour to make themselves more attractive to others. Puberty sometimes presents as a second opportunity for persons with autism to become attached to others and to develop relationships, even with their parents. It is not that these relationships are themselves sexual, but that the sexual impulse has provided the interest and motivation for them to occur.

However, just as people with autism and sld do not understand their own emotions and behaviour, so they will not recognise these signals of sexual interest in others, nor be aware of how their own behaviour may be affecting them. This may lead to harassment of others whose friendly smile they take to be a sign of sexual acquiescence, or, alternatively, vulnerability when their own naïve behaviour may give off signals of acquiescence they do not intend. These issues are dealt with below as issues of exploitation, but the point here is that there needs to be continued education about their own and others' emotions, so that they are better equipped to manage or avoid these problems. They will also need to learn how to deal with rejection (as indeed we all have to—unless we are extraordinarily fortunate in our life experiences), both in terms of actual behaviour (a distracting enjoyable, preferably physical, activity is best) and in terms of the emotions aroused. Just like the rest of us, being rejected can lead to low self-esteem and it is not helped if one has a poor sense of self-efficacy and does not understand the reasons for the rejection. People with autism and sld will need help in coming to terms with these emotions, and in developing skills to minimise future rejections, while trying to make sure they understand that asking that involves another's feelings cannot guarantee accept-ance, and the notion of two possible outcomes to asking (accept-ance, or the fall-back alternative activity) should be taught from the beginning.

Masturbation
It is hard to lay down hard and fast rules about this, since attitudes towards it will vary so much, according to moral and religious views and cultural (and subcultural) factors. On the one hand is the recognition that people with autism and sld are still people, with the need (and right) to develop and express themselves as sexual beings. Since the likelihood of a full sexual relationship with others is unlikely in all but a minority of cases, masturbation is the natural outlet for such expression. For some parents this may simply be unacceptable, and then there is the thorny ethical problem of whose needs and rights must prevail. Where people with autism and sld are able to express an informed view, then it is clear that it is their needs and rights that are paramount. But in the majority of cases an informed view is not possible and then the role of advocates (which may well be parents) becomes important. It is doubtful if it can ever be entirely satisfactory to go against the expressed wishes of parents in matters such as this, but parents may need counselling to help them accept their 'child's' sexual identity and needs, and to make them aware of the possible undesirable consequences of ignoring or denying those needs.

As will be seen in the section on exploitation below, people with autism and sld are very vulnerable and so part of their education about sex should help them to distinguish what they might like from what might be unpleasant, even painful. They also need an alternative way of dealing with sexual arousal, if they are not to be engaged in exploitative relationships nor to get very frustrated, with the consequent results in disturbed or difficult behaviour. Masturbation can be one such alternative, although, because it cannot be used in every situation, the person will also need to develop other strategies for reducing arousal and getting rid of frustration.

The most important restraint on the use of masturbation is that it should be a private activity. The person with autism and sld will need firm and clear rules showing permitted areas and times for masturbation, based on the principle of always teaching the positive rather than prohibitions. With adults in leisure time, it might well be appropriate to teach them to communicate their need to go somewhere private to masturbate if something has aroused them; it would not be appropriate, however, for them to be permitted to do this during a work activity, at meal-times or in a public place. In such situations they need help in lowering their level of interest and arousal through some distracting activity, until a more appropriate opportunity arises. Just as it would be unreasonably restrictive to say they should never indulge in any sexual activity, it is equally unreasonable to give them the idea that they can do this as and when they please; such licence is liable to lead them into trouble with others and even the law.

Once the notions of being private and at an appropriate time and place have been resolved, adults with autism and sld may need some assistance with the act of masturbation itself. It is neither necessary nor appropriate to teach people, who show no interest in masturbation, how to do it. However, some people with autism and sld may engage in masturbation frequently and frantically, and yet never achieve orgasm, and so remain aroused but frustrated; this is when they may become angry and lash out at themselves or others. They may also make themselves dangerously sore in their attempts to achieve orgasm. The reasons for this difficulty in achieving orgasm are not straightforward. The person may be on medication that affects the achievement of orgasm, or it may be the fact that they cannot use fantasy aids (thinking of, or looking at, very attractive members of the opposite—or same—sex).

In any case, it is usually in their best interests to help them achieve orgasm but there are problems in the logistics of this. Parents, quite understandably, feel uncomfortable in this role, as may young staff, and there is always the danger of permitting (or appearing to permit) abuse. In some European countries such a role is taken by a specialist sex therapist, but that is not a service available in the UK or in many other places. The advice to staff would be to make sure there is a policy and a specific treatment and care plan related to this, and to keep meticulous records of all teaching and progress. Teaching the use of mechanical sex aids can ease the problem by making it easier to teach, more likely to be successful, and less likely to lead to abuse or accusations of abuse. It is also likely to be the case that people with autism develop sexual interest in certain objects, rather than people. Where convenient, these can be given to the person while masturbating, to make orgasm more likely. Sometimes, however, the items are somewhat bizarre (soup ladles, cling film, for example) and, in seeking them out, challenging behaviour may arise. These need to be treated as other cases of challenging behaviour, regardless of the initial sexual motivation.

As with many other areas in autism, there is also the danger that masturbation may become a problem because it becomes an obsessional activity. This can then be particularly challenging since it is hard to think of an alternative behaviour to try to teach to compete with this obsession. The pleasure is, or can be, intense, and it is not possible to 'take away' the obsessional activity in order to get the individual to follow a sequence of 'work then play'. Even so, these are the same principles that have to be applied. A visual sequence needs to be provided to show the individual when (and where) they will be able to masturbate and what they will have to do first. This can work if the person is used to postponing what s/he wants to do and to work for the privilege of access, as a matter of routine. It is more likely to work if the 'work' chosen in the sequence is in fact something else that that person really enjoys doing, so that it is functioning as a distraction from masturbating. If the person can be 'caught' in the early stages of getting worked up, rather than when in the grip of a strong emotion, this will also maximise the chances of getting the behaviour under control.

Ethical issues

As indicated above, parents and carers may find the whole area of dealing with another person's sexual development very hard to handle. For parents there is the natural intergenerational embarrassment and the natural reluctance to see one's 'child' (exacerbated when the adult has learning difficulties of any kind) as a functioning sexual being. For professional carers, who may be very young, the difficulty may come from not having fully adjusted to themselves as sexual beings yet and the stress and responsibility of making these important quality of life decisions for someone who may in fact be older than themselves. It is easy to see what needs to be done when someone's needs are for food, comfort and physical care, even for occupation, but it is far more difficult to see sexual needs in the same kind of way. As a generalisation, by no means true of all cases, parents are more likely to want to deny the sexual needs of the adult with autism and sld and young carers are more likely to assume sexual needs, even when that is not the case.

However, there are genuine ethical dilemmas when dealing with the sexual needs of adults with autism and sld, which go beyond learning to identify those needs more realistically. If one has someone who is unlikely to form long-lasting emotional and companionable relationships with another person (which is the case in the majority of cases in this group), then teaching that person how to go about having a sexual relationship with someone is tantamount to saying that it is all right to treat other people as a means of gratifying one's desires. In effect, it is teaching adults with autism and sld to use others in ways that are not acceptable to most people's codes of morality, even if their behaviour often falls short of such codes. Even young men, who may espouse the doctrine of having as many sexual experiences as possible, usually mature into a more considerate and socially aware attitude, albeit that that may have something to do with the fact that it coincides with some loss in their own physical attractiveness and thus ability to continue to act in this way. Most people have an ideal of a loving as well as a sexual relationship, in spite of, in some cases, a wish for an occasional dangerous liaison. It is after all, only 'dangerous' and the stuff of so much literature, because we recognise that a casual affair seldom compensates for an enduring loving one. It is not surprising, therefore, that helping adults with autism and sld enter a sexual relationship fills many people with unease.

Yet there are as many ethical qualms about adopting a contrary position. If we do not help the person with autism and sld acquire and manage a sexual relationship (once, of course, we have ascertained that is what they want), then is this not a denial of pleasure to a group for whom life may offer precious few other pleasures? What right have we to impose our moral code on others? Why should we insist on a standard of moral behaviour in this group that is certainly not generally practised among their peers? All these are genuinely ethical problems and as such have no easy pat solutions. All that can reasonably be asked is that staff and parents are aware of these issues, that they are discussed and shared with all who are involved with the adult, including siblings, who may often be able to take a more realistic and age-appropriate attitude than the parents and mediate between staff and parents. Where possible, the adult him or herself should be involved, although this must be handled carefully to avoid disturbing and confusing the adult further. The goal would be to have an ethical policy with which all concerned agree and which informs the practice of sex education in the service.

Exploitation and abuse

As indicated above, people with autism and sld are particularly vulnerable to exploitation and abuse, and yet they too may also be perpetrators. They may misunderstand emotional and social signals and may give the wrong signals themselves in terms of their dress, manner and behaviour. Equally they may have a very literal understanding of the sex education and the codes of conduct they have been taught so that they may learn that you have to ask if someone wants sex, and go somewhere private, but they are not always taught that they must wait for, and pay attention to, the answer, especially if it is 'no'. On the receiving end, they may have had insufficient teaching in how to be assertive, how to recognise what it is that they do in fact want, have little idea of exactly what they may be consenting to, or even be unaware that they could object. If they have spent much of their life in school learning that they must comply with requests whether they want to or not, it is unrealistic to expect them to suddenly understand that this is a request where they do not have to comply. In such cases we cannot claim that failing to object, or even agreeing, constitutes a real and informed choice, and we then have an educational task in trying to make sure that such informed choices are possible. This process is made easier if the adult has been exposed to similar teaching when much younger, learning about making choices and how to recognise and assert one's needs.

The solution does not just lie in learning how to respond to sexual advances, however, but also in learning how to avoid provoking such advances through inappropriate dress or manner. This is not, of course, to say that it is in any way their 'fault' should they be molested but it is only kind to make sure they are not continually exposed to such stressful encounters by some unintentional behaviour on their own part. Siblings or other young people may be enlisted, for example, to help children with autism to dress more appropriately for their age group, rather than like their parents, as they get older. This can work well, but may backfire if, for example, a sister is going through a stage of testing her own sexual charms, dressing provocatively, but being very aware of the effect she is having, knowing many strategies for avoiding or getting out of difficult situations, and having support from friends, all engaged in the same 'game'. This is fine for the sister but may be disastrous for the girl with autism and sld, especially if she is allowed, perhaps, to accompany her sister but without the resources to support her. This does not mean that the process of copying needs to be abandoned altogether but it must be modified. Parents, carers and the sister all need to be aware of the dangers and pre-empt provocative dressing as being too risky, even with others present.

Other inappropriate behaviour may result from earlier teaching,

especially where behaviours have been taught without understanding or knowledge of their effects on others. A very young
child may have been taught to accept cuddles from others and
even to return them, as a way of encouraging social interaction
and bonding with loved ones. This usually has a good effect and
can be used as a basis of developing later more age-appropriate
behaviour as the child matures. Occasionally, however, it may
take a long while for this behaviour to become established, so
that children are only learning to respond in this way, and to
initiate cuddles, as they approach their teens. At that stage, the
upsurge of sexual feeling may increase this behaviour and make
it difficult to control. This is especially likely where the family
may be responding very positively to these advances, quite understandably, because they represent the first signs they have had
of a loving relationship with their child. It is not true that all
behaviour does not generalise in autism; sometimes there is the
reverse in that there is a lack of discrimination. If young people
are going around cuddling anyone they take a fancy to, then this
is clearly a situation that makes them both vulnerable to abuse
from others, and may lead them into acts that can be construed
as sexually harassing. As with other challenging behaviour, in
spite of its initial positive effects, this needs to be replaced by
positive teaching about appropriate ways of greeting and con-
tacting others.

Another taught response that can lead to later trouble is that
of eye contact, without any understanding of meaning or how to
make and break it according to the social situation. In such situations, one of the interpretations that may be given to deep long
looks into a stranger's eyes is of a sexual advance. As with
provocative dressing, this is not a situation that can be allowed
to continue. It is very important to begin a programme of teaching
the person the meaning of eye contact, of how it is used as a
signal and, especially important in this case, how a safer way of
looking at strangers is to look at their face, rather than eyes, and
even then, not to do that for very long. The best solution, of
course, is for schools to ensure that they always teach for meaning, and not to encourage meaningless rituals.

People with autism and sld may become vulnerable simply

because they have a strong desire to have a 'friend' or even to marry, without really understanding the implications of either of these relationships. Many exploitative relationships have been started with adults with autism because they are offered friendship (perhaps to go and listen to music, or to follow another interest they have) and then they find themselves in a situation of sexual demand that they cannot handle. They may be desperately unhappy (and some have been shown to be physically damaged and in obvious pain) but they do not know how to communicate their distress to others nor to get out of the situation. Such exploitation can go on for years, as it may in any situation where one of the 'partners' is at a power disadvantage to another (which may just be that the other person understands more), so parents and staff must be alert to the possibility and look for signs, not waiting for a complaint from the person. In this case, the additional sld may help in that such people usually have closer supervision, but that may not always be the case where staff have rigid ideas about not invading personal space and the adult resists attempts to assist with intimate care (or is judged to be competent in these areas and so does not need help).

Where it is the person with autism and sld who is sexually harassing others, he or she will need to be taught that *both* parties in a sexual encounter should actively want to participate, and that being friendly does not mean the same as wanting to have sex, in spite of what they might see on television. In the same way, if they are living with equally vulnerable people (as they may well be in a residential home for people with autism or for people with learning difficulties), then it may not be good enough for them to be taught that they must ask, implying that someone who does not object, or who says yes is giving informed consent. As we saw above, this is not a sufficient guard against exploitation in such situations and, unless they can (in rare cases) be taught to recognise and respond to true expressed feelings, and the other person can be taught to be assertive and express those true feelings, it is safest to have a system with the staff of checking sexual 'dates', as (one hopes) they can better judge whether this is a consenting relationship.

Summary

Increasing independence enhances the capacity for a full and happy life by allowing personal choice and a degree of autonomy. People with autism and sld should be allowed to attain adult status, regardless of the levels of support they may need to manage the roles and responsibilities that are the markers of that status. Sexual development and the nature and extent of sex education remain problematic, in particular because of the specific challenges raised to cultural and ethical views and the practicalities of supporting adults with autism and sld into full sexual identity. However, there are positive features as well as particular challenges in assisting in this development.

Further reading

MORGAN, H. (1997). *Adults with Autism.* Cambridge: Cambridge University Press.

12 A Productive Life and Sources of Help

A productive life

Opportunities for work

As explored above, work should not be created for its own sake, but meaningful work can help structure time and add to the individual's quality of life through this and through additional income, thus providing a certain amount of independence. In the UK there may be no economic necessity for paid employment and, while that is of course right in terms of society providing for those who need it, it has also led to low expectations of the work potential of this group. In societies without such a welfare system, there is a greater emphasis placed on training individuals with autism and sld to engage in paid supported work in normal workplace situations. The downside of this is that the child may start to be trained to do menial tasks in school with a view to later employment. It may be realistic to assume that the kind of jobs the person is most likely to fulfil is to pack plastic cutlery for airlines or to clean people's houses, but spending years training them to do such tasks is not very fulfilling for the person concerned nor the teacher. In truth, notions of what can be achieved by this group in terms of work are more often determined by what is available in a society rather than the actual abilities or disabilities of the individuals concerned.

Difficulties in workplace situations arise more often from social and communication difficulties, or from rigidity in thinking and behaviour, than they do from failures to manage the actual work involved. Some of the problems experienced by this group and the wider group of individuals with autism are explored in Howlin (1997), as are some ways of avoiding or dealing with these difficulties. In general one should be wary of situations where the individual will have to process a lot of information (especially social information) at the same time, or will have to make decisions in situations that cannot be anticipated. Beyond that, most of the restrictions will depend on individual characteristics. Some will be very disturbed by highly stimulating environments, others will be very distracted when favourite items like computers are around and may get obsessional about doing their own thing (i.e. playing a particular computer game) rather than the job they are supposed to do. Some will not manage a situation where they have to meet the public, but others may manage if, for example, they are 'protected' by a counter which people can only approach one at a time.

It is not only autism that will affect the capacity to take up, and persist in, job opportunities; sld will present barriers to certain kinds of jobs or to the capacity to adapt and take in new information, especially at speed. Nevertheless, the problems presented by learning difficulties are more predictable in advance and more generalisable across individuals. Many tasks, which would be impossible if presented as a whole can be broken down into manageable steps and put together again into a meaningful whole. This is helped if the whole sequence is represented in the form of picture symbols and the individual is trained to work towards this visible goal, performing the last little bit only as a first step and then the bit before that and so on, in a process of 'backward chaining'. Visual cueing of the task will be as important in the work situation as it was in the school or home.

Examples of work situations with adults with autism and sld

The following are meant as examples of the range of work that may be accomplished. It is not intended to imply that all people with autism and sld are capable of all, or indeed any, of these examples. Each case will depend on the individual's talents, capacity to learn, and degree of interference from the autism, as well as the quality and quantity of their preparation for the work and the ability and willingness of the work place to adapt to their needs. Some are very particular to an individual, but are given to show that one cannot make rigid judgements of suitability just from knowing that the person has autism and sld. Others are more likely to suit many people with autism and sld.

Helper in a nursery school
This represents, perhaps, the extreme of what would be considered unlikely jobs for a person with autism and sld; many such people do not like the unpredictability and messiness of little children and would find this very stressful. However, there is a young man with autism and sld (Colin) who has always been interested in little children and very gentle with them. He began some work experience in nursery situations when he was at school and managed very well, with the supervision of a helper. As he became an adult and moved to a residential home for adults with autism, it happened to be very near this nursery for under-five-year-olds, in which he had had this earlier successful experience. Staff at the adult home, therefore, decided to work with the nursery school, and with him, to train him to act as a helper in the nursery. It was a relatively simple matter to train him to perform simple duties, preparing snacks and drinks and feeding the younger children, preparing paint, collage and other play activities and helping children dress and undress when going outside or back inside. He was also taught specifically that he must do what the nursery leaders told him, and that he could only take the children anywhere if he checked first with one of these helpers.

The tasks to perform varied from day to day, but there was always a structure to the routine of the nursery and he was given this structure in pictorial form. Thus, he knew that nursery started with a group time on the mat and he was to help bring children to sit down on the mat as they arrived. After that there would be an activity time and he was given one of the activities (painting, playing with trains, the home corner, reading, playing with play dough, building bricks, playing on the indoor activity equipment and so on) to supervise. Then there would be snack time followed by a period of outdoor play (weather permitting) or indoor group games where his job was to help the children join in the activities and enjoy themselves. Finally, the morning ended with another group time, this time in a circle of chairs, where there might be a group story, some music and songs and some nursery rhymes. Mostly his job was to help the children settle to this activity, but he would lead one of the songs once a week (his favourite), and sometimes act out a familiar story with puppets which he (and the children) also enjoyed very much. There was also a regular period for toileting and he might be given the responsibility of taking a particular child to the toilet at regular intervals, if a child was on a toileting programme. Nursery finished at twelve noon when Colin helped to clear away, and then he had finished, since he only worked part-time (four hours a day, five days a week).

Colin got paid for most of this time, but the hours of paid work were adjusted, so that he did not lose the benefits to which he was entitled. However, he worked a proper half time 'shift', because this was of more use to the nursery and better for him to make sense of, in that it coincided with the time the morning nursery operated. For Colin, his time at work was a joy and he did not like holiday periods at all, counting obsessively on a calendar until it was time to start back at work. He liked the routine of the nursery with the very familiar activities, many of which were not considered age-appropriate for him; thus this time at nursery was his one opportunity to engage in such tasks. He loved 'helping' with the puzzles (and really loved clearing up at the end and putting all the pieces back in place) and building bricks, playing trains, playing simple musical instruments and above all engaging in gentle rough-and-tumble and chasing with the children. Watching him rolling around on the mats and being tickled by little children and loving it so much, made it clear that he had the opportunity that other young men only get when they become fathers—to act as a child again. Sometimes, in our efforts to treat people with autism and sld with dignity as adults, we forget that they also have needs to behave in childlike ways, and they may not have the outlets that others do in 'messing about' with their friends and as fathers, romping with their children.

The only potential problem came from how others, and particularly parents of the children at the nursery, might react to knowing that their children were being cared for by someone with autism and sld. This is not a category of disability that would preclude a person working with young children, but clearly the nursery wanted to allay any fears and to be open and honest about what was happening. Prior to Colin being taken on to work in the nursery, he came for a morning and was allowed to do what he had been trained to do, including playing with the children. This was videoed and then parents were invited to an evening when the video was shown and Colin's position explained. Parents were reassured that he had always loved being with young children and had never had a history of violent or destructive behaviour. Moreover, he was being thoroughly trained and supervised and, although the plan was to phase out the staff from the adult centre in terms of attendance with Colin, they were to continue to monitor the placement and to be on hand (literally three minutes away) should any difficulty arise. Above all, parents were assured that, although the work was of great value to Colin, the needs of the young children would always come first and the work would terminate if ever it was felt not to be in their best interests. All this did help, as did the willingness of the staff from the adult centre to answer questions openly and the invitation to parents to come and see their work. Yet what really made the difference was the video. Very few parents could fail to see for themselves how mutually beneficial was Colin's involvement with their children, and some even shed a tear or two to see such innocent joy in playing with these young children.

Horticultural assistant

Sarah enjoyed tending plants. She had her own little garden in the corner of her parents' garden and she had attended a special needs further education course after leaving special school, where she learnt more about how to grow and look after plants, indoor as well as outdoor. She was not able to read or write and could not understand any of the technical or academic side of horticulture, but she was able to recognise different plants and could remember well how each should be cared for. She could also pick out the signs of certain problems, such as over-watering, being pot-bound and certain deficiencies and diseases, not at a theoretical level but at the practical level of knowing what to do. She could also perform various tasks such as pruning, planting, pricking out, potting, and training plants to climb over trellises and up walls. Straightforward gardening tasks such as digging and mowing the grass were no problem, although weeding was a source of difficulty. Sarah had no problem in identifying common weeds, but she would get frustrated because it was seldom possible to clear a patch entirely of weeds and she would not like it when her supervisor told her to finish when she felt there was more to do.

In general, then, Sarah had developed good skills in horticulture, although she would not be able to function independently. The special career officer suggested that it might be possible to find a job in a supported employment scheme run by the local borough. Sarah, who lived at home with her parents, joined a group where there was a supervisor who knew about horticulture but also had training in special needs. He had a team of three adults working with him, the other two having learning difficulties alone and Sarah having autism and sld. In addition to his training, the supported employment scheme ensured he had access to additional training in autism and that there was back-up support for any difficulties that might arise. The team worked for a local authority, growing and looking after plants for local parks and public gardens and indoor plants for council offices. There were additional workers in teams that were not part of the supported employment scheme. Sarah worked a full week and received a full wage, the costs of the support she received being met through funding for the supported employment scheme. It worked very well, except for three days each month when Sarah's period started. Her co-workers were all male and Sarah still needed some support in order to manage. She also became emotional at this time and it was felt to be better for everyone if she took the time off, with her pay being reduced accordingly. She was given a contraceptive pill to reduce the time of incapacity and any discomfort involved.

Craft work in a centre for adults with autism
Many specialist centres for adults with autism encourage their 'clients' to develop their interests and skills to produce work that can be sold to the public. This might be done through a retail outlet that the centre also runs, through direct marketing by

advertising in specialist journals, or just through contact with friends and relatives of the people in the service. It is seldom that enough money is made to provide a living wage, but it is common for state funds to pay for living costs and for money earned in this way to be spent on luxuries or treats like holidays and outings. Some people with autism and sld are very good at pottery, for example, and so it is easy to sell their work to the public. Even if people have very severe learning difficulties and limited talent, however, many centres have been ingenious in finding meaningful productive work for them to do. Papiermâché craft work or recycled paper provides ample opportunities for the person who just enjoys tearing paper, there is a market for wood 'sculptures' which are in fact found pieces of wood which may be dried, sanded down and varnished, none of which requires great skill, and so on. Many objects so produced are beautiful and/or useful in their own right and there is the added fact that people are contributing to a good cause.

Factory workers
Factory work would not normally be the most suitable for someone with autism and sld, but one centre for adults with autism was located near an industrial estate and put great emphasis on the therapeutic value of engaging adults with autism in productive work. A special member of staff was employed by the centre to seek out suitable job placements, to analyse the job requirements, select someone from the centre who could, or could be trained to, meet those requirements and then organise the support that would be needed to enable that person to do the job. The person would be paid the rate for the job, but the cost of providing the support would be deducted, leaving the person with money additional to their living allowance. This had to be registered as a special work scheme in order to manage the complications of employment legislation, tax arrangements, and the benefits system, and also to make sure that employers were not exploiting the situation to get cheap labour. In spite of all the potential problems, however, they were able to support the employment of several adults with autism and sld.

One successful venture was with a very small company who

had not yet taken on their work force when they were approached by the centre. They had set up a small cleaning and respraying workshop, to recycle prefabricated buildings after use as temporary selling offices (on a new housing development, for example) or as offices on building sites or exhibitions. There was room for eight workers only in a room where the prefabricated sections would arrive in containers. The containers had to be unpacked, each section placed on a conveyor belt and allowed to pass through a cleaning machine. Once out of the machine, they had to be inspected and either passed through again or allowed to pass on to the drying machine and then the paint-spraying machine. Once through the paint-spraying machine there was another inspection to see if a second coat was required or not. After another dying process, the sections were finally taken from the end of the conveyor belt and stacked in a container ready for transport.

None of these tasks was itself very skilful but they did require two people to act together (the panels were too heavy to be lifted alone). They needed those two people to act together on an agreed decision involving a judgement at two stages: they required precision in the placement of the panels to go through the machines, and they needed strict adherence to safety regulations in handling dangerous machinery. Staff trained selected individuals on similar tasks back at the centre, then in the factory without the machinery running, then with close supervision in the real task, and finally they were able to reduce supervision to two staff for the eight people with autism and sld involved. What was impressive was the way that these workers, who had been described at school as having short attention spans and who normally spent a lot of unstructured time dancing around, flicking their fingers and picking up bits of fluff and so forth, were able to show concentration for the full work period (two hours) between breaks. What is more, far from being exploited, there was every sign that they enjoyed these work periods and were always happy to mark off the calendar after a weekend or holiday and know that the next day would be work.

Canteen assistant

Marie also lived in a specialist centre for adults with autism. She had additional sld and a language impairment, so not only did she not speak but she could follow very little of others' speech. She had enjoyed cooking from schooldays onwards and a part-time job was found for her in a small works canteen, helping to prepare a lunch and snacks menu. This involved an early start but, once Marie had been trained to do the job, it was only necessary for the centre staff to put her on the early morning bus. Other canteen workers used the same bus and were prepared to supervise Marie both on the bus and at work. Staff from the centre had visited the work place (of a company whose managing director had pledged his support in finding work for people with autism) to talk about autism and about Marie in particular. They explained how to manage her and promised to be at the end of a phone to deal with any problems or queries, as they arose. They also explained how to communicate with Marie, using the simple gestures she had been taught and the picture signs she would have access to. They explained how they would set up a visual sequence for her to follow, so she could do the various jobs required, and promised to return to establish a similar sequence if the job changed or new jobs were to be undertaken. Marie already knew how to do the various tasks involved (peeling and cutting vegetables, washing up, loading dishwashers, making sandwiches and so on) but the visual sequences would act as a reminder to keep her on task. Marie proved a popular and hard-working member of the canteen staff and even became 'friends' with some of the women, who would take her home for tea (they only worked until two o'clock) or for an outing they thought she would enjoy. Marie seemed to enjoy the attention, although she had not been sociable as a child, and she also appeared to look forward to going to work.

Other adult occupation

Work is not the only way of being engaged productively. The arguments for leisure opportunities, that were made in Chapter 9 about children, apply when it comes to adult life. Either as an alternative, and certainly as a complement, to work, should be opportunities for personal development and pleasure through educational and leisure pursuits.

Leisure opportunities
A few adult establishments have some in-house sources of leisure and certainly there should be access to media, to computers and to expression through arts and crafts available as part of the daily living experience. However, there is also value in using community resources in that they offer better facilities and the additional opportunity of developing or improving social and daily living skills. At one level there should be access to whatever sports activities they might enjoy, albeit with some support. The attitude should not be about what the person is currently unable to do, but what support and/or teaching would be necessary to help the person enjoy this activity, and how that can be arranged. Where activities are risky, there will need to be a proper risk assessment undertaken, but people with autism and sld have the right to experience thrills and excitement as much as anyone else, as long as sensible precautions are taken.

Thus adults with autism and sld regularly enjoy swimming, trampolining, tandem cycling, canoeing, rock-climbing, running, walking in the countryside, snooker, music making, line-dancing, kite-flying, running steam-engines, aerobics, aromatherapy, painting, doing puzzles, watching television soaps, watching quiz shows, riding on buses, watching videos, going to concerts, going out for a meal, going to theme parks, going on holiday, camping, and many, many more activities and pastimes. In other words, they enjoy (or some of them enjoy) almost everything that other people enjoy doing to relax or to get stimulation. They may not enjoy the more social activities nor be capable of more intellectual pursuits, but otherwise it is hard to make any generalisations. Sensitivities to a person's wishes and providing safe and structured ways of gaining new experiences should underpin the provision of leisure opportunities.

Further education

Adults with autism and sld, like the rest of us, are capable of lifelong learning. In the UK they are entitled to access to further education, geared to vocational opportunities, but this is interpreted widely. Thus an assessment of needs that includes communication, social and life skills teaching may well be accepted for Further Education Funding Council funding, as long as it is couched in terms of increasing employability. In response to the availability of these funds, many colleges of further education are developing some expertise in catering for adults with autism and sld in their special needs courses. Careful planning and support is necessary to ensure success (Morgan, 1996), but, once this is organised, much can be achieved. Some may even pursue particular talents in mainstream courses, although they are likely still to need support to enable access and to cope with free times, the large dining hall and the comparative lack of structure when compared to school. IT courses can often be managed, even when other skills suggest severe learning difficulties, at least up until the person is required to make his or her knowledge and skills explicit.

Diets and supplements

As mentioned in earlier chapters, there are theories about the causation of autism (or at least about one avenue of causation) related to food intolerance. Such theories would not preclude a genetic base, but would assume that the genes related to lack of enzymes or enzyme deficiency, or problems in maintaining the body's defences against toxins entering the brain and interfering with brain functioning. There are other possible reasons for such difficulties from environmental hazards such as immunisation, agricultural chemicals and over-use of antibiotics. There is no uncontroversial scientific evidence for any of these theories, although there are some interesting preliminary investigations which are being tested.

In spite of the lack of full scientific proof, many parents are convinced enough of the evidence in relation to their own particular child to try one or more of a number of diets and/or food supplements to try to remedy these conditions. There is now in production a helpful protocol which guides parents in doing this systematically, and without endangering the child through lack of nutrition or toxicity from too many vitamins (Shattock & Whiteley, in preparation). The most promising results from parental reports (Whiteley *et al.*, 1999) relate to behavioural calming, and greater ability to concentrate and be sociable. Some of the diets are difficult and expensive to follow but they are a better alternative than medication and a healthy diet can do very little long-term harm. In this area, as in others, however, parents should be aware of charlatans selling either dietary supplements or offers of 'analysis' of the child's chemistry in ways that are scientifically dubious. A dietician (not a nutritionalist, unless they have a proper qualification, since anyone can claim that title) should always be consulted before placing any child on a diet, and parents should be aware of the management problems such diets may pose, especially where other family members may not be on the diet.

Sources of advice and support for families and carers

Parent-led organisations

The most useful form of advice and support usually comes from a parent organisation, some of which have become professionalised or work in collaboration with professionals. Most countries will have at least one national organisation, although sometimes political squabbles have led to breakaway groups forming. National societies often produce their own publications and keep data bases of members, helpful professionals and services throughout the country. Some also run services themselves, diagnostic, educational, care (adult and children's respite), parent training and vocational, although they may only run some of these. In addition, they may have development officers, working with local authorities to help them plan and develop their own services, parent and family support workers, an information service, befriender services for families or individuals with autism or Asperger's syndrome, community support workers and educational officers who may liaise with and support schools or help families in the process of assessment and obtaining statements or records of need. Some may run their own training conferences.

Local branches of the national organisations offer these services at a local level, drawing on the centre for support. Independent or networked local societies may provide some or all of these avenues of support and information, depending on size and ethos. Parent support groups usually operate semi-independently within the structure of a national or local autistic society and may hold regular meetings (with or without a speaker), occasional conferences, and mutual support services like baby-sitting or play schemes and outings in school holidays. Sometimes a specialist school may be the focus of a similar range of support services or an independent group of schools may set up an advice and information centre. They may also help to run support groups for siblings of children with autism or for partners of people with Asperger's syndrome themselves. They may sell publications, conduct or support research, and operate a library and video rental service.

In the UK, the National Autistic Society (NAS) set up a quality assurance Autism Accreditation programme which provided autism-specific quality standards and had a review process to monitor how schools or adult services were meeting those standards. This was a peer review system, operating independently of the NAS but has recently (2002) changed to an NAS programme, that operates now in a more inspectorial way. Other autism-specific quality assurance systems are being developed. They are meant as additional to the services in the UK, in that they are concerned with the particular way in which autism affects those services.

In the wider field, there are growing federations of societies into international bodies. These function to provide a voice at international forums, to affect legislation in bodies (such as the European Parliament), where that is appropriate, and to organise and run international conferences on a regular (often four-yearly) cycle. They may also publicise autism and the work of their member organisations in their own publications, or in the media. They may also be a way of channelling funds from international bodies to support development in less well developed countries (with respect to autism services). It is also becoming increasingly common for societies in countries like the UK, where services may be comparatively well developed, to form a link with societies in countries that have no services to share experience and expertise in helping them to develop their own services. Sometimes this is done purely from good will, but at other times there may be a development grant to support the initiative.

Statutory sources of support

In addition to these parent-led initiatives, countries like the UK have welfare provision to support the needs of the person with autism and sld and also to support the family. However, the availability and quality of these services varies greatly across the UK, even when it is supported by legislation. The problem may lie with the lack of knowledge or understanding of autism in key professionals, employed by these bodies, and this is even worse when the professional involved is not aware of his or her own ignorance and so does not seek to find the information that is available. This can happen at any level of the services that should be available to a family or a person with autism and sld. The best services seem to occur where there is multi-agency co-operation in the sharing of information and the delivery of services.

Diagnosis

In the UK, a national group (NIASA) has been set up by the main professional bodies, and with the support of the National Autistic Society, to review practice and make recommendations on diagnosis, screening, assessment and interventions for children with autistic spectrum disorders. The aim is to make sure that there is a good standard of practice across the country, and the report is due to be published in the summer of 2002.

Diagnosis is a medical concern and is separate from (although it should lead into) the assessment of the individual for educational or care needs. In the UK, therefore, the normal route of access is through a general practitioner referral to a child psychiatrist (or adult psychiatrist, as appropriate) or paediatrician. In some cases clinical psychologists and/or speech and language therapists may make a diagnosis. Educational psychologists will only usually be involved with a diagnosis (as compared to an assessment of educational need) if a school makes a referral or a parent refers a school-aged child. This local diagnostic route should be the one for most clear cases and a medical diagnosis should be followed or accompanied by full assessment of the individual needs of the person, including intellectual functioning, language and communication ability, and behavioural characteristics. This full diagnosis and assessment information should be put in a verbal and written report to parents, which also explains the condition and gives information about local professional and other support and advice which should now be available. In addition, health authorities have a duty to inform educational and social services, so that all necessary provision and support services can be put in place.

If the case is more complicated and outside the experience or expertise of the local diagnostic team, there may be referral to a regional diagnostic service. The same range of professionals may be involved, but this time they would have some expertise in differential diagnosis, especially related to autistic spectrum disorders. They would also take longer over the diagnostic process, probably using one of the instruments specifically designed to test for autistic spectrum disorders. At regional level, they should still be sufficiently aware of local services to be able to recommend and involve local support and services in their report and recommendations.

When there are very puzzling cases, usually when the autism is mild or (as with the population described in this book) when there are accompanying sld, there may be referral to a national centre with particular expertise in autistic spectrum disorders. This is likely to be thorough and may result in very useful multidisciplinary assessments and detailed reports, but there is less likely to be any contact with, or information on, local services or support networks. Recommendations may, therefore, be general, and it is usually up to the parents to renegotiate with local services to get these recommendations accepted and put into practice. It may still be the case that the local authority may seek their own assessment, but this is understandable, in that a diagnostic assessment does not give much information on how the child or adult is functioning, and what support they will need in local provision (or what local provision, if any, will meet their needs).

Pre-school

As outlined in the chapter on daily living skills and parental support, there are different forms of parent support available at this stage. Educational psychologists should be key advisers to the family, especially in matters relating to education. The different agencies involved might be:

- *Speech and language therapists*: work with the child in a clinic, provide a home-based programme, provide or assist in parent-training through, e.g., PECS, Hanen, or EarlyBird

- *Education*: home-visiting teachers, Portage workers, support for other home-based interventions, specialist or mainstream nursery with support, nursery class in special school, educational psychology support and advice

- *Social work*: parent workshops (in conjunction with education and/or health), family support including sibling support groups, supported place at day nursery, social worker advice on benefits or home adaptations, respite or shared-care arrangements

- *Community health and hospital clinics*: nursery nurse visits and advice on play, nursery provision within a child development centre, parent workshops, sibling support groups, therapy sessions (music, art, play, sensory, physiotherapy, psychotherapy, behaviour), clinical psychology as home support adviser or running workshops, dietary advice from dietician, medical advice from paediatrician or child psychiatrist.

School-aged

Statutory rights to education and to support for access, paid for by Education. If a school is outside an education authority provision, they will still pay fees unless they can show that their own provision is able to meet the needs of the child. If a school is residential, care costs will only be borne by Education if the need for a twenty-four-hour curriculum is established. Otherwise a place may be jointly funded with social services. Therapy services may continue as part of provision provided by Health and delivered at school, or separately as clinic provision outside school. Again, educational psychologists should be the prime link between parents and educatonal services, although in some areas there are interdisciplinary autism outreach teams.

Post-school and adult
Education may continue to provide funding in schools after the school leaving age if the person can benefit. In colleges of further education the Further Education Funding Council will fund places and full access as long as a proper assessment is made beforehand, the person completes and 'passes' the course, and the course can be seen as contributing to vocational training (interpreted widely to include independence training). Social services will pay for residential care and may pay for supported living arrangements, befrienders, support for work and leisure. However, this funding is dependent on a full needs assessment and the entitlement is agreed from that. Individuals can claim pensions and disability allowances and will have support and advice from social services in making these claims. Health will be involved in providing normal health care cover to a community home or to an individual and may have special arrangements for health inspections, dentistry, eye tests and so on. Any mental health needs will be met by Health professionals such as psychiatric nurses, general practitioners (usually selected for particular knowledge or interest in this area), psychiatrists or clinical psychologists. The latter may advise services on behaviour policy and provide training in management and may do the same for matters relating to sex and sexual identity. A social worker will normally be the person linking a family with the sources of help available.

Useful contact addresses
Autism-Europe, Avenue E. Van Bacelaere 26B, bte 21, B-1170
   Brussels, Belgium
tel: +(0)2 675.75.05
fax: +(0)2 675.72.70
e-mail: autisme.europe@arcadis.be
url: http://www.autismeurope.arc.be/

Autism Cymru, PO Box 31, Machynlleth, SY20 8WN

Autism Society of America, 7910 Woodmont Avenue, Suite
  300, Bethesda, MD 20814-3015, USA
tel: +800-3AUTISM extension 150
   +301-657-0881
fax: +301-657-0869
url: http://www.autism_society.org/

Autism Society of Canada, 120 Yorkville Avenue, Ste 020
  Road, Toronto, Ontario M5R 1C4, Canada
tel: +416 922 0302

The Irish Society for Autism, Unity Building, 16/17 Lower
  O'Connell Street, Dublin 1, Ireland
tel: +353 1 874 4684
fax: +353 1 874 4224
e-mail: autismer@iol.ie

The National Autistic Society, 333 City Road, London EC1V
  1NE, UK
Tel: +(0)20 7 833 2299
fax: +(0)20 7 833 9666
e-mail: nas@nas.org.uk
url: http://www.oneworld.org.autism_uk/

Parents and Professionals and Autism (PAPA), P.A.P.A.
  Resource Centre, Knockbracken Healthcare Park, Saintfield
  Road, Belfast BT8 8BH, Northern Ireland
tel: +(0)2 890 401 729
fax: +(0)2 890 403467

Scottish Society for Autism, Hilton House, Alloa Business
  Park, Whins Road, Alloa FK10 3SA, Scotland
tel: +(0)1 259 72 00 44
fax: +(0)1 259 72 00 51

Summary

People with autism and sld continue to develop and learn well into adulthood, and need opportunities to occupy themselves productively, to continue to develop their skills and understanding, and to enjoy life to the full. A busy happy life, through its result of stress reduction, is the best way to reduce any challenging behaviour and to enable more self and social awareness. As has been emphasised throughout the book, people with autism and sld are individuals with their own strengths and weaknesses, personalities, interests, talents and level of skill and understanding. Thus, what they can do, and choose to do, can be as varied as with any group, and guidance and support should be directed to enabling access to whatever ambition and desire dictate (within legal and moral limits).

Throughout their lives, these individuals with autism and sld will need a level of support commensurate with their needs. Very few, if any, will manage to live independently, and not without continuing back-up support. Families will continue to have a continuity of care and concern, but statutory authorities will need to take over more of these as the person moves through adulthood. All individuals will need to be prepared to live their lives without the support of parents.

Further reading

HOWLIN, P. (1997). *Preparation for Adulthood.* London: Routledge.

References

AIRD, R. & LISTER, J. (1999). Enhancing provision for pupils with autism within a school for pupils with severe learning difficulties. In Jones, G. (Ed.) *GAP: Good Autism Practice.* Issue 1 Birmingham: University of Birmingham School of Education.

ATTWOOD, A., FRITH, U. & HERMELIN, B. (1988). The understanding and use of interpersonal gestures by autistic and Down's syndrome children. *Journal of Autism and Developmental Disorders, 18*, 241–257.

BARON-COHEN, S. (1995). *Mindblindness: An Essay on autism and theory of mind.* London: MIT Press.

BEYER, J. & GAMMELTOFT, L. (1999). *Autism and Play.* London: Jessica Kingsley.

BIKLEN, D. (1990). Communication unbound: autism and praxis. *Harvard Educational Review, 60*, 291–315.

BLUNDEN, R. & ALLEN, D. (1987). *Facing the Challenge: An ordinary life for people with learning difficulties and challenging behaviour.* London: Kings Fund Centre.

BONDY, A. S. & FROST, L. A. (1994). The Delaware autistic program, in Harris, S. L. & Handleman, J. S. (Eds). *Preschool Education Programs for Children with Autism.* Austin: Pro-Ed.

BRECHIN, A. & SWAIN, J. (1990). Communication: participating in social relationships. *Open University Workbook.* Milton Keynes: Open University Press.

BRUNER, J. & FELDMAN, C. (1993). Theories of mind and the problem of autism. In Baron-Cohen, S., Tager-Flusberg, H. & Cohen, D. J. (Eds). *Understanding Other Minds: Perspectives from autism.* Oxford: Oxford University Press.

CHRISTIE, P., NEWSON, E., NEWSON, J. & PREVEZNER, W. (1992). An interactive approach to language and communication for non-speaking children. In Lane, D. A. & Miller, A. (Eds). *Child and Adolescent Therapy: A Handbook.* Milton Keynes: Open University Press.

CLEMENTS, J. & ZARKOWSKA, E. (2000). *Behavioural Concerns and Autistic Spectrum Disorders.* London: Jessica Kingsley.

COPELAND, J. (1973). *For the Love of Ann.* London: Arrow Books.

DEPARTMENT OF EDUCATION AND SCIENCE (1970). *The Education Act.* London: HMSO.

DEPARTMENT FOR EDUCATION (1994). *Code of Practice.* London: Department for Education.

DONNELLAN, A. LAVIGNA, G. W. NEGRI-SHOULT, N. & FASSBENDER, L. (1988). *Progress Without Punishment: Effective approaches for learners with behaviour problems.* New York: Teachers' College Press.

GEDYE, A. (1989). Episodic rage and aggression attributed to frontal lobe seizures. *Journal of Mental deficiency research* 33, 369–79.

GERLAND, G. (1997). *A Real Person.* London: Souvenir Press.

GILPIN, R. W. (Ed.) (1993). *Laughing and Living with Autism: A collection of 'real-life' warm and humorous short stories.* New York: Future Horizons.

GRANDIN, T. (1995). How people with autism think. In Schopler, E. & Mesibov, G. B. (Eds). *Learning and Cognition in Autism.* New York: Plenum.

HARRIS, J., COOK, M. & UPTON, G. (1996). *Pupils with Severe Learning Disabilities who Present Challenging Behaviour: A whole school approach to assessment and intervention.* Birmingham: BILD.

HOBSON, R. P. (1993). *Autism and the Development of Mind.* London: Erlbaum.

HOWLIN, P. (1997). *Autism: Preparing for adulthood.* London: Routledge.

HOWLIN, P. & MOORE, A. (1997). Diagnosis in autism: a survey of over 1200 patients. *Autism: The International Journal of Research and Practice,* 1. 135–162.

IRLEN, H. (1995). Viewing the world through rose tinted glasses. *Communication*, 29, 8–9.

JORDAN, R. R. (1990). *Report on the Observer Project for the Evaluation of the Option Institute.* Hatfield Polytechnic National Autistic Society. pp. 35.

——(1989) 'Understanding and use of speaker addressee pronouns by autistic children'. *Brit. J. Disorders of Communication.* 24, 3, 169–179.

——(1997). *Education of Children and Young People with Autism.* Paris: Unesco Ed 98/WS/7.

——(1999). *Autistic Spectrum Disorders. An introductory handbook for practitioners.* London: David Fulton.

JORDAN, R. R. & JONES, G. (1996). *Educational Provision for Children with Autism in Scotland: Final report of a research project for the SOEID.* Birmingham: University of Birmingham School of Education.

——(1997). *Interchange: Educational provision for children with autism in Scotland.* 46. Edinburgh: SOEID.

JORDAN, R. R., JONES, G. & MURRAY, D. (1998). *Educational Interventions for Children with Autism: A literature review of recent and current research.* Sudbury: fee,

JORDAN, R., MACLEOD, C. & BRUNTON, L. (1999). Making special schools 'specialist': A case study of the provision for pupils with autism in a school for pupils with severe learning difficulties. In G. Jones (Ed.) *GAP: Good Autism Practice.* Issue 1 Birmingham: University of Birmingham School of Education.

JORDAN, R. R. & POWELL, S. D. (1994). Whose curriculum? Critical notes on integration and entitlement. *European Journal of Special Needs Education*, 9 27–39.

——(1995a). Factors affecting school choice for parents of a child with autism. *Communication*, Winter, 1995 5–9

——(1995b). *Understanding and Teaching Children with Autism.* Chichester: Wiley.

KANNER, L. (1943). Autistic disturbance of affective contact. *Nervous Child*, 2, 217–250.

KAUFMAN, B. (1994). *Son Rise: The miracle continues.* California: Kramer.

KEENAN, M., KERR, K. P. DILLNBURGER, K. (2000). *Parents' Education as Autism Therapists*. London: Jessica Kingsley.

KRAIJER, D. (1997). *Autism and Autistic-like Conditions in Mental Retardation*. Abingdon: Swets & Zeitlinger.

LAVIGNA, G. W. & DONNELLAN, A. M. (1986). *Alternatives to Punishment: Solving behaviour problems with non-aversive strategies*. New York: Irvington.

LIBBY, S., POWELL, S., MESSER, D., JORDAN, R. (1998). Spontneous play in children with autism: A reappraisal. *Journal of Autism and Developmental Disorders*. 28, 487–497.

LOVAAS, O. I. (1981). Teaching Developmentally Disabled Children: *The me book*. Baltimore: University Park Press.

——(1987). Behavioural treatment and normal intellectual and educational functioning in autistic children. *J. of Consulting and Clinical Psychology*, 55, 3–9.

LOVAAS, O. I. SCHAEFFER, B. & SIMMONS, J. Q. (1965). Experimental studies in childhood schizophrenia: Building social behaviours by use of electric shock. *Journal of Experimental Personality Research*, 1, 99–109.

LOVAAS, O. I. & SIMMONS, I. Q. (1969). Manipulation of self destruction in three retarded children. *Journal of Applied BehaviourAnalysis*, 2, 143–150

LOVETT, H. (1996). *Learning to Listen: Positive approaches and people with different behaviour*. London: Jessica Kingsley.

McGEE, J. J., MENOLASCINO, F. J., HOBBS, D. C. & MENOUSEK, P. E. (1987). *Gentle Teaching: A non-aversive approach for helping persons with mild retardation*. New York: Human Sciences Press.

MESIBOV, G. B. (1997). Formal and informal measures of the effectivene of the TEACCH program. *Autism: The International Journal of Research and Practice*, 1, 25–35.

MORGAN, H. (1996). *Adults with Autism: A guide to theory and practice*. Cambridge: Cambridge University Press.

NIND, M. & HEWETT, D. (1994). *Access to Communication*. London: David Fulton.

NOENS, I. & VAN BERCKALAER-ONNES, I. (2004). Making Sense in a Fragmentary World: Communication in People with

Autism and Learning Disability, *Autism: The International Journal of Research and Practice*, 8, 197–218.

OLIVER, C. (1986). Self-injurious behaviour. *Taking Sense*, 33, 23–24

PARK, C. C. (1986). Social growth in autism: A parent's perspective. In Schopler, E. & Mesibov, G. B. (Eds). *Social Behaviour in Autism*. New York: Plenum Press.

PEETERS, T. (1997). *Autism: Theoretical Principles into Practice*. London: Whurr Publications.

PEETERS, T. & GILLBERG, C. (1999). 2nd Edition. Autism: Medical and Educational Aspects. London: Whurr.

PEETERS, T. & JORDAN, R. (1999). What makes a good practitioner in the field of autism? In Jones, G. (Ed.) *GAP: Good Autism Practice*. Birmingham: University of Birmingham School of Education, pp. 85–90.

POWELL, S. D. & JORDAN, R. R. (1992). Using photographs to develop autobiographical memory in children with autism. In: Shattock P. (Ed.). *Proceedings of International Conference on Research in Autism: The individual, the family and the community*. Sunderland: Sunderland University Autism Research Unit/National Autistic Society.

PREVEZER, W. (1990). Strategies for tuning in to autism. *Therapy Weekly*, 18.10.90, 4.

RANKIN, K. (2000). *Growing up Severely Autistic*. London: Jessica Kingsley.

ROEYERS, K. (1995). A peer-mediated proximity intervention to facilitate the social interactions of children with a pervasive developmental disorder. *British Journal of Special Education*, 22, 161–164.

RUSSELL, J. (1996). *Agency and its Role in Development*. London: Erlbaum.

SCHOPLER, E. & OLLEY, J. G. (1982). Comprehensive educational services for autistic children: The TEACCH model. In Reynolds, C. R. & Gutkin, T. R. (Eds). *Handbook of Social Psychology*. New York: Wiley.

SHERRATT, D. (1999). The importance of play. In Jones, G. & Morgan, H. (Eds). *Good Autism Practice*, Issue 2 Birmingham: The University of Birmingham School of Education.

SHIELDS, J. (in press). NAS EarlyBird programme: Partnership with parents in early intervention. *Autism: The International Journal of Research and Practice.*

SKINNER, B. F. (1957). *Verbal Behaviour.* New York: Appleton-Century Press.

STRAIN, P. S. & CORDISCO, L. K. (1994). LEAP preschool. In Harris, S. L. & Handleman, 1. S. (Eds). *Preschool Education Programs for Children with Autism.* Austin: Pro-Ed.

SUSSMAN, F. (2000). *More than Words: a revised HANEN programme.* New Brunswick: The Hanen Centre.

TREVARTHEN, C., AITKEN, K., PAPOUDI, D. & ROBARTS, J. (1996). *Children with Autism: Diagnosis and intervention to meet their needs.* London: Jessica Kingsley.

WALKER, M. (1980). *The Makaton Vocabulary (revised).* Camberley: The Makaton Development Project.

WATSON, L. (1985). The TEACCH curriculum. In Schopler, E. & Mesibov, G. (Eds). *Communication Problems in Autism.* New York: Plenum Press.

WATSON, O., LORD, C., SCHAFFER, B. & SCHOPLER, E. (1989). *Teaching Spontaneous Communication to Autistic and Developmentally Handicapped Children.* New York: Irvington Press.

WETHERBY, A. M. (1986). Ontogeny of communicative functions in autism. *Journal of Autism and Developmental Disorders,* 16, 295–316.

WHITAKER, P., BARRATT, P., JOY, H., POTTER, M. & THOMAS, G. (1998). Children with autism and peer group support: Using circles of friends. *British Journal of Special Education,* 25, 60–64.

WHITELEY, P., RODGERS, J., SAVERY, D. & SHATTOCK, P. (1999). A gluten-free diet as an intervention for autism and associated spectrum disorders: Preliminary findings. *Autism: The International Journal of Research and Practice,* 3, 45–66.

WILLIAMS, D. (1996). *Autism: An inside out approach.* London: Jessica Kingsley.

WIMPORY, D., CHADWICK, P. & NASH, S. (1995). Musical interaction therapy for children with autism: An evaluation case study with a two year follow up. *Journal of Autism and Developmental Disorders,* 25, 541–552.

WING, L. (1988). The continuum of autistic characteristics. In Schopler, E. & Mesibov, G. B. (Eds). *Diagnosis and Assessment in Autism*. New York: Plenum Press.

WING, L. (1996). *Autistic Spectrum Disorders*. London: Constable.

WING, I. & GOULD, J. (1979). Severe impairment of social interaction and associated abnormalities in children: Epidemiology and classification. *Journal of Autism and Developmental Disorders*, 9, 11–29.

WOLFBERG, P. (1999). *Play and Imagination in Children with Autism*. New York: Teachers College Press.

ZARKOWSKA, E. & CLEMENTS, J. (1989). *Problem Behaviour and People with Severe Learning Difficulties: The STAR approach*. London: Chapman & Hall.

Index

Also published by Souvenir Press

THE HUMAN HORIZONS SERIES

This highly-acclaimed series is now established as the pre-eminent list for people with disabilities, the elderly and the afflicted, and those who care for them.

A library of books valuable as they are to teachers, therapist, social workers and the medical profession, the series is deliberately planned with the needs of families in mind, avoiding technical jargon, presenting material in a way that makes it easy to use and adapt at home.

All the authors are authorities in their fields, and many have international reputations for their practical pioneering work.

"It was far-sighted to establish this series to provide information for a wide range of individuals on many topics to do with disability."
                                                        BRITISH MEDICAL JOURNAL

"In a short period of time the Human Horizons Series has established itself as a valuable source of help for the handicapped, filling a gap for parents who wish to help their children but feel that existing sources of advice are too professional."
                                                        TIMES EDUCATIONAL SUPPLEMENT

"Good, well-illustrated, beautifully produced and reasonably priced . . . The books are directed towards teachers, social workers, doctors, nurses, health visitors, psychologists, welfare officers, mental health workers and, also but not least, the parents and families of the handicapped . . . full of useful ideas."
                                                        NEW SOCIETY

"All the authors are involved with the field they are writing about as parent, patient or worker. This gives their writing a vividness and conviction born of actual experience . . . Each book is constructive and informative."
                                                        THE HEALTH SERVICES

"One of the few series of such books with a consistently high standard of real service to the suffering and disadvantaged and above all their helpers . . . it is difficult too highly to praise the straightforward and real assistance to teachers, social workers, nurses and anyone concerned with people in difficulties, of this collection."
                                                        THE TABLET

What is means to be autistic. A very rare book, a beautifully
written autobiography

A REAL PERSON
Life on the Outside

Gunilla Gerland
Translated by Joan Tate

From her earliest years Gunilla Gerland knew that she was 'different' – constantly fearful, preferring solitude because it was safe
and unchanging, given to obsessive behaviour that provided a
certain relief, scolded for things she could not help. Gunilla writes
simply and frankly about herself and her attempts to find a way
for herself when everything she felt and did seemed at odds with
everyone else. Only at the end of the book does she come through
and realise that, despite her difficulties and differences, she is in
fact 'a real person'. Here, written with an outstanding ability to
convey inner thoughts and feelings, is an account of autism from
the inside.

A Real Person will be of immense value to families and professionals striving to understand autistic people in their care. But
it also stands firmly on its own as a work of the highest literary
quality. Its appeal is universal, its honesty devastating.

Gunilla Gerland was born with Asperger syndrome which was
not diagnosed until she reached adulthood. Throughout her childhood she felt herself lost in a strange and hostile world where
she was 'different' from everyone else. Eventually, through the
help of a psychotherapist, she came to terms with her condition
and was encouraged to use her gift for writing to tell her own
story. This book is the result.

216 x 135mm   256pp   0 285 63398 8

- An unique first-person account of autism.
- Serial rights under negotiation.
- Author tour.
- Specialist advertising.

Sexuality and the disabled.
At last a major work that addresses the issues and practice
with authority and humanity

HOLDING ON LETTING GO
Sex, Sexuality and People with Learning Disabilities

John Drury, Lynne Hutchinson & Jon Wright

Sex and sexuality are sensitive, complex issues when a parent has a child with learning disabilities. When that child grows into an adult, these issues become fraught with anxiety. While parents have a duty to protect their child from abuse, that child is also a 'sexual' being, with a right to be so. Is your need to protect your child's vulnerability criticised as over-protectiveness? Should you be holding on, or letting go?

This realistic book has been written specially for parents and carers facing these dilemmas, to help them get to grips with sexuality issues. After defining what they mean by 'sexuality' and 'sex', the authors, who are all experienced workers in this field, suggest a number of strategies to enable parents to face their fears, define their hopes and concerns, cope with professionals and find ways of working in partnership with them. They then examine the rights and realities of people with learning disabilities as sexual beings: their right to grow up, to know, be sexual, not be at the mercy of care-givers' differing sexual attitudes, the right to a dignified and humane environment, and not to be abused. They consider positive ways to enlarge the personal resources of the child and adult with learning disabilities and lessen their vulnerability. Sexuality education programmes are discussed, along with the importance of tailoring these to the individual's needs. It is hoped that this book will help many parents to view the future of their children who have learning disabilities with more confidence, and to share in empowering them to lead the best lives they can. Although aimed particularly at parents, this book will also be of enormous interest to professionals.

John Drury worked in the L'arche Community for four years, first in France and then in India. He worked in residential and day services for Brent for seven years and joined Barnado's nine years ago on their Queen's Road Project, Bradford.

Lynne Hutchinson has worked in the area of disability since the age of 21. Working for Barnado's since 1993, she has focused on developing understanding and skills in the area of sexuality and people with learning disabilities.

Jon Wright has been a social worker since 1982, specialising in learning disabilities.

216 x 135mm   208pp   0 285 65378 6

A pioneering book that meets a real need in social work

AM I ALLOWED TO CRY?
A Study of Bereavement amongst People who have
Learning Difficulties

Maureen Oswin

This is the first book to tackle a tragic and very real problem which exists in relation to people with learning disabilities. The book not only points out how people with learning difficulties have been mishandled in relation to bereavement, but gives very clear guidelines for staff training, understanding and dealing with people in their care.

It offers specific guidance to those who work with bereaved people, showing how they can be helped to cope with their grief. The fact that the subject has been tackled will reassure parents who worry about what will happen to their child when they die.

Maureen Oswin formerly worked for 14 years at a long stay hospital in Surrey, teaching children who had cerebral palsy. From 1975 she worked at the Thomas Coram Research Unit, Institute of Education, part of London University. She also undertook research into the services available for disabled children, and has published six books and numerous articles.

Her research for *Am I Allowd To Cry?* occupied four years. Maureeen Oswin is now retired and recently received a Millennium award voted by the readers of Community Care to have "made the greatest contribution to modern social care".

216 x 135mm   160pp   0 285 65096 3

A classic in special needs now revised and updated again

CHILDREN IN NEED OF SPECIAL CARE

Thomas J. Weihs
Revised by A.M. Hailey, M.J. Hailey, & N.M. Blitz

Recommended for anyone working and caring for children with special developmental needs, *Children in Need of Special Care* was first published in 1971 and has long been considered a classic by those in the field. Taking a radically holistic and child-centred approach, Dr Weihs believed that childhood disabilities should be described not only as a 'pathological condition' but in terms of a child's total development and environment. He also placed importance on the self-knowledge of the parent, carer, educator or therapist, as essential in the process of helping a child with disabilities.

While this new edition remains true to Dr Weihs' timeless approach, this edition has been extensively rewritten to reflect these changes and the tasks facing curative education today, to provide insight and guidance for all those currently living and working with children with special needs.

Latterly as superintendent, Dr Weihs worked at the Camphill Rudolf Steiner School in Aberdeen for over forty years. Through his work there, inspired by the teachings of Rudolf Steiner and by Karl Konig, he gained extensive experience of treating, teaching and living with children with special needs. This led him to develop his unique philosophy. He was born in 1914 and died in 1983.

Anthea and Michael Hailey have both lived and worked with children with special needs for over 25 years as houseparents and teachers, from 1988 to the present at The Mount Camphill Community in East Sussex. Dr Nick Blitz is the Medical Adviser for the Camphill Communities of Ireland.

216 x 135mm   192pp   0 285 63569 7

Completely revised and updated – the new edition of a
highly-praised book

MAKING SENSE TOGETHER
Practical Approaches to Supporting Children who have
Multisensory Impairments

Rosalind Wyman

This warm and highly practical book draws on the author's own
experience of working closely with parents to develop the abilities
of children who have multisensory impairments. The children
may have total or partial deafness, be blind or partially sighted,
and may have additional physical disabilities or learning difficulties.

Working with children ranging from a few months old to the
teenage years, the author describes a holistic approach that will
develop communication, self-help skills and, above all, confidence in their ability to explore their world in a positive way.
The many children's programmes described in the book show
what changes may be wrought with the right stimulation and with
full parental involvement.

Rosalind Wyman is Senior Practitioner with SENSE South East
and was for many years Head of the Ealing Family Centre.
Through her adopted son, Alexander, she has gained many
insights into the way children with sensory impairments perceive
the world.

216 x 135mm   288pp   0 285 63510 7